*Effective Church Accounting*

# Effective
# Church
# Accounting

*RICHARD J. VARGO*

1817

*Harper & Row, Publishers, San Francisco*

New York, Grand Rapids, Philadelphia, St. Louis
London, Singapore, Sydney, Tokyo

Exhibits 4-1, 4-2, 4-3, 4-4 courtesy of Safeguard Business Systems, Inc., Fort Washington, Pennsylvania. Reprinted by permission. All rights reserved.

Exhibits 4-7, 4-8 courtesy of Membership Services, Inc., Irving, Texas. Reprinted by permission. All rights reserved.

Exhibit 4-9 courtesy of Lowell Brown Enterprises, Ventura, California. Reprinted by permission. All rights reserved.

Exhibit 4-10 courtesy of Romar Systems, Elkhart, Indiana. Reprinted by permission. All rights reserved.

Exhibits B-1, B-2 reprinted from *Management Accounting*, U.S.A., August 1982. Copyright by National Association of Accountants, Montvale, NJ. All rights reserved.

FIRST EDITION

**Library of Congress Cataloging-in-Publication Data**

Vargo, Richard J.
  Effective church accounting.

  1. Church finance.  I. Title.
BV770.V37  1989      254.8         88-45699
ISBN 0-06-068861-0

89  90  91  92  93  RRD  10  9  8  7  6  5  4  3  2  1

# Contents

# Introduction

In the mid-1970s I was teaching a graduate course in governmental and nonprofit accounting at the University of Texas at Arlington, a large school whose students came mostly from the Dallas–Fort Worth area. To complete the course the students were required to read a large textbook, solve many intricate accounting problems, and prepare a written report on an accounting topic related to nonprofit organizations. Fully 30 percent of the students decided to report on the accounting and financial reporting practices that were being used in their churches. The popularity of this topic surprised me, as we had never discussed churches during the entire semester. The focus had been on federal, state, and local governments, school districts, hospitals, universities, museums, and so on. As I reviewed the reports submitted to me at the conclusion of the semester, I wondered why I had never before read any material on church accounting. It seemed to me that as a university professor of accounting, I should have had some exposure to church accounting. I reflected on my educational and professional background.

My accounting education started at Marietta College in Marietta, Ohio, where I majored in accounting and completed seven accounting courses. The courses had intimidating names and were rigorous, but in four years not one minute was spent discussing the unique world of church accounting. I earned my M.B.A. at Ohio University in Athens, Ohio, where I had several additional accounting courses as part of a two-year program. Once again, I never studied church accounting. My formal education culminated with a Ph.D. in accounting from the University of Washington in Seattle, Washington. My three years in

1

residence at that institution were devoted to studying very complex accounting issues, none of which related specifically to churches.

Further, until I taught at the University of Texas, nothing that occurred after the start of my professional career encouraged me to study church accounting. As an auditor with a large international accounting firm, I audited big banks, brokerage houses, and manufacturers—not churches. After all, very few churches are multimillion dollar enterprises. In my work preparing people to pass the uniform certified public accountants (CPA) examination, I discussed such esoteric topics as interperiod tax allocation and the disposition of the operating loss carryforwards of purchased subsidiaries, not church accounting. Why the absence of churches? There are simply no questions on the CPA examination that deal directly with churches. As a member of various consulting groups, I had been retained by businesses to answer very specific accounting questions and to solve highly technical problems to improve profitability. No church had ever inquired about consulting services, even to ask if some services could be provided free of charge. I have discovered that this is because many church officials don't know which questions to ask, don't know if their accounting records are accurate, and feel that they can "get by" until their successors take over.

Thus, as a consequence of the students' interest in church accounting and a deficiency in my own background, I began to seriously study churches. Employing a mailed questionnaire, I gathered extensive data on the accounting and financial reporting practices and procedures being followed in hundreds of churches of all denominations in the area. I followed this up with both telephone calls and personal visits. I talked with financial secretaries, treasurers, members of finance committees, and pastors and priests, as well as people affected by accounting information, such as music directors, education directors, and youth directors. Then I read everything I could obtain on the subject of church accounting. As a result of several years of investigation, I reached a few conclusions. First of all, few people preparing accounting information for churches knew whether they were doing it properly. Most preparers stated that they generally followed what previous preparers had done with regard to the books and financial statements. The facts that their systems of keeping the records were cumbersome, sometimes involving more than a thousand accounts, and their financial reports were lengthy, sometimes more than twenty pages, troubled them. But they did not know how to change their accounting methods. Second, the users of accounting information did not understand the financial reports, which should have been useful to them in planning and controlling operations and in decision making. Users of accounting information routinely had to ask for clarification and assistance. If none was forthcoming, they tended to ignore the accounting information. Some of the difficulty resulted from the lack of a business or accounting background by many users; some was caused by preparers of information not recognizing that nonaccountants would be using the data. Third, unlike the subjects of dieting, exercising, cooking, and auto repair, very little material has been published on the subject of church accounting and financial affairs. As nonprofit accounting has been the stepchild of the accounting profession, church accounting has been the stepchild of nonprofit accounting.

Encouraged by several church accountants who recognized these same problems, I developed a one-day, interdenominational, continuing education seminar entitled "Church Accounting" for both current and prospective church accountants. The response was overwhelming. Since it was introduced in the late 1970s the seminar has been offered twenty-eight times by eight universities in three states. Almost all of the participants who attend it note that the seminar is their first class on the topic. Interestingly, some people have been serving their churches for decades. The attendees come with the zeal that generally accompanies people working for the church in either volunteer or paid positions. Yet they seem fearful that some esoteric academic will present material in an incomprehensible way and then chide them for not understanding it. A few bring calculators, ready to compute something if necessary; others bring a sample of their financial reports for me to review in confidence during the day. Most of the participants are preparers of accounting information: financial secretaries and treasurers. Some are beginners who have just taken over for someone; others are seasoned veterans. Regardless of experience, however, the attendees don't know what to expect. By the conclusion of the seminar, they are an excited and determined group of "movers and shakers." This book is an outgrowth of that seminar.

You may feel uncertainty and apprehension as you read these introductory remarks. Rest assured that this book is down to earth and will bring new skills and perspective to your role in the church accounting process. I subscribe to the KISS principle—Keep it simple, stupid. Additionally, I have no intention of making this book the complete, unabridged encyclopedia of church accounting, encompassing all situations that may occur during the existence of your church. To do so would distract you from the main elements of effective church accounting, presume that you have an interest in all areas of accounting, and violate the KISS principle.

The reason for the preceding discussion was not a desire on my part to talk about my background, credentials, or philosophy, but a desire to point out that I entered the field of church accounting by accident and started from ground zero. That's probably just the way you got involved as well . . . by accident. Few people are trained to handle the accounting and financial reporting responsibilities of churches. Members volunteer and serve perhaps because no one else comes forward. I often hear the comment, "Well, someone has to do it, and I had some time to spare." I should also note that the certified public accountants from whom many of you are either officially or unofficially seeking advice did not learn about church accounting in school either; it's still not in the curriculum. In effect, they too have come to serve the church by accident. Except for those very few people trained in church financial administration, we all enter this field with little, if any, formal training. Somehow it helps to know that almost everyone else has the same problem.

As you read this book, keep in mind that many people involved in the church accounting process suffer from a disease called psychosclerosis, or the hardening of the attitudes. This is a terminal illness if not detected early and immediately corrected. Symptoms of this disease can easily be spotted in comments such as, "It may work in California, but it won't work in _____" or "It may work in a small church, but not in our large church" or "It may work in a newly organized church, but we've developed our procedures over a _____ year period" or "It may work for the _____, but it won't work in our denomination." I hope you have none of these symptoms and will keep an open mind throughout the book. You will be exposed to hundreds of new ideas and approaches in the chapters that follow. An open mind will better enable you to consider the ideas and approaches that are presented and then decide which ones can be implemented at your church.

CHAPTER **1**

# *Effective Church Accounting*

## AN OVERVIEW

The foundation of effective church accounting is the idea that those with responsibility for generating accounting and financial information within the church should have one goal in mind—to assist members, church administrators, and other interested parties in all of their planning, controlling, and decision making activities. In this approach accounting is not viewed as an end in itself. It is instead considered an integral part of yearly activities, such as the budgeting process. It also monitors operations and assesses progress, thus safeguarding assets and assisting in both short-term decision making (Should we purchase a new photocopy machine?) and long-term decision making (Should we expand the church's facilities?). Thus effective church accounting is a broad, comprehensive philosophy of accounting.

Effective church accounting is not new and revolutionary. It has been present in the business world, particularly in large, successful corporations, for many years. Its application within churches, however, has been almost nonexistent. As a consequence those people responsible for church accounting, whether financial secretaries or treasurers, typically believe that their role is simply to keep the books. This is a very limiting, Bob Cratchit, green-eyeshade view of the accounting function. With this narrow approach, treasurers and financial secretaries are measured according to their ability to 1) place transactions in the proper accounts, 2) achieve a set of books that balances, 3) be neat, and 4) be punctual in furnishing financial reports accurate to the penny. Although the accountant may be receiving high marks for his or her performance in keeping the books, the church may be wasting its resources, failing to prepare a budget properly, losing cash to an embezzling money counter, using an antiquated accounting system, or furnishing reports that no one can understand. Today's church accountants cannot adequately serve the church if they fail to see the association between accounting and the entire financial side of church affairs. If financial secretaries and treasurers are not instrumental in solving these problems, they must be held partially responsible for the existence of these problems. If they pass the buck by claiming that budgeting is done by a budget commit-tee, that internal controls and the accounting system were installed by someone else, and that it's the readers' responsibility to understand financial reports, they are not serving their churches very well. Effective church accountants should be involved in all areas that have financial implications and should work to provide relevant, timely, and com-prehensible information to people who need it.

The transition from a narrowly defined role for accounting within a church to a comprehensive approach may not be easy or quick. Years of tradition are not overcome in a matter of minutes, either by users of church data or by church accountants. But with perseverance and a plan of action, all of those affected by the changes should eventually conclude that the church accountant's role within the church must be expanded, because it will benefit the church. Managers in large corpora-tions would never think about making top-level decisions without an accountant's analysis and the accountant's attendance at key meetings. I hope churches will soon follow suit.

Exhibit 1-1 provides an illustration of the accountant's responsibility to the church. Observe that many areas of involvement for the church accountant go beyond the traditional role of processing data and issuing financial reports. Note the accountant's role in resource allocation and budgeting, internal control of assets, the management of accounting systems and information processing, and, finally, the communication of accounting information via the financial reports. Each of these topics is discussed separately in the chapters that follow. A brief overview here of each topic serves as a foundation for later material.

### Resource Allocation: Planning and Budgeting

Churches' resources are generally very limited and, in most cases, represent precious funds entrusted by the congregation to maintain the church and help fulfill its missions. Therefore church officials are responsible for spending those funds wisely. It is paradoxical then that most churches have developed budgeting, accounting, and financial reporting systems that prove only that the churches spent the money, not that the money was wisely spent. Accountability is much more than

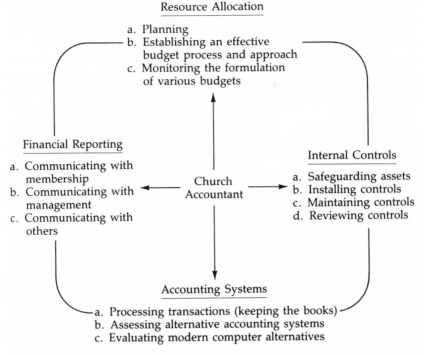

Resource Allocation

a. Planning
b. Establishing an effective
   budget process and approach
c. Monitoring the formulation
   of various budgets

Financial Reporting

a. Communicating with
   membership
b. Communicating with
   management
c. Communicating with
   others

Church
Accountant

Internal Controls

a. Safeguarding assets
b. Installing controls
c. Maintaining controls
d. Reviewing controls

Accounting Systems

a. Processing transactions (keeping the books)
b. Assessing alternative accounting systems
c. Evaluating modern computer alternatives

**Exhibit 1-1   The Role of a Church Accountant**

recording expenditures in the proper account. As a prelude to spending funds, a church needs both a short-term plan and a long-term plan. Planning will result in the identification of needs, the drawing up of a statement of measurable goals and objectives, and the establishment of priorities. In such an environment the accountant becomes responsible for periodically evaluating the church's progress toward reaching its goals and objectives.

With or without adequate planning, churches typically prepare an annual operating budget. The process of budgeting should not be taken lightly. In fact, the budgeting process is as critical as the resulting numbers. Suffice it to note here that churches can benefit greatly or be seriously damaged by how the budgeting process is carried out. It is imperative that budgeting be done for the right reasons, be accomplished in a manner that elicits the support of all parties for its attainment, employ an approach that allows for the evaluation of church programs, and embody realistic expectations of resource inflows and outflows. Unrealistic assumptions defeat the entire purpose of budgeting. With regard to the inflow of resources, budget preparers need to look beyond cash contributions and consider, among other items, restricted gifts, tuition from educational activities, amounts provided for the pastor's discretionary fund, the value of items donated to the church, and even the value of services donated by church members. All are resources; all need to be budgeted and accounted for. Considering only regular cash offerings is simple, but fails to develop a comprehensive picture of resources entrusted to the church.

The church will benefit when the church accountant is sufficiently involved in and informed about the preparation of the operating budget that he or she can help make sure it is done correctly. In the process the accountant needs to be alert to the games some people play at budgeting time.

Allocation of church resources through planning and budgeting is covered in chapter 2.

### Internal Control of Assets

The protection of the entity's assets is a basic management requirement of all organizations. Unfortunately, in most churches the internal control of assets, especially cash, has traditionally been weak. As a consequence it is estimated that about 15 percent of all churches, or more than fifty thousand churches, have been, are being, or will be cheated by an employee or member. Millions of dollars of cash and other church assets are involved each year. Most cases are never even brought to the attention of the congregations whose assets have been plundered. Honest errors also account for significant losses. Because most church assets come from the congregation, church accountants have a special obligation to make certain that all funds are received, deposited, and spent properly.

Safeguarding the church's assets, particularly cash, is the primary objective of the church's internal control system. This means that proper controls for the handling of all cash receipts and disbursements should be developed, maintained, and periodically reviewed for compliance. Church accountants can be instrumental in all three phases. The controls will guard against the understatement of cash receipts and the overstatement of cash disbursements, whether intentional or unintentional.

By recognizing the main causes for internal control problems among churches and instituting some action, the church accountant can significantly lessen the likelihood that funds will be misappropriated or records will be unreliable. For example, incompatible duties may be separated, the organizational structure may be made more formal, better qualified personnel may be attracted, an accounting procedures manual may be prepared, and audits may be undertaken, either by an internal committee or an external accountant.

Internal control of assets is discussed in chapter 3. Included in chapter 3 is a self-test of fifty internal control practices to allow you to assess the quality of your church's internal control system. The test will also provide you with many ideas for making improvement.

## Accounting Systems and Information Processing

Every church has an accounting system to process its transactions and to generate the information that goes into its financial reports. Accounting systems differ in shape, size, complexity, and efficiency. Some were designed professionally for use by the church; most just evolved over time from what the first church accountant began with years ago.

The general objectives of the church's accounting system are to measure and control financial activities, to provide financial information to church officials, and to provide financial reports to members of the congregation and others. In attaining these objectives every church should follow established guidelines of systems design. If the guidelines are not followed, the system may fail to serve the church as it should. For example, the system may not leave an audit trail, which is used to locate errors by tracing transactions through the accounting records. Also the system may lose data, thereby producing unreliable financial reports.

Church transactions can be processed manually or by computer. Presently 80 percent of all churches use manual processing because of the low cost of operation. The "write-it-several times" or the more efficient "write-it-once" systems are commonly used manual systems. There are pros and cons for each of these systems. Computers are presently used in about 20 percent of churches, but are being considered by many churches as the alternative to a manual system. By the year 2000, only the smallest churches will employ a manual system.

Yet computers offer both opportunity and danger. They offer opportunity because they can provide so much processing capacity and information at increasingly reasonable costs. They offer danger because the computer selection and implementation process is littered with traps, curves, explosives, delays, and dead ends. Planning is critical in establishing a computer system for a church. A computer committee needs to be organized and to adopt an agenda of steps that will lead to success. Two of the biggest decisions the committee will make are 1) whether to use an outside computer service bureau to process church accounting data or to purchase an in-house computer, and 2) if the latter, which vendor to select.

The church accountant will play a pivotal role in making certain that the church's accounting system is efficient and effective. Where deficiencies exist the church accountant will likely be the champion of improvement. When computers are being considered, the church accountant will probably be a member of the computer committee and take an active role in any selection and implementation. After all, no person is in a better position to evaluate the church's accounting and financial reporting requirements.

Chapter 4 deals with accounting systems and information processing. It presents an overview of general types of church accounting systems, including an extensive discussion of computer alternatives. Particular attention is given to the in-house computer option. One hundred questions to be asked by members of the computer committee are presented. An appendix to chapter 4 reviews several alternative accounting systems used by churches, including general ledger and fund accounting systems. Detailed explanations and examples are provided.

## Financial Reporting

Reporting financial information is the final step in the accounting process. If church budgeting has been done properly and the accounting system has correctly processed data into information, users of the financial reports can be reasonably sure that the information is good and can be used for planning, control, and decision making. For example, if the annual operating budget for utilities expenses is well planned, actual costs can be effectively compared with budgeted amounts. But if the budget was prepared without enough thought, detailed comparisons between budgeted costs and actual costs will be pointless. Informed people will simply scan the actual figures looking for items that appear abnormally high or low. Unfortunately, the actual amount spent on utilities expenses may be out of line because of wasteful practices, yet not high enough to warrant review. Similarly, if users of the financial reports routinely receive information that is several months late or full of errors because of sloppy processing, lost data, or mathematical errors, they will begin to plan, control, and make decisions without using the financial reports. You can't blame them. Thus it is critical that financial report users receive timely, accurate, and meaningful information.

Also all financial reports prepared by the church accountant either for use by the administrative board or for distribution to the congregation should be organized so that users can understand the information. It is not the responsibility of users to learn what all the accounts, comparisons, schedules, footnotes, and so on, mean. It is the responsibility of the accountant to make certain that the information can be understood. Why keep the books and issue financial reports if no one understands them? Comments such as, "Why do they have to make these financial statements so difficult to understand?" and "What good are financial reports if no one understands them?" are common in churches. I've heard them hundreds of times. Imagine the confusion among baseball fans if the score could not be relied upon to determine the winner of the game! In a sense this happens within churches when the financial report is distributed and people can't understand what it means. In such situations it is the church accountant who must change. Educating the users is a far more difficult task. Experimenting with different formats for and terminology within financial statements is in order. Further, if the preparer of the financial statements must be in attendance when the reports are distributed, so he or she can answer questions or prevent readers from reaching erroneous conclusions, the preparer needs to improve the clarity and organization of those financial statements.

Chapter 5 discusses financial reporting, the end product of the accounting process. Emphasis is placed on the need to communicate through financial statements so that users can plan, control, and make decisions. An appendix to chapter 5 presents a brief review of the key accounting principles and practices developed by the American Institute of Certified Public Accountants (AICPA) for certain nonprofit organizations, including churches. Examples of church financial statements that follow the AICPA's principles and practices are provided. The appendix is included for the more advanced church accountant.

## A PACKAGE: BOOK AND NEWSLETTER

This book presents the principles of effective church accounting. Except for the technical material contained in the appendix to chapter 5, which may be modified by future pronouncements of the AICPA, all presentations, examples, and suggestions contained in the book should be as timely to your successor as they are to you. In fact, I hope that this book becomes part of your church's library of administrative aids and gets read by the many church accountants likely to follow you.

In order to maintain timeliness, topics where change frequently occurs are not included in this book. These topics include details of computer services for churches and taxes. In the case of computers, new companies, products, capabilities, prices, and addresses are weekly events. If such information were provided in this book, it could be obsolete before publication. In the case of taxes, there always seem to be questions relating to payroll taxes for employees, nonemployees, and clergy—especially in the areas of filing requirements and social security. Further, clergy typically have income tax questions dealing with such things as the parsonage and other allowances, professional expenses, retirement programs, and how their gross income is determined. But the income tax code has been in a state of flux for several years as new laws have been enacted by Congress. This is compounded by the continual interpretation of the code by the Internal Revenue Service and the results of tax court cases. As with the details of computer services, I did not want you to read stale information.

To obtain this type of time-sensitive information, you may elect to receive the annual *Effective Church Accounting Newsletter* for two years at no charge. The newsletter will contain current information that will assist you in completing your responsibilities to the church. The *Effective Church Accounting Newsletter* will be published and distributed in January of each year, starting in 1990, by Harper & Row, Publishers. You will receive the two free annual newsletters by completing and returning the information card found at the back of this book.

Assisted by a package composed of the book and the annual issue of the *Effective Church Accounting Newsletter*, church accountants can always be in a position to offer up-to-date service to their churches.

## TERMINOLOGY

Up to this point I have referred to those serving their churches in an accounting capacity as church accountants. But few churches have a "church accountant." Most churches have a treasurer or a treasurer complemented by a financial secretary, who assists the treasurer in the processing of routine transactions. Different churches may use different titles for persons having identical financial responsibilities. Further, the manner in which accounting and financial information moves up the hierarchy is different among churches. In order to facilitate the presentation of material, however, roles have to be defined and an organizational structure presumed. With this structuring, when reference is made to a financial secretary, for example, all readers will visualize the same position. Exhibit 1-2 presents the organizational structure used in this book.

The responsibilities and duties include:

*Financial Secretary*—Maintains the accounting records (books) by recording all income and expenditure transactions, prepares disbursement checks for authorized signatures, and prepares financial reports. Found in large churches; often a full-time, paid position. Reports to the treasurer.

*Treasurer*—Responsible for safeguarding church assets, analyzing church programs that have financial ramifications, signing checks, and issuing financial reports. In large churches oversees the work of the financial secretary. Serves also as the financial secretary if none exists. Reports to the finance committee.

*Finance Committee*—Oversees all financial activities. Receives financial reports and analysis from the treasurer and subcommittees that deal

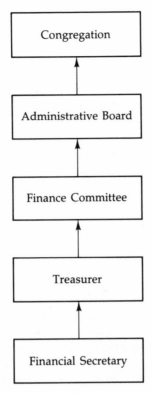

**Exhibit 1-2   Organization Chart**

with specific financial matters, such as budgeting and computer selection. Makes recommendations on financial issues to the administrative board.

*Administrative Board*—Oversees all church affairs. Receives reports from the finance committee as well as all other committees, such as the worship committee, Christian education committee, youth committee, buildings and grounds committee, and so on. Clergy often hold membership, perhaps ex officio, on this board. Reports to the congregation.

The minister or pastor is not shown on this organization chart because different churches position that person at a different level of authority. You may add your minister or pastor to the chart at the place appropriate to your own church.

# CHAPTER 2

# Resource Allocation: Planning and Budgeting

All organizations, whether organized for profit or not for profit, have a finite amount of resources with which to work. Thus IBM, school districts, the corner pharmacy, city government, local clubs, families, and churches all have at least one financial element in common: the need to achieve their objectives with limited resources. Just as you must exhibit some restraint in your personal expenditures in order to provide funds for food, clothing, shelter, savings, children's education, and so on, churches too must be cautious in allocating their resources among projects. Unfortunately, since the beginning of the Christian church there have always been more hurts and hopes to address than resources available. Because church resources are limited and, in most cases, represent funds entrusted to the church by the congregation, church officials have the responsibility of making sure that every nickel of these funds is spent wisely.

Spending money wisely is not the same as spending money. Most churches have a budgeting, accounting, and financial reporting system that proves that they planned for the expenditure and spent the money. Accountability is proven by having the expenditure show up in the correct account in the financial statements. Some finance committee members spend hours poring over the reports to make certain that all expenditures have been correctly recorded and presented on the statements. God help the financial secretary or treasurer who misclassifies an expenditure! What we see in such situations is an incorrect notion of what accountability means. Accountability involves the measurement of whether the church's resources have been successfully allocated to its programs. Churches can usually show that they have programs and that budgeted funds have been spent and correctly accounted for, but they typically cannot show whether the funds have been wisely spent. Spending money wisely involves both establishing specific, measurable goals and objectives and, after spending precious resources, evaluating whether the goals and objectives have been reached. To illustrate this point, let's presume that the church started a hot lunch program for elderly people in the community and budgeted $12,000 for this purpose. Further, assume that during the period involved, $9,700 was spent by the program coordinator. When the financial report is received by the finance committee, many members are likely to praise the coordinator's ability to operate the program under budget. But would the committee be as kind if, for example, it also found out that only eight people a day were served and that the meal was always steak and lobster? Alternatively, would they be pleased if only oatmeal was served? Such a program would need better definition of purpose and some goals and objectives. For although only $9,700 was spent for food, and the elderly did receive some benefit, one could argue that the church's funds were not spent wisely. A nutritionist would have a field day testing whether either menu described complied with dietary standards. Thus we can see that a preoccupation with a historical account of money spent can be misleading. When used properly, accounting includes budgeting, control, and evaluation dimensions.

### Meeting at St. Chaos Church

In the following pages you will be eavesdropping on the annual budget meeting of St. Chaos Church.[1] Although this hypothetical church probably does not allocate its resources in exactly the same way that your church does, some similarities may exist. In fact some church officials have accused me of secretly attending their meetings! As the meeting progresses, I will provide a running critique of the activities.

The chairperson of the finance committee begins. "Thanks for coming out on such a rainy day. As Notre Dame and the University of Southern California are playing for the national football championship later today, let's try to wrap up our discussion of next year's budget as quickly as possible."

(As will be discussed in this chapter, the budget process should be done carefully and over several months. For instance, planning

---

[1] The idea for the budget meeting comes from a similar meeting presented in "The Evaluation of Resource Usage in the Not-For-Profit Environment," written by Loudell O. Ellis and published in *The Woman CPA*, v. 37, April 1975, 6–8.

for an annual calendar year budget should start at least six months in advance. Preparing a budget quickly is bad administration. Yet countless churches get in the habit of doing their budgeting before sporting events, before picnics, between services, in one evening, and so on. Such haste could taint all future accounting and financial reporting done for the year.)

The program leader of the buildings and grounds committee requests a 5 percent increase over this year's operating budget plus $40,000 for a new roof and $30,000 to repave the parking lot. No report on the current year's activities is provided, the amounts for the roof and paving are rough estimates, and no details of the budget year activities are provided. "The buildings and grounds look magnificent; let's help to keep them that way," voices the finance committee. "Your operating budget is approved. But we don't have enough funds for both a roof and repaving, so we'll give you $30,000. Either get the parking lot repaved or get a cheaper roof."

(There are several problems with this allocation of funds. First and foremost, all programs being funded need data on past results accomplished versus money spent. Also, any request for an increase in funding must be justified. And the committee must know the expected results from next year's allocation of funds. It may be that more volunteers could be attracted to help with buildings and grounds. Certain projects might be handled by special groups, such as teens or retired members. Perhaps more projects could be completed within the budgeted amount. Questions need to be asked about such matters; they don't get asked if the operations and goals for the next period are not discussed. Note that the program leader presented no information needed to evaluate the current and future situations. In some churches no data means no money. Second, the need for a new roof and repaving was never established, and the amounts involved were just rough estimates. For such items the program leader should prove the need and obtain detailed estimates by licensed contractors. Third, for such major work, the finance committee should not give such freedom of choice concerning the use of the funds. Although there are only two choices involved, there's a hint of "Here's the money, do what you want with it." Fourth, if $40,000 is really needed for a new roof, the $30,000 allocated is insufficient to do a quality job. The church might be better off by waiting a year or two to obtain the necessary roof.)

The program leader of the music committee requests a 10 percent increase over the current year's amount. The request includes $1,000 for music books, $750 for organ repairs, $500 for podiums, $2,000 for new instruments, and $30,000 for miscellaneous items related to committee activities. "Approved," says the committee.

> (First, to recapitulate, the committee needs data on current activities to determine if this year is going satisfactorily. Also, the next period's expenditures must be justified. Why new books? What's wrong with the organ? Why new podiums and instruments? Second, "miscellaneous" should be the smallest of all items requested, not the largest. Obviously this amount needs to be questioned.)

The financial secretary then submits a report on the acquisition of a small business computer to handle the church's accounting needs. She had been asked to prepare the report by the finance committee. She concludes that the church needs to spend about $10,000 for a computer and related software programs. Her analysis of the currently available computers and computer programs is very thorough. "Thank you for the report," says a member of the finance committee, "but that's a lot of money for a computer. For the moment let's shelve the report. In the interim we can appeal to the congregation for a donated computer."

> (There are several mistakes in planning and budgeting here. First of all, if someone has taken the time to prepare a report for the meeting, the report should be reviewed, as a courtesy to the preparer. If reports get used the committee will receive more reports. If they are quickly discarded, few people will go to the trouble of preparing them. Second, getting a donated computer may be exactly what is not needed. Looking to the congregation for a computer may take the decision out of the hands of the finance committee. Donations are great, as long as the item acquired is what is needed. Using unsuitable computers, typewriters, photocopiers, vans, station wagons, and so on, because they are donated may actually turn out to be a waste of resources.)

At this point a member of the finance committee has second thoughts about the allocations of funds to the buildings and grounds committee and the music committee. "Don't get me wrong. I'm all in favor of maintaining our facilities and enhancing our great music program. But shouldn't we first consider the amount of funds we will have available next year before we start to divide it up among the various programs? I think we have put the carriage in front of the horse." "Possibly so," says another member, "but this congregation has always supported the programs approved by this committee. Don't worry, the Lord will provide." "I guess I was out of order," says the questioning member. "Forget my comments."

(Actually the questioning member is making a valid point. Each church has a limited amount of resources with which to work. To maximize the possibility of success, those resources should be directed toward predetermined goals and objectives. You need to know the amount of resources available before becoming committed to various programs, some of which may turn out to have long-term high-budget needs.)

The next budget request comes from the program leader of the Christian education committee. The request is well documented with data, and justifications are provided for all increases. But the committee continues to request funding for a preschool program that has been funded for several years but has never been started. The committee believes that continued funding will encourage someone to finally do something. "Sounds reasonable," says the finance committee. "Approved."

(Funding a nonexistent program is dangerous. For one thing, there are no assurances that the program is needed. It has been funded before and nothing happened. There's a message there. Further, why should a program be funded before its mission and goals have been approved? Also, the existence of this budgeted amount may cause the committee to think of this money as a reserve fund in case other educational projects are over budget. The Christian education committee could get sloppy. Additionally, funding of a nonexistent program will not be overlooked by the other program leaders. If they are short of funds later in the year, astute leaders will request that the unused funds in the preschool program be spent in their areas. Endless debates could occur at each future meeting of the finance committee.)

The next request comes from Susan Hubbard, who wants to do something for the elderly members of the community. She's vague on exactly what to do, how to do it, and how much it will cost. More than anything else, she wants the church to take a position on the matter by earmarking $950 for the program. "You've got it, Susan," voices the committee.

(Although Susan Hubbard is probably a fine person, she simply does not have a program yet. One approach is to tell her that she needs to talk with others and develop a clear-cut program of assistance, together with monetary needs and program goals, and present this at a future meeting of the committee. An alternative might be to allocate a nominal amount of seed money for her to investigate the need for a program. She may incur expenses for long-distance telephone calls, postage, or local travel in the preparation of a proposal. On the one hand, you don't want to discourage new ideas for programs. On the other hand, you cannot use the church's limited resources without expecting specific results.)

The worship committee is requesting a sizable increase in its budget for next year. Its leader is convinced that a new computerized telephone reminder system will secure a 90 percent attendance of all members at weekly worship services, up from 45 percent this year. "Approved; great idea."

(One problem here is unrealistic expectations. Churches having normal attendance of less than 50 percent of members would need the proverbial miracle to double attendance in a year, regardless of what was done. Rather than fund a standard that cannot be attained and doom the group to failure, it would be more realistic to have the group commit to lower expectations, say 60 percent. Another problem may be the incongruity of goals between the worship and stewardship committees. If people are coerced over the telephone to attend church, weekly donations could actually decrease.)

At this point in the meeting, a request is heard to make a special gift to a state university that has a museum of church artifacts. "Great school, great basketball team, great museum," note several members of the finance committee, "but do we have the responsibility of funding a state university?" "That's a thought," says one member, "but the museum relates to us, and we should show our support." "Well, okay, it's only a small amount. Approved."

(The problem here is that no one is quite sure if making the special gift is an appropriate use of church funds. Essentially the members of the committee are searching for directives to guide their action. If none are available they are on their own. Several odd proposals are likely to be brought before the finance committee each year. Without specific goals and objectives to refer to, some of these requests could be funded inappropriately.)

Youth programs are handled by Tony Smith, a nice guy who is not terribly effective. Parental support and youth involvement have decreased in recent years because of his lack of leadership. He asks for a 5 percent increase over this year's budget for new activities, which "will create great interest." Everyone knows that it won't help, but the request is approved.

(The finance committee just knowingly committed itself to wasting some of the church's valuable resources. A change in program leadership is needed, an unpleasant thought in most churches. But those churches addressing this issue will have more resources for other purposes.)

Time is running short, but Les Sullivan, from the finance committee, interjects that interest rates on bank certificates of deposit (CDs) are near an all-time high. "Why not put some of our funds in CDs and earn some interest for the future? How are we ever going to build a parsonage if we don't save any money? How about the purchase of the adjoining land for a larger parking area? How about future generations of members? I'm afraid that by approving all of the requests, however worthy, we are draining the church of its resources. As a conservative person, I think we should invest $50,000 in CDs to ensure the future of the church."

"You have a point there, Les. I think we should scale back all of the approved requests by 10 percent and more critically evaluate the several other proposals yet to be discussed," notes the chairperson. "All agreed? Yes? Great. Did all of the program leaders hear that? Tony had to leave? I'll tell him on Sunday."

"Moving on, the next committee is missions . . . ."


## PLANNING: THE BIRTHPLACE OF SPECIFIC, MEASURABLE GOALS AND OBJECTIVES

Many churches unfortunately skip the planning phase of the accounting and financial reporting process. Many of the problems at St. Chaos related to poor planning and a consequent lack of clear-cut goals and objectives. The finance committee of St. Chaos was simply not ready to allocate the church's resources among programs. They didn't know where they were headed or how they were going to get there. An analogy may be helpful.

Assume that you visit the corporate headquarters of XYZ Company, a manufacturer of chemicals and other products, to question employees on the firm's goals and objectives. During the course of your investigation of various departments, you hear many comments on the need to increase sales, cut costs, increase productivity, advertise more effectively, increase market share, and so on. But on closer inspection you find that all of these comments relate to the objective of increasing the profits of the firm. Rightly or wrongly, employees are promoted, laid off, retired early, or fired based on how they contribute (or fail to contribute) to the "bottom line." That's the way it is. Few persons working for profit-seeking businesses fail to grasp the key business objective. The capitalist system efficiently focuses the attention of all personnel on a common, measurable objective.

In nonprofit organizations, churches included, no such common focus exists. Thus each organization must force itself to spend time in planning and, as an outgrowth, developing its own goals and objectives to guide its every action. Then programs can be developed to achieve these goals and objectives. Without adequate planning and the fruits of planning, you can easily slide into a situation like the one illustrated by St. Chaos. For example, in a recent "Church Accounting" seminar, I asked all attendees (treasurers, financial secretaries, pastors, assistant pastors, board members, and so on) to list the five main goals and objectives of their churches in decreasing order of priority. Several people laughed. Several people leaned over to see what their friends had written. Several people thought it an appropriate time to go to the restroom or have a cigarette. Those few who were mentally committed to the task had great difficulty beyond the first few goals. After several minutes we shared the results of the exercise by discussing the lists. Typically, the initial goal and objective related to the continued belief and support of Christian principles, including the Bible as the word of God. Beyond that the responses became more scattered and were often expressed as generalized activities such as evangelism, youth activities, helping the elderly, or membership growth. Further, even when five goals and objectives were given, few attendees could establish priorities for their lists. Comments such as, "They are all important" were common. Yet, faced with limited resources, church officials need to handle high-priority objectives before low-level ones. Not a single objective discussed at this seminar was measurable. The answers implied that merely having activities that addressed social concerns was the measure of success. Yet addressing problems can be quite different from achieving results.

Without proper planning, goals are dreams, objectives are hazy, programs are vague, priorities are confused, and evaluation of results is impossible. In such an environment accounting is relegated to the role of making sure that any funds spent are accounted for properly, not that the funds are spent wisely.

As Kennon Callahan notes in *Twelve Keys to an Effective Church,*

> Indeed, the first and most central characteristic of an effective, successful church is its specific, concrete, missional objectives. . . . "Specific" refers to the fact that the local congregation has focused its missional outreach on a particular human hurt and hope—for example, by being in mission with alcoholics and their families, with homebound elderly, or with epileptics and their families. Missional outreach is not best accomplished by developing a purpose statement or some generalized approach to a given age group in the surrounding area. Nor is mission best accomplished by the church seeking to engage in helping everyone with everything. The church that does that ends up helping no one with anything. . . . Objectives refers to missional direction stated in a sufficiently clear fashion that it is possible to know when they have been achieved. . . . The local congregation that is effective . . . has moved forward toward the substantial accomplishment and achievement of very clear, intentional goals. The effective congregation is not engaged in wishful thinking with a generalized purpose or goal statement that just lists its sentiments to do something noble, worthwhile, and helpful.[2]

Operating as they do in the nonprofit sector, and with possibly a large cadre of volunteers who need focus, it is imperative that churches receive the direction that results from planning and that is defined by:

identifying needs

stating goals—statement of intent, general purpose, or broad direction

stating objectives—the desired ends that are to be achieved in a specific period of time

being specific (as opposed to generalizing)

establishing priorities

being able to evaluate progress toward reaching goals and objectives

considering both short-term and long-term perspectives

---

[2] Kennon L. Callahan, *Twelve Keys to an Effective Church* (San Francisco: Harper & Row, Publishers, 1983), 1, 2.

## Evaluation of Progress

Because churches do not deal in tangible products or services, evaluating the progress of churches in achieving their objectives is not an easy task. What is the value of a worship service enhanced by beautiful choral music, the value of pastoral counseling to a teenager in difficulty, or the value of a summer Bible camp? Yet we cannot sidestep the difficulty of measurement by claiming that all of the church's programs must be effective because members' contributions have steadily increased. After all, contributions may have been received from people who attended just a few services, or perhaps the church just happens to be located in the path of growth and would show increased revenue regardless of its programs.

As evaluation of progress is necessary, and as direct measurement of value from church programs cannot be easily accomplished, a substitute, or surrogate, must be employed. Using surrogates for performance indicators is not perfect, but it's far superior to no evaluation. Surrogates need to be identified by each program leader and discussed with the finance committee at the time of funding. Surrogates for evaluating program success could include, for example, attendance at the summer Bible camp, worship services, Sunday school, preschool, Bible study programs, or picnics. Or it could be that the number of classes in Sunday school and other educational activities is a superior surrogate for measuring success. The surrogate could be expressed as a percentage of the membership rather than as absolute numbers, such as attracting a certain percentage of the members to nonholiday worship services or to Bible classes. Surrogates can also be used to spur on those persons involved with community relations and publicity to, for instance, increase the number of column inches given to those activities in the local press. The surrogate selected should be the one that best measures the program activity being evaluated. Only your imagination will limit the development of appropriate surrogates.

Sometimes, however, even commonly used indicators of success must be employed carefully. For example, percentage of active membership at worship services is often used to measure the success of the worship program. Yet congregations facing changes in pastors during the year might find that such a surrogate is an unsatisfactory indicator until the new pastor assumes full control.

Some activities and programs of the church may not lend themselves to this type of evaluation. Some of the activities of the pastor and the office staff could fall into these categories. Rather than inventing a contrived surrogate, it is more realistic to recognize that such unmeasurable areas exist. In such cases obtaining a clear statement of goals and objectives for the activities is the best that can be achieved.

## Long-Range Planning

Most churches are geared to establishing their plans and allocating resources for a specific calendar year or fiscal year. Almost as important is to plan even further into the future. Churches must be constantly alert to changing conditions that may alter their goals, objectives, and programs. Without such a perspective they may find themselves in financial difficulty. For instance, many inner city churches failed to recognize soon enough that their constituency was changing and income sources were eroding. As a consequence some activities were carried on when they could have been dropped or scaled back. Today a large percentage of inner city churches are operating at a loss and are being bailed out by income on their investments and their denomination's central organization. Long-term planning might have helped to alleviate some of the pain of change in these situations.

Other churches are more fortunate to be in the path of growth. But here too, valuable resources and opportunities can be squandered without adequate long-term planning. For example, one Texas city had its population grow from 72,000 to 175,000 in eight years, thanks in large part to the mid-1970s national oil shortage. Churches serving a hundred or so members in the rural outskirts of the city were quickly transformed into churches that needed to serve thousands in the bustling suburban housing tracts. Those churches that had done their long-term planning by acquiring sufficient land for buildings and parking and that had always built with future expansion in mind thrived. Some who were not prepared for the growth, those who had bought and built small, found themselves continually modifying one thing or another to make do. One congregation even decided to sell their church and start all over again about ten miles away—in the rural outskirts of the city.

All churches need some sort of long-term planning. One way churches can avoid the unexpected is to prepare a five-year, continuous master plan. The plan is continuous in that a new year is added as the current year is completed. A continuous five-year plan offers the advantage of forcing church officials to continually think about the future. Using this approach, preparation of a five-year plan is not just done one year for the following five-year period, but becomes an ongoing, stabilized activity.

There is no one correct way to prepare a five-year plan. The plan should, however, identify 1) the needs to be served in the future and how those differ from the needs of the current situation, 2) the goals, objectives, and programs (including building and capital improvement programs) that are likely to be needed, and 3) the anticipated sources of income necessary to carry out the programs over the five-year period. Such a plan would enable the church to develop a long-term fundraising strategy, which could help generate the momentum necessary for increased contributions. When planning and thinking are oriented toward one-year programs and fundraising efforts, this kind of momentum never has the chance to develop.

Churches need to plan for both the short term and the long term. Planning is the prerequisite and basis for budgeting. Preparation of the annual church budget without the benefit of proper planning makes the budget a less valuable tool in guiding church affairs. Preparation of the annual church budget with proper planning makes the budget a vital link in the church's quest to reach its goals and objectives.

## BUDGETING

If done correctly, budgeting is a time-consuming and arduous process. An in-depth look at the future requires numerous assumptions, much uncertainty, and often considerable cooperation and compromise among people. Furthermore, participants must frequently turn their thoughts away from pressing personal and business problems to devote full attention to the budget effort. With all these unattractive features, the question arises, Why budget? For the vast number of churches, the benefits of sound budgeting outweigh the associated problems.

There are ten reasons why budgeting is important for churches.

1. *Formalizes planning.* As already discussed in this chapter, budgets are an outgrowth of the planning process. Budgets force people to study the future so that they can develop a formal plan. To get an idea of the benefits of a plan, imagine building a church parsonage without architectural drawings. Walls may be plastered or encased in plasterboard, and then you discover that electrical outlets and heating vents were forgotten. Or the foundation may be laid and then you find that it's over the property line. The building process would be chaotic at best. Similarly, the lack of a formal plan leads to considerable "fire fighting" on the part of management, thereby hampering the church's attainment of long-run goals and objectives.

   With a budget churches can anticipate potential problems and introduce preventive or corrective action. In this manner the operations of the church can be continued without distraction. The eventual outcome of planning is a direction-oriented church program that is achieving its goals and objectives.

2. *Reduces emotion-charged discussions.* Churches operating without budgets (or with budgets that are known to be very flexible) are

prone to spend their money erratically. Emotional pleas for special, extra, once-in-a-lifetime funds will be heard each month by the finance committee. Members of the committee will either have to approve the expenditure of funds, thereby reducing funds needed for other programs, or deny the request, an often emotional act causing misunderstandings and hurt feelings. Churches having heated monthly battles about spending their money should take a serious look at their resource allocation systems.

With a firm one-year operating budget, programs and activities are funded prior to the start of a calendar or fiscal year, and program directors are expected to live within their budgets for the period. Truly exceptional circumstances may dictate a reexamination of a program allocation, but that should be rare. As a consequence monthly meetings of the finance committee can be devoted to determining if the church is progressing toward its goals and objectives and if the financial situation is as anticipated. One church treasurer noted that, "A good budget means that eleven acts of war can be eliminated, because one battle is substituted for twelve skirmishes."

3. *Is a basis for performance evaluation.* If church officials are to have insight regarding the church's progress toward its goals and objectives, continual evaluation of programs is necessary. Performance evaluation commonly involves the preparation of a financial report in which budgeted amounts are compared with actual amounts. Variances, or deviations from the budget, are often separately noted. Thus budgets provide a foundation for the evaluation of programs. Keep in mind, however, that such an analysis only compares dollars budgeted versus dollars spent; it does not show if the dollars were spent wisely. Using surrogate measures of success, as discussed earlier, program expectations must be contrasted with program results at that same time.

Performance should be measured against a budget for the same period. Although the budget relies on numerous assumptions, the finance committee can adequately appraise performance if care has been exercised in the formulation of the budget and if all available information is considered.

4. *Is a basis for control.* By using budgets to evaluate performance, control can be exercised. If variances from the budget—either under or over budget—are out of line, inquiries can be made and corrective action can be taken. Corrective action may be in the form of seeking additional contributions, cutting costs, or changing personnel. Such control helps the church keep on target in terms of

achieving the original plan. Control not only assists in eliminating deviations from budgets, but it also renders valuable perspectives for the next round of the planning process. By closely monitoring church operations, members of the finance committee get a better feel of the church's business affairs, which, in turn, leads to more effective management.

5. *Assists in communication and coordination.* A church is involved in many diverse activities. These activities are handled by many different committees and leaders. The budget process serves as a gigantic blender to communicate, integrate, and coordinate all of these activities to achieve the church's goals and objectives. Obviously, in any process where different views are represented, there must be some compromise to achieve a successful result. If each activity or program attempted to satisfy its own objectives regardless of its impact on others, the church would suffer continuous infighting and poor overall performance. The process of establishing a budget allows the communication that is necessary for compromise.

6. *Gets members involved.* As will be discussed in greater detail in a later section, budgeting should involve as many members of the congregation as possible. By getting members to share their ideas, thoughts, opinions, and dreams about what activities and programs the church should sponsor, you improve the chances for program success. Comments such as, "It's their program" will turn into, "It's our program."

7. *Increases the commitment to giving.* When people have participated in the formulation of the budget, they are more apt to make sure that the budgeted results occur. Stated differently, the stewardship commitment increases with the amount of involvement in the planning and budgeting process. This point is often missed in churches that have highly centralized budgeting approaches. Involved, committed members are much more likely to contribute than are members who are kept distant from the financial affairs but then asked to contribute.

8. *Generates confidence in the church's leadership.* Picture the situation over at St. Chaos. Without goals and objectives, the budgeting process was a travesty. Operating in such a financial climate, the clergy and top-level lay leaders would need special divine guidance to have successful programs. Their jobs are made harder by a defective planning and budgeting process. Alternatively, when both long-term and short-term goals and objectives are prepared and sound budgets are established and followed, programs are

more likely to be successful. In such an environment calls by the leadership for greater participation, changes, new missions, special donations, and so on, tend to be taken seriously.

9. *Allows for continued operation when cash receipts and disbursements are mismatched.* Many churches have a cash flow situation in which excess funds are available to the church for several months of the year, but the excess must be retained to cover the fixed costs of operating the church during the summer months, when attendance and giving are traditionally lower. Without appropriate budgeting, excess funds could be committed by a finance committee after hearing an emotionally charged plea for funds. Summer bills may go unpaid; summer programs may be suspended. Thus budgeting helps those churches having mismatched inflows and outflows of cash.

10. *Allows time to lend or borrow prudently.* A church's annual operating budget may show a cash deficit or surplus. If the deficit, for example, cannot be eliminated with the church's assets, the church must borrow. Churches often can obtain funds from their regional or national denominational offices. Some churches borrow at a bank. Either way, budgets help to pinpoint how much money is needed and when it is needed. The situation of having a surplus of funds is more pleasant. But here too, the budget allows the church to determine the appropriate investment vehicle to balance return and risk. Without proper time to plan investments, the church is not likely to get the best return or understand all of the risks involved.

You can see that it is vitally important that a church prepare a budget and use it to guide its operations. Failure to recognize the importance of budgeting has caused churches to experience severe financial distress. This failure may even contribute to a church's demise.

### The Name of the Committee

Even in our casual American society, a title carries an air of power, prestige, and responsibility. Organizational leaders are expected to carry themselves with a certain dignity and provide thoughtful, measured decisions. Lower level personnel, on the other hand, can get away with being more pragmatic and impulsive. Recognize, however, that it usually takes leaders years of training and experience to develop full understanding of their organizations and of their roles and responsibilities in them.

No such training tends to accompany the selection of people asked to serve on the committee that allocates church resources through the budgeting process. Whether the group is called the budget committee, administrative committee, board of directors, finance committee, or something else, people are typically selected on the basis of their willingness to serve and their business acumen. No training is required; no certification is necessary. As a consequence members of these committees often do not know how to carry out their responsibilities. Thus, using common sense, members of a budget committee, for example, will unilaterally determine that their job is to budget. But no one tells them exactly how to budget. Similarly, members of a finance committee will determine that their job is to monitor the church's financial situation. But, again, no one tells them precisely how to monitor the financial situation. An analogy to this process is the placement of an individual in the middle of a game with which he or she is not familiar. You may have had similar experiences yourself when joining a ball game or a card game. Remember the uncertainty you felt before someone made the rules clear to you? You may have even held up play until you were satisfied that you wouldn't make a mistake. Picture the situation if no one in the game really knew the rules, and your requests for information were met with silence, stares, and shrugged shoulders. Unfortunately many church financial committees operate just that way.

Committees who don't know how to carry out their responsibilities cause some interesting outcomes. For example, some finance committees believe that their only job is to check on the activities of the financial secretary or treasurer. They demand extensive monthly financial reports, sometimes as long as twenty pages, which provide breakdowns of all revenues and expenses, by program or budget unit, in dollars and cents. They believe that their responsibility is to make certain that all moneys are accounted for and in the proper accounts. I offer my sympathy to those financial secretaries and treasurers working for such groups. Obviously such finance committees need to become redirected and to start monitoring the performance of the church in meeting its goals and objectives via the receipt and spending of money.

Another common occurrence involves the transformation of aggressive businesspeople who serve on resource allocation committees. Successful local businesspeople are often appointed to the finance committee because tough decisions need to be made. After all, in these situations could anyone function better than a businessperson, who routinely makes tough decisions? Unfortunately no one considers that, as discussed, the profit sector is clearly focused on goals and objectives related to achieving a large profit, whereas the nonprofit sector has no such built-in focus. Hence businesspeople often find 1) that the church has no stated long-term or short-term goals and objectives, 2) that success in programs is either not measured or hard to measure, and 3) that the process of selecting among human needs programs is more emotional than selecting new lines of merchandise. When this occurs a businessperson can quickly change from an action-oriented, hard-nosed decision maker into an extremely accommodating person who can't wait to finish out the term. The transformation occurs because no guidance is provided as to how the committee's responsibilities should be carried out. And rather than rock the boat in the church and community, a businessperson will keep a low profile.

I have concluded that it does make a difference what the finance committee or its equivalent is called. You *can* give guidance through a name. By labeling the committee the finance and program evaluation committee, for example, you provide members of the committee with a perspective that might not occur to them. You want more than programs, more than allocating funds, more than a periodic monitoring of dollars spent. You want all programs continuously evaluated to make sure that their objectives are being met. After all, only successful programs will permit the church to reach its goals and objectives. The name change, therefore, is not merely cosmetic. Real changes could result. Exhibit 2-1 portrays the role of the finance and program evaluation committee.

Some churches separate the duties of resource allocation/finance from program evaluation. This division is satisfactory as long as both functions are being performed, and both groups are kept well informed. For instance, if a program is considered unsuccessful in one year, the program evaluation committee should advise the finance committee to reduce, eliminate, or maintain next year's appropriation of funds. I am more concerned that many churches never evaluate the programs that have been funded. If changing the name of a committee helps, it's a small price to pay for the additional direction. If program evaluation is part of the committee's name, indicating that it is part of the committee's responsibility, perhaps members who have hounded the financial secretary and treasurer for accounting data to audit will begin to see the light. Similarly, businesspeople serving on such a committee will find evaluation to their liking, because it provides a focus previously not present.

One final thought on this topic is in order. Because a finance and program evaluation committee is likely to take a broader view than a typical finance committee would, its composition needs to be thoroughly considered. Selecting members for this committee in the traditional manner may exclude certain segments of the church that should be involved in the evaluation of programs. Having all bankers, merchants, and CPAs on such a committee, for instance, may be satisfactory

**Prior to the Budget Period**
Review requests for funds
Review program goals and objectives
Evaluate the consistency between program and church goals and objectives
Determine methods of measuring performance

**During the Budget Period (Monthly or Quarterly)**
Compare interim dollar results against budgeted expectations
Evaluate program performance
Recommend ways to improve program results

**At the Conclusion of the Budget Period**
Compare total dollar results against budgeted expectations
Evaluate program performance for the full period
Report on program performance to next year's committee—recommend changes in budget amounts, program goals and objectives, methods of measuring performance or program leadership, and so on

Exhibit 2-1 The Role of the Finance and Program Evaluation Committee

when discussing financial issues, but unsatisfactory when discussing churchwide program issues.

**Budget Flows**

Budgets can be prepared in two directions: top down or bottom up. Each direction has important advantages and disadvantages.

*Top-Down Approach*

With the top-down approach virtually all budget development takes place at the upper echelons of the church, usually by a committee handpicked by church leaders. The budget is imposed on all members of the church, who rarely become involved in the construction process. The congregation may be asked to vote on and approve the budget, but time for discussion is purposely kept short, answers to questions may be sketchy, and the motion and second to adopt the budget are quick. On paper the top-down approach offers the advantage of sound budget preparation, reflecting all of the overall goals of the church. Preparation in this instance is carried out by those who have the best view of church operations, that is, the church leadership. Further, this approach is efficient for both budget preparers and other church members. Preparers save months by not having to sort through diverse ideas from the membership, and other church members are spared the difficulty of coping with financial information and reports.

But in most cases these apparent advantages give rise to a significant problem. When the budget is imposed from above, people not involved in the budgeting process often feel bad because their opinions and perspectives were not solicited. Although those in the general membership are asked to support the budget with their contributions, they are not asked to contribute their ideas. As discussed earlier in this chapter, obtaining members' involvement and financial support may be difficult. Those program leaders whose activities will be evaluated against the budget may also be upset. As a consequence, this approach generally is met with resentment or the feeling that the budget is the property of the finance committee, neither of which bode well for budget achievement.

### Bottom-Up Approach

Unlike the top-down approach, bottom-up budgeting centers on broad-based participation in the development process. Standing committees are asked to prepare their own budgets. Ideas for new programs are solicited and budgets are prepared. Office personnel are asked to submit their requests for new equipment and operating supplies. Teachers are asked to think about their needs and submit requests. Clergy is similarly involved, as the amounts for housing, transportation, secretarial assistance, and other operating expenses need to be anticipated. The idea in the bottom-up approach is to get as many people involved in the budgeting process as possible.

The bottom-up approach usually begins with the issuance of general budget guidelines, including the due dates, by church leaders or the finance and program evaluation committee (or equivalent). Written budgets and requests for funds, prepared by many different people, go to the finance and program evaluation committee for review. This group thoroughly reviews the needs for funds and invites the people and committees seeking funds to present in person their budget/request and goals and to answer questions. Sessions are businesslike but friendly, and open to all. Budgets/requests are accepted, rejected, or modified by this group. The rationale for any modifications or rejections is clearly stated by the committee and understood by all in attendance. In this environment members could leave disappointed because their favorite program was not fully funded or not funded at all, but they will not leave angry because they were not heard. In its deliberations the committee constantly points out that it must carry out its responsibility to the church as a whole, not to individual programs, activities, or people.

The bottom-up approach is not 100 percent bottom up; there is some direction and coordination from above. Nevertheless, the bottom-up approach offers several distinct advantages over a budget that is handed down from above with a "here it is, meet it" attitude. First, bottom-up, participative budgets are really self-imposed. By consulting with and incorporating the opinions of a large number of members, greater strides are made toward budget achievement. In other words, individual members know that their views are valued by church leaders and others. Morale and satisfaction are greater with this approach, so extensive efforts are made to meet budgeted targets. Second, the budget is constructed by people who are close to the action and who know the ins and outs of programs and activities. The same cannot be said for a budget that is prepared solely by a select group of church officials. The bottom-up approach usually results in more realistic goals.

But the bottom-up approach is more time consuming and cumbersome to administer than the top-down approach, because of increased member involvement. Despite these problems participative budgeting is an effective tool among progressively administered churches. Because the broad perspectives of church leaders are used in conjunction with the detailed operating knowledge of program leaders and others working within the church, a powerful budget is created, one that encompasses the views of all ranges of the church hierarchy and indeed all members.

The participatory approach to budgeting and other church decisions can be carried to an extreme. As Callahan points out,

> The process is participatory whenever it is open and inclusive rather than closed and restricted. That does not mean to suggest that every person in a congregation should be forced to participate in every decision that needs to be made in that congregation. There existed some years ago a fad for total consensus for every decision. Pastors and key leaders of congregations should disabuse themselves of the notion that everyone in the congregation should be included in every decision—or that everyone in that local congregation even wants to be included in every decision. In fact, most people do not. Rather, they want the sense of openness and inclusiveness that makes it easy for them to share their own judgment and wisdom on a given matter if they want to do so.[3]

---

[3] Callahan, *Twelve Keys*, 56–57.

At this juncture let's put your understanding of budget flow approaches to the test by referring to the information for First Church:

### First Church

First Church operates on a calendar-year basis. It begins the annual budgeting process in late August, when the budget committee, composed of key church leaders, establishes targets for total contributions and expenditures for the next year. Built into the targets is an increase in the church's bank savings account desired by leaders to cover any contingencies.

The stewardship committee is given the target for contributions and is expected to devise methods for achieving the goal. On the expenditure side, budgets for all programs, activities, and functions are developed with the targets of the budget committee kept in mind.

None of the areas has achieved its budget in recent years. Contributions typically do not meet the target. When that occurs each area is expected to cut costs so that the savings objective can still be met. But the church can rarely increase its savings account, because the revenues have already been spent, are in the process of being spent, or cannot be cut. In fact, many costs are higher than the original budget, and the church usually has to draw on its dwindling bank account to get through the year. Church leaders, disturbed that First Church has not been able to meet its targets, is thinking of hiring a cost control consultant to rectify the problem.

In analyzing the situation at First Church, consider first how the budgeting process employed by the church contributes to its failure to meet the targets. The budget at First Church is a top-down budget, which fails to consider the need for realistic data and the human interaction essential to an effective budgeting/control process. True participation in the preparation of the budget is minimal, limited to a mechanical gathering and manipulation of data. This suggests that there will be little enthusiasm for attaining the budget.

Leaders at First Church do not provide any basis for their targets, so no one knows whether the targets are realistic. But the targets anticipate a small surplus and the church repeatedly expends more than anticipated, so perhaps the targets are unrealistic. Perhaps there is a genuine long-term financial imbalance. The church may need external assistance more immediately with fundraising, not with cost control. On the other hand, the programs that continually spend more than their budget, unless the budgets are too low, are candidates for a cost review.

What should First Church do? First Church should consider the adoption of a bottom-up budget approach. This means that all people responsible for performance under the budget would participate in the decisions by which the budget is established. Such participation includes setting targets. Although time consuming, the approach should produce a more acceptable, effective goal/control mechanism. This involvement encourages "ownership" of the budget and a cooperative attitude throughout the budget period. The budget becomes self-imposed, not imposed by others. The dynamics involved in all members working toward common goals will greatly enhance the church's ability to meet its targets.

## Budget Approaches

Three approaches to the preparation of the church's annual operating budget are 1) incremental budgeting, 2) program budgeting, and 3) zero-base budgeting.

### Incremental Budgeting

Incremental budgeting, often called line item budgeting or traditional budgeting, is based on the age-old question, How much did it cost last year? Most churches follow this budgeting approach. Incremental budgeting takes this year's budget as the basis for next year's budget and makes adjustments for anticipated cost or activity changes. For example, assume that the Bible school served the needs of 100 children this year at a cost of $1,000 ($10 per child). Further assume that the Bible school anticipates serving 125 children next year and, because of inflation, the cost per student will rise to $11. Using the incremental approach, next year's budget for the Bible school will be $1,375 (125 × $11). Incremental budgeting gets its name from the fact that the budget changes incrementally from year to year. An abbreviated hypothetical example of an incremental budget is presented in exhibit 2-2.

The incremental approach has several points in its favor. For a preparer, it is an easy one with which to work. For a user, it is easy to understand. These twin advantages are important to many churches, especially small ones. But the approach has two serious inherent flaws. One problem is that the budgeted amount is almost automatic—that is, you take the past and adjust for the future. Little attempt is made to judge operating efficiencies by analyzing prior activities and costs. It is therefore conceivable that a church could be continuing its ineffective and inefficient ways from one year to the next and, curiously, be willing to pay more and more money to do so. Ineffective practices could be perpetuated. Stated differently, the incremental approach presumes that the church is already spending all of its money wisely and that no improvements are necessary for next year. This presumption, however, is never critically examined. The second problem is that the approach

## Proposed Expenditures Budget for the Year 19X2

|  | 19X1 | 19X2 |
|---|---|---|
| **Salaries** | | |
| Pastor | $18,000 | $19,000 |
| Youth director—part-time | 2,000 | 2,000 |
| Church secretary | 9,000 | 8,800 |
| Financial secretary | 4,000 | 4,200 |
| Janitor | 6,000 | 6,200 |
|  | $39,000 | $40,200 |
| **Operating Expenses** | | |
| Utilities | $ 5,000 | $ 6,000 |
| Insurance | 2,000 | 3,000 |
| Office supplies | 500 | 600 |
| Postage | 750 | 1,000 |
| Continuing education | 800 | 1,000 |
| Automobile expense—pastor | 1,500 | 1,200 |
| Computer—new | | 4,000 |
| Flowers | 400 | 500 |
| Maintenance supplies | 800 | 900 |
| Miscellaneous expenses | 150 | 250 |
| Bus expenses | 1,500 | 2,500 |
|  | $13,400 | $20,950 |
| **Christian Education** | | |
| Literature | $ 4,000 | $ 3,500 |
| Bible school | 1,000 | 1,475 |
| Library | 300 | 300 |
| Refreshments | 1,000 | 1,100 |
| Miscellaneous expenses | 400 | 500 |
|  | $ 6,700 | $ 6,875 |
| **Youth** | | |
| Retreats—spring and fall | $    500 | $    600 |
| Juniors' Convention in Laramie | 400 | 400 |
| Teen club | 200 | 1,000 |
|  | $ 1,100 | $ 2,000 |
| **Music** | | |
| Music materials | $ 2,000 | $ 2,300 |
| Robes | 400 | |
| Piano repairs | 100 | 150 |
| Organ repairs | 200 | 1,000 |
|  | $ 2,700 | $ 3,450 |
| **Missions** | | |
| Foreign missions | $ 1,000 | $ 1,300 |
| Galt Orphanage | 3,500 | 5,000 |
|  | $ 4,500 | $ 6,300 |
| Total | $67,400 | $79,775 |

Exhibit 2-2   Our Lady of the Mountains, Denver, Colorado

relies on the past, which cannot be changed, rather than the future, which can be changed.

A problem associated with incremental budgeting is that preparers and users often fail to consider that there are several kinds of costs that behave differently in different churches under different circumstances. Variable costs vary in direct proportion to a change in the amount of activity. Examples of variable costs are the cost of literature per student in Bible school and the pastor's use of automobile fuel. More students and more miles driven would translate into higher costs. Fixed costs do not change over the year, possibly because they are the result of previous commitments. Examples are insurance and salaries. Mixed costs, such as those for utilities and telephone service, contain both variable and fixed elements. For example, there may be a fixed monthly charge for utilities plus a certain number of cents per kilowatt hour. Further, the rate per kilowatt hour is likely to rise dramatically with increased use, because state utility commissions want to discourage extravagant consumption of energy. Understanding the mixed cost nature of utility costs may cause some churches to redistribute the costs to programs based upon usage. Finally, step costs tend to increase in chunks. For instance, a new classroom teacher needed in the early childhood school program would cause the education budget to increase by the full amount of the salary. As a consequence of understanding the behavior of costs, churches may be able to accomplish more with no additional costs or 40 percent more activities with a 10 percent budget increase or 10 percent more activities with a 40 percent budget increase. It all depends on the church and how its costs will behave with the change in activity level. Thus churches looking only at the rate of inflation on items to get from one year's budget to the next are financially naive.

### Program Budgeting

As we have discussed, traditional budgeting focuses on expenditure classifications, such as salaries, materials, and other costs. As a result decision making comes down to increasing, decreasing, or eliminating individual line items. Another approach to preparing the annual church budget is program budgeting. With this approach costs are identified with the specific programs being carried out by the church. Of importance is the fact that each program indicates its goals and objectives prior to funding. Program budgeting operates on the premise that programs operate to achieve certain purposes, and by clearly establishing these purposes the church can improve both the use of its resources and the effectiveness of programs. This approach to budgeting forces the church to do its planning before preparing the budget.

The program-budgeting process begins by requiring the church to identify each program (activity) it conducts and the needs it serves. Next, each program leader examines his or her own program in terms of how well it is achieving its purposes. If improvements are indicated, an assessment of the benefits to the church, as well as the cost implications, is made by the program leader. Finally, an estimate of the resources needed to operate the program for the next year is developed. (Churches using multiyear budgets would have data prepared for a several-year period.) Each program leader then compiles the data into a program budget format that includes a statement on the purpose of the program, a description of the services provided, program goals and objectives, the amount of money needed, and the benefits and costs of any program change requested. In performing this step each program leader receives information on how much of the common costs (costs that are allocated among programs) should be included in his or her budget. The final step involves review by the finance and program evaluation committee, which evaluates the costs and benefits of each program.

The benefits of program budgeting are well documented. First, program budgeting provides a better understanding of what each program is attempting to do. Also, because the purposes of each program are specified, the costs of each program can, at the end of the period, be compared with the benefits achieved. Second, this budgeting approach directs program leaders' attention to program achievement. Remember that traditional budgeting emphasizes the disbursement and control of expenditures, such as those for salaries, utilities, and so on. As a consequence, the purposes of the programs can easily be overlooked. In program budgeting, program purposes and annual goals and objectives are stated up front, so they are not likely to be forgotten when program success is measured.

For church members, program budgeting offers them a clearer picture of what their contributions are supporting, and provides them with numerous opportunities to become involved in the process. Both points can help to generate a higher level of member support for the church's activities.

On the negative side, program budgeting takes considerably longer than incremental budgeting. But the extra time spent is not wasted with trivial matters. It is spent in planning, in establishing measurable goals and objectives and thoroughly evaluating what programs should be and how they should operate. Put differently, incremental budgeting can be done without the planning process discussed earlier in this chapter.

Program budgeting, on the other hand, cannot be done properly without planning.

An example of a program budget prepared for a youth program is shown in exhibit 2-3. Data from Our Lady of the Mountains from exhibit 2-2 is employed and recast into a program-budgeting format. The youth program, of course, is just one church program; budgets need to be prepared for all programs. In reviewing exhibit 2-3, notice that costs charged to the program are 1) direct costs, or costs that are easily traceable to the youth program, such as the salary of the youth director, and 2) indirect costs, such as the pastor's salary, which are spread among several programs, based on estimates of time and usage. So the pastor's salary of $19,000 must be allocated to programs based on the amount of time spent on each program. Therefore if the pastor spends 5 percent of his or her time on youth activities, $950 ($19,000 × 5%) of the pastor's salary is added to the youth budget. Alternatively, if 25 percent of the pastor's time is spent preparing the weekly sermon, 25 percent of his or her salary is attached to the worship program's budget. The operating expenses are similarly divided up among the various programs. For example, if the new computer is used 10 percent of the time on teen activities, $400 ($4,000 × 10%) is attached to the youth budget. Vehicle use, such as use of buses, can be budgeted using estimates of cost per mile. Comparing the budget for youth activities prepared using the incremental approach with that using the program-budgeting approach is revealing. First, the program budget includes a statement on program purpose and measurable goals and objectives, whereas the incremental approach of exhibit 2-2 states nothing about these critical matters. Next, users of the incremental approach are led to believe that the 19×2 budget for youth activities amounts to either the $2,000 total shown in the youth category or $4,000 if the salary of the youth director is included. Using the program approach and by allocating all church costs to programs, it becomes apparent that 19×2's total cost for youth programs amounts to $7,515, a whopping difference. This amount may be more than members of the finance and program evaluation committee want to spend. Further, the program approach directs program leaders to detail the cost of changes made to their programs. In this case increasing the size and scope of the Teen Club would cost the church $1,800. Again, church officials may not want to spend so much money. On the basis of their analysis and review, they may ask that parents of the teenagers cover more of the expenses.

Given the benefits of program budgeting, churches not using this method should give thought to switching. It is superior to the traditional incremental method of budgeting.

**Program Budget for the Year 19X2**

## Youth Program

Purpose:   To involve children of church members and, in some cases, nonmembers in activities at or sponsored by the church.

Objectives:   The program intends to hold two retreats at Camp Lockeford in May and October, serving twenty-five youngsters up to age twelve on each retreat; to select and accompany four high school students to the annual Juniors' Convention in Laramie; and to increase the size of the weekly Teen Club so that it has between eight and twenty members, by introducing computer games and weekend fishing, bowling, and ski trips.

Amount needed:

|  | 19X1 | 19X2 |
|---|---|---|
| Youth director | $2,000 | $2,000 |
| Pastor's time—5 percent est. | 900 | 950 |
| Church secretary's time—5 percent est. | 450 | 440 |
| Janitor's time—5 percent est. | 300 | 310 |
| Utilities—5 percent est. | 250 | 300 |
| Insurance—5 percent est. | 100 | 150 |
| Postage—2 percent est. | 15 | 20 |
| Computer—10 percent est. |  | 400 |
| Maintenance supplies—5 percent est. | 40 | 45 |
| Bus expenses—30 cents per mile | 300 | 900 |
| Retreat expenses | 500 | 600 |
| Juniors' Convention | 400 | 400 |
| Teen Club | 200 | 1,000 |
| Total | $5,455 | $7,515 |

Total funds needed in 19×2 exceed those budgeted in 19×1 by $2,060. Of this amount, $1,800 relates to the planned increase in size and scope of the Teen Club. Details of the additional costs for teen activities are as follows:

| | | |
|---|---|---|
| Computer use | | $  400 |
| Bus use | | 600 |
| Teen Club expenses | | 800 |
| | Total | $1,800 |

**Exhibit 2-3   Our Lady of the Mountains, Denver, Colorado**

### Zero-Base Budgeting

A third budgeting approach, one that has been tried by several large churches, is zero-base budgeting. Unlike the two other approaches, zero-base budgeting does not use last year's information as a starting point in determining this year's budget. Instead, each program leader is asked to start from scratch ($0) in formulating his or her budget, as if the program were beginning anew. This procedure forces program leaders to take an in-depth look at their programs and how they carry out their activities before funding requests can be honored. Nothing is taken for granted. Every aspect of every activity is reviewed to see if it's justified. For example, in zero-base budgeting the director of the preschool program would critically evaluate the need to use a paid teacher and teacher's aide in each of the four rooms used by the school. The director may conclude that a better approach would be to have two larger classes each staffed by a teacher and an aide and use the other two rooms, each staffed by a teacher, for special activities, such as motor development, music, or art. In the process the need for two teacher's aides would be eliminated and higher quality special activities could be provided. Presumably, ineffective methods will be identified and either improved or eliminated in the process. Zero-base budgeting offers the further benefit of participative management, by involving many people in the budget construction process.

The zero-base approach is not without its problems, however. In-depth reviews are time consuming, and the amount of paperwork generated justifying every expenditure can be immense. Critics note that because of these problems, zero-base budgeting should not be attempted every year. Many say once every five years is sufficient. In any case, zero-base budgeting should be used only if the anticipated benefits exceed the cost of implementation. Small churches not involved in many programs beyond worship services, as well as professionally managed churches, may not need this budgeting exercise. Older churches, whose programs and methods of operation may have been carried forth from one generation to another without question, and less-than-efficient churches should consider this budgeting approach.

## The Operating Budget

Whichever budgeting approach or combination of approaches is used, an operating budget for the annual or fiscal year still needs to be constructed. Anticipated inflows of resources need to be matched against anticipated outflows of resources. It is important that the operating budget contain detail on both inflows *and* outflows of resources. This point is often missed by churches, and consequently they do not include inflows of resources in their budgets. For such churches the budget is a detailed list of anticipated expenditures by functional category (salary, utilities, and so on) or by program. The rationale for omitting the inflows of resources has been expressed to me in many ways, including, "The Lord has always provided," "This congregation always digs deeper if necessary," "We don't obtain pledges," "Individual and total pledges are confidential and handled by a committee other than the finance committee," "We solicit and receive only anonymous pledges," and "Pledges are unenforceable." But I believe a church should not commit itself for expenditures, particularly those long term in nature, without having a good handle on the anticipated inflow of resources. Imagine yourself purchasing a home, entailing substantial monthly payments, with the understanding that the money will come from somewhere because it always has. Most of us would not make such a commitment until the funds necessary to pay for it either have been saved or can be realistically anticipated. Those people living a certain way of life without being fairly certain where funds will come from are apt to get into financial difficulty. Some churches have followed this pattern. It is just good common sense that the operating budget should include both anticipated inflows and outflows of resources.

### Budget Estimation

By its nature a budget is a series of future estimates. These estimates should not be arrived at haphazardly. Instead, significant care should be exercised in their determination.

Normally budget estimates are based on both the past and the future. That is, historical information is often a good starting point for prediction. But any changes in the church or its community of members mean that a budget trend may change. As an example, suppose a church is attempting to budget its contributions for the year. Assume that member giving has increased steadily at the rate of 4 percent per year for the past five years. Should economic and membership conditions remain stable, the church would be correct in anticipating a 4 percent increase for the upcoming period. If, however, the town's main employer recently cut its work force by 20 percent or if the church has a new pastor, this factor must be taken into account. In this situation it may be prudent to anticipate no increase in contributions for the upcoming year.

In constructing the yearly operating budget, two kinds of estimation difficulties can surface. In large, well-endowed, growing churches, there is slack. Slack may be introduced in several ways, but typically it is an overstatement of the cost necessary to purchase, for example, a piece of equipment or to operate a program or activity. Thus when the actual expenditure is tabulated and is found to be less than the budgeted amount, no one can criticize the program leader or administrator. In fact, he or she looks like a hero for spending less than the amount budgeted. Slack, therefore, provides some leeway to those who spend the church's money. Slack may permeate the entire budgeting process and can perpetuate itself if people to whom funds are allocated adopt the "use it or lose it" attitude found in government. Slack creates a difficult problem for budget makers and may be hard to correct. Slack is inherently wasteful for several reasons. First, the leeway provided program leaders and administrators allows them to be casual in their spending. Second, if actual costs are less than budgeted amounts, the church has lost an opportunity to use the funds for something else during the year. Third, financial discussions could be reduced to bickering over which activity has slack that could be reallocated to those programs in real need.

Another type of budget problem is commonly found in poorer, inner city churches and small churches located in agricultural areas, which have experienced a gradual erosion of their membership. The problem here is often overly optimistic estimates of yearly member giving. Many churches annually overstate their anticipated resources by 25 percent. They develop and approve a $100,000 budget and, when contributions lag behind this ideal target, programs and activities are cut back, bills are paid more slowly or are deferred to future months, and equipment or improvement projects are deferred to future years. A finance committee meeting in this kind of church focuses on monitoring the cash balances and approving bills to be paid. Purposely using highly optimistic targets may have merit for one year as the church strives for the unreachable in that short time frame. But repeated annual failures and a constant battle to cut, defer, and monitor will cause most church members to recognize that the budget target is fabricated, and they will not feel a commitment to help meet it. To correct this problem the budget needs to be attainable under *normal* operating conditions. Budget preparers should consider what members have given in the past and should make a realistic assessment of those active members who will support the church. Phantom members cannot be relied upon for support.

Although it is easier said than done, budget estimates should be realistic, shying away from excessive optimism or pessimism. Unrealistic assumptions defeat the purpose of budgeting.

### The Annual Budgeting Process and Timetable

As we have discussed, good budgeting takes planning, patience, and time. Often a treasurer will ask me if his or her annual budgeting process and timetable is satisfactory. This is a difficult question to answer without knowing the dynamics of the particular church. But assuming the church has done its planning and has stated both short-term and long-term goals and objectives, the following approach, used by the hypothetical Atherton Church, is a reasonable one for most churches.

### Atherton Church

The Atherton Church uses the program-budgeting approach. The budget process begins on July 1 for the next calendar year with an invitation to members to submit budget requests for programs, activities, capital improvements, and equipment. Ideas for new programs are solicited. Participation by all members is encouraged. From July through September members of the finance and program evaluation committee prepare a tentative budget by making a realistic projection of expected annual giving and anticipated expenditures, sorting through all requests, and meeting with program leaders and others to discuss their specific goals, objectives, and methods of operation. In this process some items may be cut back or deferred. In October the committee conducts its annual pledge month, requesting all members to indicate their expected giving for the next calendar year. To obtain the required commitment for funds, the tentative expenditure budget is given to the congregation as the basis for pledging. In November, after the pledges are received, the total of pledges is adjusted downward by a small percentage to reflect the fact that not everyone can or will honor his or her pledge. On the basis of the adjusted pledges, the tentative budget is revised and becomes the final budget. Differences between the tentative budget and final budget are typically small and involve the addition or deletion of a few pieces of office or educational equipment. The final budget is approved by the committee in November and approved by the congregation at a general church meeting in early December.

Although the six-month timetable at Atherton may seem too long, the committee does not work forty hours a week on the budget. The committee may meet only once or twice a month. Given the normal inefficiencies, absences, and interruptions that committees often experience, six months is a good rule of thumb. Churches not allowing sufficient time for budgeting are easy to spot. They are the ones groping around in January or early February without a budget for that calendar year or the ones, like St. Chaos, preparing a budget before a ball game.

### Budgeting for the Inflow of Resources

Church treasurers often express the size of their churches by indicating the size of their budget. You'll hear that one church has a

$100,000 budget, another has an $800,000 budget, and so on. Because most churches try to remain financially viable from year to year, these statements usually mean that cash equal to the stated amount will be raised and then dispensed for various purposes. The figure used typically includes only cash resources and sometimes not even all cash from church-related and church-derived activities. In order to determine the total resources entrusted to the church by its members, the budget should include not only member giving but inflows from restricted or designated gifts, bazaars, car washes, bake sales, bingo, special canvasses and drives, tuition from educational activities, amounts provided to the pastor's discretionary fund, the value of items donated to the church, and the value of donated services.

Because of this oversight most churches do not know the total value of the resources being provided to the church. Stated differently, most churches do not know what it would cost to operate for a year and pay cash for everything received. The need for such information is particularly evident during recessions, when volunteers or low-paid church personnel have to find jobs or better-paying jobs in order to assist their families in meeting their own budgets. Churches unprepared to pay for help that had been free or to pay market wages to attract qualified personnel will break their traditionally prepared budgets. In the recession of 1981–1982, some churches used up their entire calendar year budget by July, because their women volunteers had to find employment and the churches had not anticipated paying for the services they had provided. With a full-picture financial resources budget that includes all items, church financial leaders will know that, for example, of total resources of $250,000 provided, $100,000 may come from weekly member giving, $20,000 from restricted gifts, $15,000 from funds earmarked for the pastor's discretionary fund, $40,000 from tuition at preschool and Mother's Day Out, $10,000 from miscellaneous church activities, such as bake sales, $20,000 from the in-kind donation of equipment, and $45,000 from the value of donated services. Using a full-picture approach, this church's operating budget would be $250,000. Yet in many churches the budget would be stated as $100,000, if only weekly giving was considered, or $110,000, if weekly giving and miscellaneous church activities were considered. The difference can be sizable.

Armed with the knowledge of how important some of these other items are to the church, financial leaders will not merely assume these items will occur and will not treat them as immaterial. For example, with tuition included in the budget, someone is certain to question whether it covers all or a satisfactory portion of the cost of educational activities. Notes to encourage the donation of noncash items and personal time to the church could be included in the church bulletin or sermon. Miscellaneous activities that generate cash may have an appointed coordinator just to make sure that they are completed successfully. After all, they can represent a significant percentage of the budget. Without including such items in the budget, tuition may not be reviewed, special appeals for donated items and services may be forgotten, and several miscellaneous activities could be deferred.

The rationale for including some of these resources in the annual budget needs to be explained. First, there is the matter of restricted or designated gifts or offerings. Many churches do not include these items in their budget, because the funds received must be spent according to the wishes of the member-donor or are collected with a special purpose in mind. They are not available for the payment of regular church expenses and are essentially in-and-out items. But the failure to include such restricted gifts and offerings in the budget disregards the resources provided by these church members to missions, to outreach programs, or for special items within the church. Restricted funds that are to be paid out within the year would be shown as a restricted disbursement in the expense section of the same budget. If the funds are to be disbursed in the following year, they would be shown as a restricted disbursement in the expense section of the next year's budget.

Many churches exclude funds given personally to the pastor by members for his or her discretionary fund. There are, however, several problems with this omission. First, if the funds are used for the pastor's routine operating expenses, the church's expense budget will be understated. This practice will contribute to confusion about what it really costs to operate the church. Second, financial leaders will understate member giving to the church, and the congregation will not get to share the good feeling that comes from recognizing that, as a group, they are helping to provide for the needs of the pastor or people in dire need. Third, omitting such income from the budget could lead to unfavorable income tax ramifications, as only the church, not the pastor, qualifies as a tax-exempt organization. Contrary to common belief, a gift made directly to the pastor for the discretionary fund is technically not tax deductible. Checks made out to the pastor should be endorsed over to the church and deposited in an account that is in the name of the church. The pastor can draw on this account as desired. For the reasons just stated, anticipated contributions to the pastor's discretionary fund need to be budgeted as resources, and later, in the expense section of the budget, as anticipated expenditures for the pastor's discretionary use. This budgeting procedure neither discourages contributions to the pastor's discretionary fund nor influences the pastor's freedom in determining how to spend the funds. The procedure merely includes in the budget the resources provided by the membership. Thus both the inflow and outflow of funds are shown in the budget.

For most churches the largest inflow of resources comes in the form of weekly envelope offerings made to fulfill a yearly, monthly, or weekly pledge. Although the subject of obtaining pledges is hotly debated in many congregations, most churches find that the pledge card is a device useful in obtaining the commitment of its members and in preparing its own budget.

If pledge cards are used, thought should be given to their design.[4] Most are small, provide little room for comments, may not even have the church's name or logo, and focus the member's attention solely on the pledge, not on the broader concept of financial commitment. The instrument used to gather financial commitments should have built-in excitement, with some color, the church name and logo, and perhaps a Scripture passage. The instrument should have sufficient room for people to express their feelings about their pledges. Some people will take this opportunity to let you know why they are supporting the church, which is valuable information. It also allows people to note why they cannot or will not make a pledge. Further, by turning the card into an instrument for financial commitment, not just a yearly pledge commitment, questions can be asked about whether the church is included in the member's will, whether tax-deductible gifts of property to the church or any of its ministries have been considered, and whether the donor would like to meet with a church representative to discuss these matters. Some churches never ask these questions and, as a consequence, lose excellent opportunities to provide for the long-term financial viability of the church. Renaming it the commitment card and redesigning its elements can enable the church to achieve greater financial support.

Even without pledges, however, most churches could make a fairly good estimate of expected income by preparing a graph of prior years' donations and assessing the trend. In fact, many churches receiving pledges maintain extensive statistics on member contributions. Valuable information can be gained by analyzing the contributions according to, for example, frequency of giving, marital status/youth, and age. Exhibit 2-4 is a partial analysis of contributions according to age.

The summary can be analyzed many different ways. One way is to relate it to the life cycle of a church. For instance, the summary reveals that those younger than 21 contributed a small proportion of church funds. But it is a healthy sign to have 144 contributors in this category. Those persons younger than 21 are the future of the church. The number of young adults, 21 to 40, indicates the church's ability to retain its youth into adulthood. This group is low in both absolute numbers

---

[4] Thomas C. Rieke, "Cards," *Church Management: The Clergy Journal*, vol. 59, no. 1 (October 1982), 10–11.

| | | Age | | | | | |
|---|---|---|---|---|---|---|---|
| | | Younger than 21 | 21–30 | 31–40 | 41–50 | 51–65 | Older than 65 |
| No. of givers (500) | | 144 | 45 | 35 | 52 | 117 | 107 |
| Total for year ($300,000) | | $5,000 | $30,000 | $20,000 | $65,000 | $110,000 | $70,000 |
| Percent of total* | | 1.7% | 10% | 6.7% | 21.7% | 36.7% | 23.3% |
| Range | No. | | | | | | |
| Less than $100 | 217 | 138 | 22 | 7 | 8 | 21 | 21 |
| $100–499 | 124 | 4 | 13 | 16 | 17 | 36 | 38 |
| $500–999 | 69 | 2 | 3 | 6 | 9 | 20 | 29 |
| $1,000–1,499 | 35 | — | 4 | 3 | 6 | 15 | 7 |
| $1,500–1,999 | 22 | — | — | 2 | 1 | 13 | 6 |
| $2,000–2,499 | 2 | — | — | — | 1 | — | 1 |
| $2,500–2,999 | 9 | — | — | 1 | 3 | 2 | 3 |
| $3,000–3,499 | 7 | — | 2 | — | 2 | 2 | 1 |
| $3,500–3,999 | 7 | — | 1 | — | 2 | 3 | 1 |
| $4,000–4,499 | 1 | — | — | — | — | 1 | — |
| $4,500–4,999 | 2 | — | — | — | 2 | — | — |
| $5,000–5,500 | 5 | — | — | — | 1 | 4 | — |
| | 500 | 144 | 45 | 35 | 52 | 117 | 107 |

* The sum of all percentages exceeds 100% due to rounding.

**Exhibit 2-4  Summary Analysis of General Member Contributions By Age**

and in contributors. Only 16.7 percent of contributions comes from givers between ages 21 and 40. The short-term future of the church may be in jeopardy when this group gets older. Those in the 41 to 50 and 51 to 65 age categories are important to churches. This is because they typically provide the greatest financial support and lay leadership. In the exhibit more than 58 percent of total giving comes from these age groups. The older-than-65 age group also has a large number of contributors. It provides 23.3 percent of total giving. This group may also be counted on to volunteer its services. But the large number of contributors in this category could indicate some future financial auster-ity for the church.

There are several other ways that churches can evaluate the level of member giving. Each has an appropriate use, depending on the church's circumstances.

Many churches, for instance, first compute their anticipated contribu-tions budget. They then analyze contributions by using the average contribution per contributor. For example, using exhibit 2-4 data, the average contribution is $600 ($300,000/500). Although this figure is easy to compute, it has a deficiency. The deficiency is that hefty gifts made by wealthy members are commingled with smaller gifts made by others. A rule of thumb is that 80 percent of funds will come from 20 percent of the contributors. Conversely, 20 percent of the funds will be provided by 80 percent of the contributors. So users of this approach may be well advised to calculate two averages. One average would be for the smaller number of large contributors. One would be for the majority.

Some churches use an average of giving based on the number of members in the congregation. Thus if the church in exhibit 2-4 had a membership of 1,000, the average contribution would be $300 ($300,000/ 1,000). This figure could be used together with an estimate of the next year's membership for budgeting purposes. (This is assuming economic conditions are stable.) A problem with this approach, however, is that many members are inactive. Those who do not participate are not apt to give. Thus there may not be a relationship between increased contributions and increased church membership.

Some churches compute the average income received based on the average attendance at worship services. This system has great merit, because it equates contributions with involvement. The causal factor to increased giving is presumed to be increased participation in worship attendance. As Callahan notes,

> Over time . . . income goes up in relation to increased participation, not increased membership. Thus, a congregation that wishes to increase its total income should work more strongly on increasing worship and church school attendance than on increasing membership. There is very little correlation between an increase in membership and an increase in giving; the key correlation is between participation and contributions.[5]

Other churches analyze member giving in terms of families. This is because in many churches the majority of contributions comes from families. It does not come from single, widowed, or youth members. Of course, using only one group when evaluating contributions lacks comprehensiveness. And in fact, many churches would find this approach inappropriate. This is because of the composition of their congregations.

Some churches analyze contributions in terms of giving units. A church using giving units recognizes that different members have different abilities to provide financial support. With this approach the total membership of the church is analyzed according to number of

---

[5] Callahan, *Twelve Keys*, 108.

giving units. Many variations of this approach are possible. In one approach one giving unit equals one family, including husband, wife, and children, if any. Other members' capacity to give is compared against this reference point. Based on historical patterns of giving, the following giving units might be relevant to a particular church:

| | |
|---|---|
| Family | 1 |
| Wife- or husband-only member | 1/2 |
| Single, employed member | 3/4 |
| Wife- or husband-only member, other spouse in another church | 1/3 |
| Retired member | 1/2 |
| College student member | 1/10 |
| Youth member | 1/20 |

So statistics must have indicated that a wife- or husband-only member will give 50 percent of what a family contributes. Therefore, forty members in this category would translate into twenty giving units (40 × 1/2). Similarly, ten college students would translate into one giving unit (10 × 1/10). With this approach, a church's membership of, say, nine hundred members might be reduced to three hundred fifty giving units.

The giving-unit approach can be used advantageously for intradenominational comparison. That is, with the number of members translated to a common capacity for giving, churches can be evaluated in relative terms and need not be concerned with differences in absolute size. This benefit becomes especially useful when comparing one church against another for regional or national purposes. Thus Church A may have twelve hundred members, and Church B may have only five hundred members. Yet by converting the membership of both churches into giving units, many financial relationships may be comparable on a giving-unit basis.

Another advantage of using this approach is that it can be used to help determine the potential of the congregation to contribute. To find this potential, the number of giving units (i.e., family-giving equivalents) is multiplied by the average family income of church members. Average family income is important because, unless there are some very large benefactors, the income of the church will mirror the income of its members. Income statistics can be obtained from federal government sources maintained at most large state university libraries, based on either taxation or census data. Governmental statistics on a town or city, however, will be representative only if the church has a cross section of members from the community. To overcome this defect smaller churches could compute average income of members by having a person expert in the wage and salary levels of trade and professional persons review the membership roll. Hence if Assembly United Church had one hundred giving units and an estimated average income per member of $30,000, total income of church members would be estimated at $3,000,000 (100 × $30,000). Based on this total a table (see the one that follows) could be prepared, which showed what the income potential of the church was with different percentages of giving.

Total giving-unit income $3,000,000

| Giving | 1% | $ 30,000 |
|--------|-----|----------|
| Giving | 2% | 60,000 |
| Giving | 3% | 90,000 |
| Giving | 5% | 150,000 |
| Giving | 10% | 300,000 |

By using this type of analysis, financial leaders can determine the percentage of the potential cash resources that the church is currently receiving. Thus if Assembly United Church can expect to receive only $60,000 in contributions during the year, it will be receiving only 2% of available annual resources. If this percentage is deemed to be insufficient to support church programs, church leaders need to think of ways to stimulate greater membership involvement and, through participation, increased giving. Or, based on the results of this analysis, church leaders may conclude that the church is receiving amounts from its members comparable with those of other churches in the same denomination. They may instead decide to augment income by attempting to increase membership through a new-member drive, a household visitation program, a church visitation program, or well-publicized activities.

### Donated Services

During the year a church receives many hours of donated services from members. Many volunteers are senior citizens who suddenly have some extra time on their hands. Others are busy mothers with little time to spare. Some people donate their time because they can't contribute cash. Other people give cash, time, and ability. Donated services represent valuable resources for the church. They are different from cash resources only in the form that they take. Resources are resources. All are needed. All need to be budgeted, monitored, and managed.

The need for recognizing this resource in the budgets and financial reports of nonprofit organizations became apparent to me fifteen years ago, when I served as treasurer and member of the board of directors of a private school in Texas. Shortly after my appointment to the position, I was asked by the school director to include a copy of our budget and latest financial report in a grant application to a large foundation for funds to be used for the development of a playground. I complied and we all waited. Several months later our grant application was returned rejected. Something in the rejection letter caught my attention. Evidently the reviewer of the grant had difficulty comparing our activities with those of other schools throughout the country requesting financial assistance. What made it difficult was that our school was a cooperative school, where parents and families donated their time in lieu of high tuition, and we were being compared with schools that operated solely on tuition. When we described our goals, objectives, programs, and activities, and then showed a paltry budget compared with comparable full-tuition schools, the reviewer must have had a hard time believing our story. The cost of the computer literacy and education program for preschoolers and K–4 grades wasn't in the financial statements, because the machines had been donated and the instructor was a student's father. The annual trip the fourth graders took to Switzerland didn't show up, because it had been funded by an extensive aluminum can and paper drive, supervised by parents. Land reclamation and improvement costs on the twenty-three-acre site were absent, because parents had done the work. In effect we were penalized for using donated services instead of charging full tuition and paying cash for our expenditures.

To show the foundation all of the resources being given to the school, I decided to impute (subjectively derive, or make up) a value for donated services. I used the following formula: 200 families × a 9-month school year × the 8 hour per month work requirement × the $25 extra tuition charged for every hour not worked. The resultant $360,000 amount was added to the cash inflow from tuition in our budget, almost doubling the budget, to arrive at total resources provided to the school. The same $360,000 was then subtracted in the expense section as "Expenses saved; donated services." In other words, the insertion and then subtraction of the value of donated services only made the budget larger. Nothing else changed. The grant application was resubmitted, identical except for recognition of the value of donated services. Several months later the grant was approved.

The example discussed has equal application to churches. Few churches adequately treat donated services as valuable resources, and virtually none include the value of donated services in their accounting records. I believe that this omission is a mistake. Resources not monitored and managed inevitably are wasted. Church leaders often incorrectly presume that because donated services are free, there's no resource involved. But volunteers' time is valuable and their contributions are worthwhile. How can it be that donated services are resources of the provider but not to the recipient? In some churches volunteers use outmoded equipment, such as manual typewriters, photocopiers that overheat, computers that belong in a museum, buses and vans that should be in a junkyard, a manual lawnmower, and janitorial equipment so bad that volunteers bring their own from home. These churches need to consider whether the cash spent for new equipment will result in a greater benefit from their donated resources. Some churches have never thought about the trade off.

I believe that records should be maintained on donated services, and that periodically people should receive thanks for their gifts of time and ability. Many approaches to keeping track of time spent are possible. If your church is presently not doing anything in this area, it is probably best to keep it simple. Use a sign-up sheet on a bulletin board for volunteers to indicate what they did, when they did it, and how much time they spent. Volunteers should decide whether to use the sign-up sheet. Some people will not want to write down anything. Some people will forget. Data received need not be checked; the honor system should be used. Records on donated services should be maintained by someone called, for example, the director of donated services. At least annually, volunteers should receive letters that indicate the number of hours they have given to their church and that thank them for those contributions. Do not place a cash value on the time donated, as some members may inadvertently deduct this amount as a charitable contribution on their federal income tax return. The value of donated services is not an allowable deduction for income tax purposes, and some members could become hostile when the IRS notifies them that they owe back taxes and interest. In addition to the letters, a growing number of churches sponsor a banquet each year where volunteers are recognized and awards or certificates are presented.

Two final questions are often raised in discussions of donated services. The first question is, Should time spent by members serving on the church's committees and projects be included in the budget as donated services, or should we record just services for which the church would have paid cash if members had not given of themselves? This is a good question. From an economic point of view, hours spent on church affairs represent resources provided, regardless of their form. Thus an hour of committee work would be equal to an hour of painting, mowing, sweeping, or bookkeeping. Another point of view, however, is that only services provided that saved the church its cash resources should be recorded in the budget. Therefore, as the church would never have paid anyone to serve on a committee, such a service should not be in the budget. Although this topic has not received much attention, I believe that most accountants would favor the latter approach for budgeting purposes: only donated services that save the church its cash resources should be included in the budget. But churches that do not wish to discriminate between types of volunteer services and that prefer to use the broader approach for recognizing the services contributed by their members need not hesitate to do so. There's no rule prohibiting this. Anything is better than the present situation of not recognizing donated services at all.

The second question is, How do you place a value on donated services? To an accountant the figure is imputed by multiplying the number of hours worked times an appropriate hourly rate for services received. Therefore the value of landscaping services may be set at $7 per hour, teacher's aides at $6 per hour, and legal services at $80 per hour. Some churches may prefer to use a single predetermined rate for all services. Some may elect to use the minimum wage. However the rate(s) are selected and however precise the amounts are, valuation difficulties should not deter you from treating donated services as a resource important enough to budget, monitor, and manage.

### Budgeting for the Outflow of Resources

The planning, budgeting, and control of church expenditures have been discussed at several points in this chapter and will not be repeated here. In fact, the majority of the material dealing with incremental, program, and zero-base budgeting concerns the outflow of resources. It is sufficient here to note that the outcome of the budgeting process should be the comparison of full-picture income with full-picture expenses for the calendar year or fiscal year. By now you know that I will recommend that the expenses named in the budget include more than just the expected cash disbursements necessary to operate the church. The expenses should also include the disbursement of benevolences, disbursement of restricted gifts, expenses of operating church-related activities such as schools, disbursements to the pastor's discretionary fund, and use of donated services, property, and equipment. A sample of a full-picture, all-financial-resources budget is presented in exhibit 2-5.

The all-financial-resources budget shows that the expected resources provided to this church total $250,000. The majority of income is expected to come in the form of cash gifts, both unrestricted and restricted, but $14,000 is anticipated from miscellaneous activities, $9,000 from interest, dividends, and rent, $35,000 is expected from school tuition, $10,000 will come in the form of gifts of property and equipment, and $30,000 is expected from donated services. On the expenditure side the budget shows that the following funds have been earmarked: $49,000 for the pastor's ministry, $48,000 for administration,

## All-Financial-Resources Operating Budget for the Calendar Year 19XX

**Income**

| | |
|---|---:|
| Pledges | $100,000 |
| Special offerings | 10,000 |
| Cash plate | 5,000 |
| Sunday school offerings | 3,000 |
| Communion offerings | 1,000 |
| Restricted gifts | 25,000 |
| Interest and dividend income | 6,000 |
| Rental income | 3,000 |
| School tuition—all programs | 35,000 |
| Miscellaneous activities | 14,000 |
| Gifts to the pastor's discretionary fund | 8,000 |
| Gifts of property and equipment | 10,000 |
| Donated services | 30,000 |
| | $250,000 |

**Expenditures**

**Pastor-related**

| | | |
|---|---:|---:|
| Salary | $20,000 | |
| Housing allowance | 10,000 | |
| Car allowance | 5,000 | |
| Educational allowance | 1,000 | |
| Pension | 5,000 | |
| From discretionary funds | 8,000 | $ 49,000 |

**Administration**

| | | |
|---|---:|---:|
| Salaries | $22,000 | |
| Supplies | 4,000 | |
| Property maintenance | 6,000 | |
| Utilities | 4,000 | |
| Insurance | 3,000 | |
| Telephone | 700 | |
| Postage | 1,000 | |
| Literature | 300 | |
| Flowers | 200 | |
| Computer—new | 3,000 | |
| Bus expenses | 2,800 | |
| Publicity | 1,000 | 48,000 |

**Programs**

| | | |
|---|---:|---:|
| School | $40,000 | |
| Youth | 5,000 | |
| Music | 4,000 | |
| Social concerns | 2,000 | |
| Worship | 2,000 | 53,000 |

**Benevolences**

| | | |
|---|---:|---:|
| National | $13,000 | |
| Local | 2,000 | |
| Foreign | 5,000 | 20,000 |

| | |
|---|---:|
| **For restricted gifts per the donor** | 22,000 |
| **Reductions in expenditures from gifts of property and equipment** | 10,000 |
| **Reductions in expenditures from donated services** | 30,000 |
| **Debt retirement fund** | 5,000 |
| **Building fund** | 10,000 |
| **Contingency reserve** | 3,000 |
| | $250,000 |

Exhibit 2-5　Community Christian Church

$53,000 for various programs, $20,000 for benevolences at all levels, $5,000 to pay off the church's existing debt, and $10,000 for the building fund. A contingency reserve of $3,000 is planned to cover any unexpected changes in income and expenditures.

Sometimes a preliminary budget indicates that expected expenses are in excess of expected income. Some value judgments then have to be made. Questions have to be answered regarding items such as salary increases for the pastor and other employees, the adequacy of the pastor's expenses (housing or housing allowance, entertainment allowance, travel reimbursement, pension, and continuing ministerial education allowance), the importance of various programs, the financial requirements of missions, the appropriate amount to add to the building fund, the possibility of deferring some expenditures until the next year, and so on. This process of reconciling expected income and expenses is, of course, an important step in the resource allocation process, because it is here that the church's operating plan for the coming year is determined. The mechanics of this reconciliation process have been discussed at several points earlier in this chapter.

In most churches the amount of budgeted inflow of resources sets the limit on budgeted expenses. Deficit spending may be popular in Washington, but it's not popular in churches. As previously noted, decreasing membership, poor location, changing religious leadership, and so on, can cause unexpected financial difficulty for some churches. But this is the exception rather than the rule. This is not to imply that churches are wealthy, just that they usually attempt to break even.

There are some instances, however, when a budget is approved showing expected revenues less than expected expenses. A church may deliberately decide to invade its accumulated savings and to spend more than it receives. This decision may be made to honor commitments and to keep the church moving toward its long-term goals and objectives. Or the church may have indications that funds equal to the shortfall will be received from denominational offices or other congregations during the year. The church should, however, attempt to attain a balanced budget as soon as possible.

Alternatively, a church could budget a surplus for the year—inflow that exceeds outflow. This may occur in well-established churches where member contributors have not yet realized, or have not yet been informed, that the church's needs have diminished. It could also happen in growth situations where spending cannot keep pace with increasing membership and affluency. It may also occur in congregations that anticipate major renovation work or that desire to build up a contingency fund for possible difficult economic times in the future.

### Games Some People Play

Because budgeting is an exercise in human interaction and debate, some people take this opportunity to play games to get what they want from the budget. One of the games used to obtain something new is called The Foot in the Door. Beware when you hear comments that a new program has hardly any costs. It may not cost much now, but wait until a constituency is built up. Another game is Getting the Pastor's Blessing. Many members of finance committees or equivalent groups have a difficult time being objective about a proposal that is said to have the approval of the pastor. Yet the proposal may be weak on its own merits. Implied Support is another game. Watch for statements to the effect that, "A lot of members want this" or "They'd never tell you but the members want this." Another ruse involves comparing the church with the one down the block or with a sister church in a neighboring city. This is the But They Do It game. A church moving forward without goals or objectives could fall for such ploys.

Games are also used to keep funding for established programs and activities. One game is called The Flood. It involves overwhelming the finance committee with more data and materials than necessary, in order to impress it. A more risky one is the Out of Town game. Here a program leader requests an amount in good faith, because an out of town trip prevented him or her from preparing anything formal. Last, there's the We've Always Done It This Way game, which is supposed to raise the item to an almost divine level, so that analysis and discussion would be distasteful. Churches operating like St. Chaos could fall prey to these games and thus allocate their resources in a particularly wasteful manner.

## Other Budgets

In addition to the annual operating budget, several other budgets may be constructed to guide the church's financial affairs. Discussed in this section are the cash budget, capital-spending budget, and debt retirement budget.

### Cash Budget

All churches could benefit from the preparation of a monthly cash budget. Rarely will the church's expected monthly cash receipts exactly match the expected cash expenditures. Although cash inflow will normally equal outflow for the year taken as a whole, a different story usually surfaces when cash flow is reviewed on a month-to-month basis.

There may be several months where the projected cash outflow exceeds inflow, and either savings must be reduced, bills paid late, or money borrowed. A cash budget serves to summarize a church's cash activities for the budget period.

To prepare a cash budget, the church's historic pattern for giving needs to be examined and understood. Unless dramatic changes are occurring within the church, the past pattern is a good indication of how member contributions are likely to be made in the ensuing year. For example, a church may find that monthly giving is stable every month except December, which is twice the monthly average. This pattern would be included in the cash budget by having each month except December budgeted for 1/13 of total expected cash giving, and December would be budgeted for 2/13 of the total. Other churches may find that giving is highest in March, April, November, and December, lowest in January, February, July, and August, and moderate in all other months. These churches would anticipate future monthly cash contributions on the basis of historical percentages. Thus if July typically accounted for 5 percent of yearly contributions, the July budget for the ensuing year would anticipate 5 percent of the expected annual amount. Whatever your church's pattern, adjustments will be necessary for situations where months in the preceding calendar or fiscal year had a different number of Sundays than in the budget year. In other words, if December had four Sundays in the preceding year and has five Sundays this year, this year's cash budget should take the extra Sunday into account.

Cash disbursements are also projected by using historical data, knowledge of any rate increases or inflationary factors, and due dates. Many of the church's obligations will be paid monthly. Some may be paid only quarterly or annually.

An example of a cash budget for All Saints' Church for a two-month period is presented in exhibit 2-6. The cash budget indicates that although the church has a small cash balance at the beginning of August and will have a larger one at the end of September, the church will run out of cash in August unless certain managerial actions are taken. This is important information. I recommend that a church prepare a cash budget for the same twelve-month period that is covered by the annual operating budget.

### Capital-Spending Budget

The capital-spending budget details the costs of renovation or building projects together with the source of funds necessary to finance the project. This budget is prepared for the asset acquisitions that have a

## Cash Budget for the Months of August and September 19XX

|  | August | September |
|---|---|---|
| Beginning cash balance | $1,000 | $ (500) |
| Add cash receipts | | |
| Envelope offerings | 9,000 | 12,000 |
| Loose plate offerings | 1,000 | 1,500 |
| Restricted gifts | 3,000 | 3,000 |
| Special offerings | | 3,000 |
| Other | 4,000 | 1,000 |
| Cash available for disbursements | $18,000 | $20,000 |
| Priest's salary | $1,500 | $ 1,500 |
| Priest's housing allowance | 1,000 | 1,000 |
| Administrative expenses | 6,000 | 4,000 |
| Program expenses | 4,000 | 5,000 |
| Benevolences | 2,000 | 2,500 |
| Mortgage payment | 1,000 | 1,000 |
| Disbursed restricted gifts | 3,000 | 3,000 |
| Total disbursements | $18,500 | $18,000 |
| Ending Cash balance | $ (500) | $ 2,000 |

**Exhibit 2-6   All Saints' Church Cash Budget**

long-term life and a high cost. Naturally, what is a high cost for a small church may be a small cost for a large church. Purchasing a computer to handle the church's financial affairs is a good example of this kind of acquisition. In some congregations the acquisition of a several-thousand-dollar computer would need to be included in the capital-spending budget. In larger congregations the purchase of the computer would be presented only in the annual operating budget, where it would be shown to be paid from current income. Some larger expenditures that are typically included in capital-spending budgets are the construction of a new church, adding on of a wing, building of a parsonage, repaving of the parking lot, putting on of a new roof, and purchase of a new van. Often churches will maintain a separate building fund to accumulate funds for such large expenditures. In exhibit 2-5 Community Christian Church earmarked $10,000 of current income for its building fund. Assuming that this church was planning to add a $100,000 addition to its main structure, its capital spending budget might look like exhibit 2-7.

As you can see from exhibit 2-7, the church is relying on outside financing for less than half of the cost of the project, because internally generated funds have been accumulated for the expansion. Those churches selling bonds and soliciting special building fund pledges to finance their large spending projects would include the anticipated receipt of such funds as sources of income in the capital-spending budget.

## Capital-Spending Budget for the Building Enlargement Project

**Uses of funds**

| | | |
|---|---|---|
| Building construction contract | | $ 87,000 |
| Architectural fees | | 1,000 |
| Licenses, legal fees, and so on | | 500 |
| Landscaping | | 500 |
| Furniture and equipment | | 10,000 |
| Carpeting | | 1,000 |
| | Total | $100,000 |

**Sources of funds**

| | | |
|---|---|---|
| Building fund balance—beginning of year | | $ 40,000 |
| From current income | | 10,000 |
| From interest on building fund | | 4,000 |
| From mortgage financing | | 46,000 |
| | Total | $100,000 |

**Exhibit 2-7 Community Christian Church**

### Debt Retirement Budget

The debt retirement budget is used to show how the church's debt will be paid off. Separate budgets could be prepared for each of the church's long-term debts, or a unified budget could be prepared for all long-term payables. As some mortgages are amortized over a thirty-year period, this budget could project thirty years into the future. Churches often have a debt retirement fund, which accumulates funds for eventual disbursement to creditors. For instance, in exhibit 2-5 Community Christian Church allocated $5,000 of its current income for the debt retirement fund.

Assuming that Community Christian Church will pay off its $46,000 mortgage by making twelve yearly payments of $5,000 for principal and interest, its debt retirement budget would appear as shown in exhibit 2-8. A review of this exhibit reveals that Community Christian Church expects to pay the first year's obligation with current income, the second year's with a special pledge drive, and the last year's with memorial gifts.

### Closing Observations

The administering of a planning and budgeting system is a difficult task. Too often financial people become overly involved with the mechanical aspects of budget construction. They lose sight of the fact that budgets are for their church, a voluntary group of members sharing common religious beliefs, rather than for a business corporation. Unless the budgeting effort considers human relations, even the most precise

### Debt Retirement Budget for the Building Enlargement Project

|                                    | Year 1   | Year 2   | .................... | Year 12  |
| ---------------------------------- | -------- | -------- | -------------------- | -------- |
| **Uses of funds**                  |          |          |                      |          |
| Mortgage payment, including interest | $5,000 | $5,000   | ....................  | $5,000   |
| Total                              | $5,000   | $5,000   | ....................  | $5,000   |
| **Sources of funds**               |          |          |                      |          |
| Current income                     | $5,000   | —        | ....................  | —        |
| Special pledges                    | —        | $5,000   | ....................  |          |
| Memorial gifts                     | —        | —        | ....................  | $5,000   |
| Total                              | $5,000   | $5,000   | ....................  | $5,000   |

Exhibit 2-8   Community Christian Church

efforts will go for naught and will be met with resistance, skepticism, or indifference. Along the same lines, many churches overemphasize the use of budgets in the control of expenditures. A budget is not carved in stone. A few changes in the annual operating budget or any other budget during the year may have to be made because of unanticipated events. These changes do not flaw the planning and budgeting process. They simply reflect the difficulty of accurately forecasting the future.

As we have discussed, plans and budgets are only as effective as the effort that has gone into their preparation. Church leaders must thoroughly support the planning and budgeting processes, or else the entire resource allocation exercise will be a lesson in futility. Also, although planning and budgeting are crucial to a church's financial well-being, they cannot replace effective week-to-week management. That is, plans and budgets cannot by themselves change the course of a faltering church. They are but tools to be used by skillful leaders.

# CHAPTER 3

# Internal Control of Assets

The protection of assets (cash, equipment, securities, valuables, and so on) is a basic management requirement for all organizations, whether large or small, profit-seeking or nonprofit. Unfortunately in most churches the internal control of assets traditionally has been weak. As a consequence about 15 percent of all churches have been, are being, or will be victimized by an unscrupulous employee or member. With about 350,000 churches in the United States, approximately 52,500 (350,000 × 15%) churches are affected by lax asset controls.

In most situations the problem has been people pocketing cash. This is not surprising because churches receive and disburse significant amounts of cash, and all too often money is handled in a casual way. Millions of dollars of cash are involved each year. Investment securities, jewels and other valuables, supplies, and equipment have also disappeared from church premises. Few of these cases appear in the newspaper. In fact, in many cases the problems are handled by the leaders of the church, and the employees and congregation never learn of the situation.

Honest errors also account for significant losses. Many church treasurers and financial secretaries have inherited a set of accounting records that contain errors and cannot be balanced. Errors may have been made years ago, which preclude the preparation of accurate financial reports. Such situations cause frustration for both the preparers and users of financial information. Further, some treasurers and financial secretaries use unusual accounting procedures that practically invite error. Although you cannot design a perfect system that detects and prevents all errors, various features can and should be built into the accounting system to minimize the probability of errors.

A discussion of internal control of assets among those involved in the church accounting process is never very popular. Most of us like to think of our fellow workers or members as being both competent and, above all, honest. This feeling is compounded in those instances where churches have never experienced embarrassment from internal control failure. Nonetheless, consider this: churches receive contributed resources from their members, some of whom would otherwise buy food or clothing with the money, to spread the word of God. Consider also the widespread nature of the problem among churches and, as will be discussed, the particular vulnerability of churches. For these reasons I believe that church accountants have a special fiduciary obligation to make sure that all church assets are protected and used properly.

## GENERAL OBJECTIVES OF INTERNAL CONTROL

Generally stated, internal control can be defined as the various procedures adopted by an organization to safeguard assets, check the reliability and accuracy of financial records, and ensure compliance with managerial policies.

In most churches the primary objective of the internal control system boils down to safeguarding the church's assets. In simplest terms this means that the church's treasurer must establish controls and procedures for handling cash receipts and disbursements and all of the other assets owned by the church. Internal controls for cash guard against understatement of cash receipts and overstatement of cash disbursements. Internal controls for other assets provide proper physical controls, accurate recording, and periodic verification.

But the need for the internal control system to help produce reliable financial records should not be overlooked. First, accurate recording of all transactions is essential for maintaining sound interpersonal relationships among those involved with the accounting process and with users of financial reports. A treasurer resents receiving reports prepared by the financial secretary that contain entries made to incorrect accounts, fail to include all items of income and expenditure, and fail to tally. Members of the finance committee have a similar problem when receiving such financial reports from the treasurer. Members are annoyed when their contributions are incorrectly reported to them or their pledges or progress toward meeting their pledges are erroneously calculated. After all, members' records of contributions may be used for income tax purposes. Members do not like to call the church office about the problem, and the church secretary would prefer not to receive these calls. Rectifying such problems takes time, which is a waste of resources and reflects adversely on the church's financial administration. Second, users of financial information need reliable reports in order to plan effectively. Finance committee decisions to, for instance, add a wing, put on a new roof, pave the parking lot, purchase another bus, grant a raise, purchase a new organ, recarpet the hall, or invest excess funds in a certificate of deposit are made based upon the reliability of the information contained in the financial reports. Sound decisions are difficult to make if the financial reports cannot be relied upon! Third, church managers need reliable data to judge the efficiency of operations against past or expected performance and to remedy any problems. Consider how you would counsel program leaders for going over their budgets if the information in the budgets was not necessarily accurate. The uncertainty caused by the absence of reliable information would temper what you would say.

## INTERNAL CONTROL PROBLEMS IN CHURCHES: CAUSES AND SOME SUGGESTIONS

Churches encounter cases of misappropriated funds and unreliable financial records as the result of six problems, which include 1) the handling of incompatible duties by personnel, 2) the lack of a crisp organizational structure, 3) the absence of qualified personnel, 4) the lack of an accounting procedures manual, and 5) the absence of any monitoring of accounting work being done. The sixth problem, and an all pervasive one, is that because people are working in a church, they let their guard down believing that distasteful incidents could never occur. Often these problems arise because treasurers and other people involved with financial affairs disregard the principles of sound internal control. The more attention church treasurers, in particular, give to the installation and periodic review of internal controls, the fewer the problems that are likely to occur.

### Separation of Duties

Many functions (duties) performed within a church pertain to financial activities. The church must provide for an adequate separation of duties in order to ensure the accuracy and reliability of financial information and protect the assets. Incompatible duties or functions must be divided; that is, they must be performed by different people.

Three basic types of financial activities are performed within a church:

Authorization of transactions

Recording of transactions

Custody of assets

Someone must first authorize a transaction, such as the payment for supplies purchased or the receipt of a special gift. Later the transaction must be recorded in the books in the form of a journal entry. In addition, because many transactions will either immediately or eventually affect an asset, the church must maintain custody of its assets. For an adequate separation of duties to occur, authorization, recording, and asset custody should be performed by different individuals. When different people handle separate aspects of the same transaction, the likelihood that an error will go all the way through the system is diminished. Each person will, in effect, be checking on the other's work.

In addition to assisting in error detection, the separation of authorization, recording, and asset custody makes misappropriation of church assets more difficult. Consider a situation where a person could steal the church's assets by altering the financial records. This situation arises if an individual who maintains custody of an asset also handles the accounting for the asset. Assume that Jennifer, a church financial secretary, has the authority both to receive cash from members who stop by the church office and to record cash transactions. Suppose that Lillian, a member of the church, arrives at the office with a $100 special donation for the church's foreign missions. If the transaction is handled properly, Jennifer would place the $100 in the cash box and, later in the day, deposit it in the bank. Further, she would enter the transaction in the accounting records by increasing the cash account and the member's record of contributions by $100.

But because duties are not separated, the following could occur. Rather than placing the $100 in the cash box, Jennifer could simply steal the cash. Obviously the cash received could not be recorded on the books, because the increase in the cash account would not be matched by an increase in the cash box. But Jennifer would still have to update the accounting records to reflect Lillian's contribution, as Lillian could become suspicious if the payment were not acknowledged. Jennifer could have several ways of accomplishing this, depending on the amount of review given her work. She could merely add the $100 amount to Lillian's contribution record without fear of being found out. And if this action could be detected by someone reconciling total contributions for the year against individual contribution records,

Jennifer might, for example, subtract $100 from the contribution record of a member who had moved to a distant state or a member who had recently died.

This example illustrates the point that incompatible duties must be separated for adequate accounting control. This scheme would have been more difficult for Jennifer to undertake if she had had access to either the cash or the accounting records, rather than both.

The principle of separating duties to establish internal control is violated in the majority of churches. It could be the single most important cause of misappropriated assets and unreliable financial records. I routinely encounter church financial secretaries and church treasurers who "do it all." They authorize transactions, record transactions, receive cash, and disburse cash. These are incompatible duties and need to be separated. More people need to be involved in the accounting process if the church wants a good internal control system.

Although the best situation is to have separate people handle transaction authorization, transaction recording, and asset custody, many churches do not have sufficient personnel to do this. At the minimum, however, all churches should separate the functions of transaction recording and asset custody. For most churches, then, the financial secretaries would be responsible only for bookkeeping and accounting. It is important that these financial secretaries not be responsible for counting the weekly offerings, receiving cash from members who come to the office, or paying the bills. The financial secretaries would instead record the details of 1) cash that has been received, counted, and deposited by the counting committee; 2) office cash received, counted, and deposited by another office employee; and 3) disbursements made by authorized persons.

### Establishment of a Crisp Organizational Structure

If you were to review a business corporation's annual report to stockholders, you would realize that its organizational structure was precise. The firm would probably be divided into various centers, such as departments, plants, territories, or divisions. Managers would be appointed to oversee individual center activities, held accountable for the operating results, and evaluated accordingly. Employees would provide reports to and be evaluated by their superiors in accordance with a well-developed and clearly understood organizational chart. Likewise, individuals hired would be given specific titles, such as the assistant controller of the Trenton plant in the eastern division of Velvet Manufacturing Company. They would perform duties specified with precision in the firm's personnel manual.

In many churches people are hired or asked to volunteer so many hours a week to "help out." Quite often church managers do not specify job responsibilities and the order in which each of these responsibilities should be carried out. Many people report to the church each day or week without really knowing what their exact duties are. Some are put to work in accounting and financial reporting without being familiar with established operating procedures. Errors can be made, omissions occur, and reports be misdirected, because the organizational structure of the church is not well defined. Such fuzziness often leads to internal control breakdowns. Precise job descriptions are just as important to churches as they are to large profit-seeking businesses. In fact, these descriptions are even more acutely needed by churches, because, as discussed in chapter 2, they do not have the readily identifiable objectives of business. Also, churches use many volunteers, who need both supervision and structure to be most effective.

### Recruitment of Qualified Personnel

A church may limit access to assets, separate incompatible duties, and install a host of sophisticated accountability procedures. Yet all of these elements of internal control will be wasted unless one other essential element is present: qualified personnel. Any system is certain to be destroyed if operated by an untrained novice. What would you think about a church that allowed someone who had never maintained accounting records to keep the books? How about a church that allowed a member whose hobby was computers to design its new computerized financial system? Or how about a church that requested its financial secretary, barely out of high school, to design a new financial report for the membership? I trust that you would shake your head in dismay at all three instances. Yet these types of incidents frequently occur.

As I mentioned in the introduction, almost all of us came to serve a church by accident and without the skills and expertise that we are now developing. If you hold a paid position, you were probably retained for your availability, personality, and reasonable wage requirements. Or you may be a volunteer. During the learning process we have made our share of mistakes and failed to note many defects in the internal control system. Church officials must recognize that many people working with the church's financial concerns are novices lacking specific skills. Church leaders need to commit themselves to a program of continuing education for those involved with accounting, just as businesses do. Church leaders need to get beyond the question of, What does it cost? and instead ask, Do the benefits of having qualified personnel outweigh the costs? Until then many churches will have a succession of under-qualified people handling accounting functions—and accompanying problems of internal control.

Professional training in church management is available through membership and participation in several organizations, both intradenominational and interdenominational. One interdenominational organization is the National Association of Church Business Administration, headquartered in Fort Worth, Texas. Certification as a fellow in church business administration (FCBA) is available through that organization. Local chapters hold meetings to further the knowledge of church staff members.

## Accounting Procedures Manual

Few churches have manuals that specify the manner in which every accounting and financial reporting function is to be handled. Usually the outgoing treasurer or financial secretary simply meets with the incoming treasurer or financial secretary to discuss these procedures. And sometimes new treasurers and financial secretaries don't receive any instructions at all! They are on their own from the start.

When exiting treasurers and financial secretaries do provide instructions to their successors, the instructions may have limited value, for the following reasons:

1. Many of the instructions are given orally; newcomers quickly forget them.

2. Some of the accounting procedures and methods used by the exiting people are not conveyed to newcomers because of an oversight or the haste with which many of these meetings are conducted. Transition in industry may take two weeks or longer. Transition in a church often takes one hour.

3. Never having seen the accounting records, many new treasurers and financial secretaries are not in a position to digest all of the instructions quickly. Some have told me that they even pretended to understand the instructions, so that they wouldn't look stupid.

The approach to transition used in many churches is comparable to granting a driver's license to a teenager after a one-hour discussion (not a road test!) of some of the driving regulations.

Given the instruction provided many new treasurers and financial secretaries, you cannot expect continuity of internal control procedures from year to year. In fact, in some cases elaborate procedures are established and used effectively one year—and totally disregarded the next year. But from an internal control standpoint, it is important that sound procedures be developed, installed, and maintained year after year.

Church financial leaders need to prepare an accounting procedures manual to guide every step of their accounting and financial reporting process. A manual provides the glue between the old and the new and allows the church to maintain high standards of internal control. Some church groups have prepared treasurer's manuals for their churches. Most of these manuals are useful, but tend to emphasize the processing aspects of accounting (which accounts to use) and financial reporting (who receives which report and when). Internal control procedures are often treated lightly, if at all. Further, the effective approach to church accounting espoused in this book is not presented in any manual that I have seen. If a suitable manual is not available, church financial leaders need to design their own manual. The manual should specify the procedures used in:

A. Preparing the budget

B. Handling transactions

Internal Controls
    1. All of the internal controls used when receiving cash or other assets, whether in the offering or at the office.
    2. All of the internal controls used when disbursing cash, whether by check or through the petty cash fund.

Processing of Transactions
    3. The forms and procedures used to record both cash receipts, including memorials or restricted gifts, and cash disbursements.
    4. The forms and procedures used to record gifts of property and securities.
    5. The accounts used to record the transactions, together with a written description of the types of transactions that should be entered in each account.

C. Assuring reliable recordkeeping

Internal Controls
    1. The procedures used to reconcile totals of cash receipts and cash disbursements against individual amounts.
    2. The procedures used to reconcile church cash records against bank records.

D. Preparing and distributing financial reports

Financial Reporting
    1. Membership.
    2. Management (finance committee, program leaders, pastor, and so on).
    3. Others (regional/national church offices, the bank, the Internal Revenue Service, and so on).

## Absence of Monitoring

In many churches no one has ever monitored the performance of any treasurer or financial secretary. Such a review may be thought to be unnecessary and, indeed, an affront to the people in those positions. I can think of many people who would become unpleasant or quit on the spot if someone suggested that the church conduct an audit of the accounting records.

Although I am sympathetic to the threatened egos of people so affected, the absence of monitoring has led to sloppy records and misappropriated assets. I hope I don't offend readers by noting that if I were a crooked accountant, I would be attracted to a situation where my work was never checked. Statistics show that people who misappropriate assets are very often "faithful" employees who perhaps have never even taken vacations, who have perpetrated their schemes over many years, and, interestingly, who have never felt guilty. Some believed that the money they had taken was a pittance compared with their value to the church. In other words, they believed themselves underpaid or underrecognized.

To provide some measure of monitoring, some churches have organized internal audit committees. These committees, often composed of former church treasurers and businesspeople and accountants from the congregation, determine whether the church's procedures and controls are functioning as originally intended. They serve to safeguard assets and to check on the reliability and accuracy of the accounting information. If nothing else, the mere existence of a committee like this is a psychological deterrent to a person considering embezzlement.

Church leadership sometimes obtains external assistance in the form of a yearly audit by a certified public accountant. An audit involves the investigation and examination of the transactions that underlie the church's financial reports and results in an opinion of those reports. In this process the auditor follows established auditing standards. A thorough review of the internal control system is included. Any defects in the internal control system are brought to the attention of church officials. Charters of some churches specify that annual audits be performed. But even when the certified public accountant performs the audit at the community service fee or during his or her slow period, many churches find that external audits are prohibitively expensive.

A church may also retain a certified public accountant to conduct a review. A review involves the inquiry and analysis necessary to provide the accountant with a reasonable basis for expressing limited assurance that the financial statements are presented fairly. A review does not involve a study or evaluation of internal accounting controls, tests of the accounting records, or other procedures ordinarily performed during an audit. But if the accountant becomes aware that information is incorrect, incomplete, or unsatisfactory, additional procedures necessary to achieve limited assurance are performed. Thus churches that cannot afford audits may want to consider obtaining reviews. Alternatively, churches presently having annual audits may want to consider alternating audits and reviews to reduce costs.

A final note on external assistance may be prudent. To laypeople, the terms *audit* and *review* can mean anything from an extensive investigation performed by an unsmiling individual to a quick check by someone not connected with the accounting records. To a certified public accountant, however, the terms mean specific services. Many church treasurers and financial secretaries think that their churches are receiving audits when, in fact, they are not. Check to see which service your church is receiving; you may be surprised.

### The Arena of Trust

Most churchgoers want to believe that anyone connected with their church is trustworthy. I frequently hear such comments as, "Who would steal from the House of the Lord?" "If I can't trust people at church, can I trust anyone, anywhere?" And "If someone takes money from the church, he or she probably really needs it." In other words, people working within a church, whether employees or volunteers, generally think of their environment as being different from other environments, where people may act dishonestly. For many people, in fact, this entire chapter will have been disturbing simply because of its topic.

In such an arena of trust, people let their guard down. They are less apt to call for strictly enforced internal control procedures. They are also less likely to monitor performance and, if necessary, take corrective action. Partially as a consequence of this trusting attitude, churches are vulnerable to embezzlement. The problem is real and cannot be ignored simply because it is unpleasant. As an accounting professional, I believe that the subject must be openly discussed.

## INTERNAL CONTROL SYSTEMS

Each church, regardless of its size, should establish a system of internal control. These practices and procedures can be tailored by church financial leaders to meet their church's specific needs. Implementation of these practices and procedures can substantially reduce but not eliminate the opportunity for misappropriation of assets and the generation of sloppy, unreliable reports. But no system is foolproof. Further, care must be taken in the design of specific controls. For example, a zealot could mandate that members personally take their weekly offerings to the bank as a way of reducing the risk of embezzlement, require five signatures on all checks to reduce unauthorized cash disbursements, and have all employees fingerprinted and photographed just for good measure. Obviously such practices would be oppressive. Controls should be selected for which the benefits outweigh the cost, both financially and emotionally.

It may be difficult to place a value on sound internal controls. But consider whether it is a benefit to the church to:

Remove temptation for misappropriation?

Prevent a cloud of suspicion from developing over the heads of honest staff members?

Save the time and expense of having to reconstruct destroyed or altered accounting records?

Improve the probability that errors, intentional or unintentional, are discovered?

Reduce the chance of having to confront a member or employee who has taken funds?

Reduce the chance of dividing the congregation or leadership into those who want to forget a misuse of funds and those who want to accuse and take action?

Reduce the chance of ever having to tell the congregation that some of their contributions have been lost?

Reduce the chance that you and other church leaders will have to feel embarrassed for allowing an incident to occur and feel guilty for not recognizing the potential for problems in time?

## Fifty Internal Control Practices for Every Church: A Test

Following are fifty internal controls that should be used by every church. The list is not exhaustive; other practices may be suitable in individual circumstances. For example, larger churches or those handling millions of dollars need to employ those controls appropriate for comparably sized commercial enterprises. Further, the practices mentioned may not be of equal importance to every church. Some may be very important to your church, and others may be of only secondary importance. I have, however, attempted to make each control relevant to every church. Thus, for example, controls related to pledges receivable are not included, because many churches do not obtain pledges. Additionally, I made no effort to weigh the importance of the different controls. Collectively they are all important, because they compose a comprehensive system of internal controls. Almost all of these internal controls can be established and maintained without significant cost to the church.

The fifty controls are presented in the form of a test of your church's current system of internal control. Each practice is introduced, its importance is discussed, and any possible violations of the control are indicated. After you read about each control, indicate in the box whether your church presently adheres to this practice. Answer yes if your church follows the internal control practice in *all* cases. Answer no if your church does not follow the practice or does not follow the practice consistently. Space for your notes is provided. Be honest with your answers; your church has a lot to gain from this self-test. Keep in mind that it takes only one no response to show vulnerability. But because the list is not exhaustive (there are probably a thousand-odd controls we could examine), fifty yes responses do not mean complete, 100 percent protection. I selected these fifty controls because they are the most reasonable for all churches, large and small, to use to reduce the risk of embezzlement and the generation of unreliable financial reports.

### Internal Controls—General

The first nine internal controls are general in nature and relate to organizational structure and the overall protection of church assets.

---

| **1** | **Are specific accounting functions handled by the individuals or groups assigned these functions in the church's organizational chart?** |
|---|---|

☐ Yes     Notes: _____

☐ No    _____

_____

_____

_____

---

There are several considerations within this first internal control practice. It is important that the church have an organizational chart that specifies the position responsible for each accounting function. Of equal importance, the organizational structure needs to be followed. Many churches have a written organizational structure, but the structure is violated almost every week. For instance, in some churches ushers who collect the weekly offering are people who are tardy for the start of the service and who sit in the last pew. Ten minutes before the offering is collected, they are recruited to be the ushers. It is unlikely that the organizational chart did not specify who was to collect offerings. In other churches the members who count the offering are recruited in an equally haphazard fashion, even though a counting committee has officially been given the task. Getting cash to the bank looks like a Laurel and Hardy movie in some churches as those people who hold the Sunday offering look for someone to take it to the bank. "Are you going to the bank?" is a common question. A small church in California lost an entire offering when it was entrusted to a visitor. He happened to stay around after the service and appeared to be a close friend of a former member.

Another aspect of this control involves the relationship between the accounting/finance area and the religious leader of the church. In many churches pastors become heavily involved with financial administration even though they are not given that responsibility on the organizational chart. They become involved for several reasons. First, the pastor is likely to spend more hours at the church than anyone else and therefore be around to make many financial decisions and inquiries. Second, the pastor is the leader of the church and is typically well respected by the congregation. Therefore his opinion is often solicited, and people comply with his requests. But typically the pastor is not trained in accounting or financial management and thus not truly able to serve as the final authority on these matters. For example, a pastor might tell a church treasurer that he or she had used a counter check at the bank to withdraw some of the church's funds for a particular purpose. Most treasurers would overlook the pastor's withdrawal of funds in this manner, even though the church's disbursement procedures were probably violated. Third, pastors routinely obtain information about the financial viability of their churches. This can inadvertently lead to increasing management and control of the financial area, including counting cash, signing checks, and, in some cases, handling the accounting records.

The writer, consultants to churches, and certified public accountants have no intention of keeping pastors from the financial information necessary to operate their churches. Information should be freely transmitted as necessary. But internal control is best maintained when those given responsibilities by the organizational chart carry out their duties precisely as planned.

| 2 | Does the church have a written, up-to-date accounting procedures manual? |
|---|---|

☐ Yes  Notes: _____

☐ No  _____

_____

_____

_____

The need for an accounting procedures manual to establish accounting procedures, place responsibility, and assure continuity was discussed earlier in this chapter.

| 3 | Does the financial secretary's or treasurer's activities involve only keeping the records of cash collections and preparing the support for disbursements? |
|---|---|

☐ Yes  Notes: _____

☐ No  _____

_____

_____

_____

The need for adequate separation of incompatible accounting duties was discussed earlier in this chapter. To reiterate, the separation of duties is the keystone of a church's internal control system. Keeping the recordkeeping function distinct from the cash handling (asset custody) function will go a long way in reducing the church's risk of misappropriation of funds.

For example, in one church the financial secretary had the responsibility of depositing Sunday offerings in the bank on Monday. The money was counted on Sunday. On Monday the financial secretary would change the figure on the deposit slip to a lesser amount and keep some money. Because the financial secretary also handled the bookkeeping, the lower amount was recorded on the books. Thus the discrepancy was covered up. Making sure that the financial secretary never had custody of cash would have prevented this.

In another case a treasurer, who was the sole signer on checks, decided to steal the church's funds. He accomplished the theft by writing checks to himself and entering the disbursements in the journal as payments for candles. To cover the ploy the treasurer would destroy the checks made out to himself when they were returned by the bank. Because the treasurer's reconciling of the cash account was never checked, the scheme went on for years. Again, if the treasurer had not had access to both the books and cash, this incident could have been avoided.

---

**4**   **Are facilities locked when not in use?**

---

☐ Yes     Notes: _____

☐ No      _____

_____

_____

_____

Securing the premises to safeguard the church's assets is just good common sense. Yet just as we read about people who go on two-week vacations and don't lock their houses, there are some churches that are not adequately secured when not in use. Exterior and interior doors may be unlocked, and windows may be left open.

---

**5**   **Are the accounting records safeguarded at all times?**

---

☐ Yes     Notes: _____

☐ No      _____

_____

_____

_____

Special physical control should be exercised over the accounting records. In large congregations all of the records are kept at the church. Safeguarding would therefore entail controls to make sure that the records are 1) not destroyed, altered, or tampered with during office hours and 2) hard to get at when the office is closed. In smaller congregations the problem is more acute, because much of the treasurer's job is performed at home. More than once church records have been stolen from the backseats of treasurers' automobiles or lost by treasurers. Any time accounting records are moved from location to location, there is added risk of loss.

Also, in the age of computers, information can easily be lost if the computer operator punches the wrong key or selects the wrong alternative. For example, diskettes, sometimes called floppy disks, contain the accounting records of most churches that use computers. New data are entered on a diskette and are merged with old data to update the records. If, however, the operator accidently clears the diskette or removes a file without having made a copy of it, data can be lost. Data can also disappear if the computer is turned off while the diskette is in the computer, or rearranged if the diskette comes in contact with a magnetic field. Further, a diskette can become bent, worn out, or contaminated. Thus churches using diskettes have to take special measures to safeguard their accounting records. This may include, for example, the computer operator making several duplicates of each diskette at the end of the day and storing them in different locations.

---

**6**   Is an internal audit committee operational?

---

☐ Yes     Notes: _____

☐ No       _____

_____

_____

_____

---

As discussed earlier in this chapter, an internal audit committee is usually made up of members with accounting or business backgrounds. They perform some tests of the accounting records. Their tests should be done on a periodic basis (possibly quarterly and annually), but tests done on a sporadic, surprise basis are also beneficial. If possible, the church's external accountant should specify which tests to perform and which procedures to follow.

There are two schools of thought on the extensive use of an internal audit committee. One group claims that audits by nonqualified members are worse than no audits at all. These people assert that the work done by the committee creates a false sense of security for both the accounting staff and the congregation. The other group, of which I am a member, holds that any review is better than no review. People perpetrating dishonest acts do not want their work reviewed by anyone. Having someone examine the records is troublesome to these people; they may get caught! Thus a working internal audit committee is both a psychological and an actual deterrent.

Of course, at times the protection afforded the church from an internal audit committee is almost laughable. To illustrate, my father, a welder by trade, once faithfully served as the one-person audit committee of his church. His responsibility was to audit the work done by the church treasurer, a CPA. Each month the CPA would spread out the books on the dining room table and instruct my father as to how his work should be audited. They would jointly reconcile the accounts and bank balances. Obviously this was a mismatch situation. But the next year my father's term expired, a new treasurer was installed, and the CPA became the one-person audit committee. Thus the mismatch became reversed. As you can see, it may be difficult to obtain full benefits from such a committee every year. But if you focus too much on the negatives, the committee may never be appointed.

---

**7**    Are the accounting records and the underlying internal controls audited annually?

---

☐ Yes    Notes: _____

☐ No      _____

_____

_____

_____

---

An annual audit offers the church several advantages. First, the fact that everyone knows an annual inspection will occur serves as a deterrent to embezzlement. Second, the auditor has an annual opportunity to evaluate compliance with those internal controls that have been established and to suggest new ways of protecting church assets. Third, in those churches that have a new treasurer every year, the church will be certain to have each treasurer's work reviewed. Thus the auditor can identify and correct any deficiencies before they become standard operating procedures. Fourth, a written policy of annual audits precludes any treasurer from feeling paranoid about the members not trusting him or her. Church leaders in those churches having only occasional audits are apt to hear this remark from treasurers in office when an audit is suggested.

As discussed earlier in this chapter, only an independent CPA can conduct a professional audit. If the cost is not prohibitive, I recommend that you use a CPA. If retaining a CPA is out of the question, the audit could be conducted by the internal audit committee or a group of members who report to this committee. Auditors may also be available from or suggested by the church's regional denominational office. Sometimes retired CPAs or former church treasurers are available for annual audits.

---

**8**  **Are new personnel screened?**

---

☐ Yes   Notes: _____

☐ No    _____

_____

_____

_____

Amazingly enough, 70 percent of all embezzlers are repeat offenders! This alarming statistic is relevant to churches for several reasons. First, few dishonest church accountants are ever prosecuted. As noted earlier, the matter is often hushed up within the church. Unfortunately, this sometimes means that the perpetrator is free to repeat the scheme in other churches. And that has occurred. In one case a treasurer embezzled cash from Sunday offerings that he counted himself. After he was caught, church leaders told him that he was never to set foot in the church again. Not two years later he surfaced as the treasurer of a similarly sized church of the same denomination twenty miles away. No one from the new church bothered to inquire about the treasurer's past. Similar cases have involved salaried financial secretaries who embezzled a succession of churches over a long (and probably prosperous) career.

Screening prospective (and probably underpaid) employees and pivotal volunteers is not a pleasant task. In most cases congregations are so happy to receive the services that they never make background checks of the individuals. Additionally, screening people to work in the church seems distasteful. Remember the arena of trust discussion. I do not advocate using the extensive screening that is routinely carried out in the business world, but some screening must occur. This screening may involve as little as a few telephone calls to references, former supervisors, neighbors, and so on. People who are careful to get several opinions on which long-distance telephone company to use, which VCR to purchase, and which supermarket has the lowest prices fail to get any opinions on new church personnel. The church's assets are certainly as valuable as a new VCR and need to be safeguarded.

---

**9**    Are all employees who have access to cash bonded?

---

☐ Yes     Notes: _____

☐ No      _____

_____

_____

_____

A fidelity bond provides insurance protection for the church if there is any lapse in the integrity of the accounting system. Various types of fidelity bonds can be purchased. Blanket bonds can cover the entire staff without people's names or the positions they hold being listed. Many blanket bonds cover embezzlement and other dishonest acts committed alone or in collusion with others. Position bonds, on the other hand, cover people who are working in selected positions, such as treasurer or financial secretary. Individual bonds cover only those individuals named in the bond.

Blanket bonds are popular with churches, because all employees may be covered. And unlike individual bonds, no personal or credit checks are conducted. Also, a uniform amount of coverage is obtained, such as

$10,000 per incident, and new personnel are usually automatically covered. Further, the insurance company typically does not have to be informed of every slight realignment made in financial positions or duties.

Many churches are unknowingly covered by a fidelity bond under an all-risks property insurance policy. Many church leaders have been pleasantly surprised to learn that they have a bond. Fidelity bond protection can also be obtained as a rider to a property insurance policy or purchased separately.

Bonding provides much more than protection, with its associated peace of mind, for the church. Bonding also gives the church a quick and easy way to handle actual or suspected cases of theft, forgery, embezzlement, or other misappropriation of assets. Imagine what you would have to go through without bonding protection. First, you would have to detect the problem, verify its existence and form, and determine the amount of money involved. After that, you would have to decide if and when to accuse the dishonest person and exactly what to say. If you were to accuse anyone erroneously, you could be sued personally and lose your own assets. Contrast this situation with the procedure if the church was bonded. In this case, if you had good reason to suspect that something was wrong, you would merely call the insurance company. Its staff would handle the rest. The insurance company would have auditors trained specifically for such situations. Their auditors would know how to approach people without incurring legal liability and how to ask for a return of the money.

### Internal Controls—Cash Receipts

The next seventeen internal controls concern the handling of the church's cash receipts.

---

**10** Are members encouraged to use offering envelopes?

---

☐ Yes          Notes: _____

☐ No           _____

_____

_____

_____

Envelopes serve to 1) protect members' offerings until they can be counted, and 2) provide the basis for recording the contribution in the church's accounting records.

The envelopes should be retained by the treasurer, similar to the handling of monthly bills, invoices, and other business documents. The envelopes are essential if total or individual contributions need to be verified by or for the church members. Such verification may be necessary for members having to support their figures on their federal and state income tax returns.

---

**11** Are members encouraged to use checks in making their offerings (and other gifts as well)?

---

☐ Yes          Notes: _____

☐ No           _____

_____

_____

_____

Even if members of the congregation are encouraged to use the envelopes the church provides, they should also be encouraged to write checks when contributing to the church. Checks, made out to the church, are much more difficult to steal than cash is. A statement in the church bulletin to the effect that checks provide proof for IRS purposes and reduce the likelihood of loss if the church were ever burglarized should suffice.

---

**12** Is the handling of offerings always controlled by at least two people?

---

☐ Yes          Notes: _____

☐ No           _____

_____

_____

_____

The key word in cash handling is togetherness. At least two people need to be involved in every step of the cash receipts process. At least two people should collect the offerings, take the money to the counting area, count the offerings, and take the deposit bag to the bank. With the togetherness principle, only collusion between the individuals or extreme carelessness will cause problems. This control not only safeguards assets but also reduces the possibility that money handlers will ever be caught up in controversy.

Several incidents involving the unilateral handling of cash have already been discussed. Recall the case of the treasurer who wrote checks to himself and that of the financial secretary who, before going to the bank, altered the deposit slips to cover her theft of cash. Several other cases can be cited. In a Texas church an usher who collected the offerings, some of which were loose bills, would say, "Elaine Johnson would like $10 change for her $20 bill." He would then take $10 out of his plate and pretend to go back to Elaine Johnson's pew while the other ushers left for the counting room. Needless to say, Elaine Johnson had not asked for change, and the cash was pocketed. The church later adopted a rule that no change would be given from the offering. In a Louisiana case an usher would pocket some loose bills from the offering when he was hidden from the congregation by large curtains. After this was detected (by a member who just happened to peek around the curtain), the church changed its collection procedure so that two persons were assigned to collect from each row. One person would collect and one person would assist.

In a case with another twist, a priest skimmed $100,000 from offering plates over a series of years and deposited the money at the local bank. Remorseful, he presented the money to his successor when he retired.[1]

---

**13** Is the handling of other receipts of cash always controlled by at least two people?

---

☐ Yes    Notes: _____

           _____

☐ No    _____

           _____

           _____

---

[1] "Church Finance Chief Tries to Balance Reality with Spiritual Needs," *Wall Street Journal*, 7 January 1986, p. 13.

Churches also receive cash from Sunday school classes, Mother's Day Out programs, preschool educational programs, operations of schools, hot lunch programs, and so on. The togetherness principle for handling cash also applies in these activities. Thus Sunday school class secretaries and program directors should not unilaterally handle the cash generated in their areas.

---

**14** Is cash counted in a secured area?

---

☐ Yes    Notes: _____

☐ No     _____

_____

_____

_____

Most churches have the offerings counted in a secured, locked room. There have been cases, however, of people counting cash in unsecured areas, such as in passageways and regretting having done so when some money disappeared.

---

**15** Do the money counters verify that the contents of the offering envelopes are identical to the amounts written on the envelopes by the members?

---

☐ Yes    Notes: _____

☐ No     _____

_____

_____

_____

Once again, using the togetherness principle, at least two money counters should open the envelopes, remove the contents, and compare the amount taken from each envelope with the amount stated on the face of the envelope. If the amounts are not identical, which may occur frequently, the actual amount enclosed should be written on the envelope, followed by the initials of the money counter. Large churches may have more involved procedures for handling the discrepancies.

Because the offering envelopes serve as the basis for posting to members' contribution records, they must be correct before being turned over to the financial secretary or treasurer. It serves no purpose to deposit a sum of money that is different from the total shown on envelopes, which is posted to the accounting records. In fact, such a practice would automatically produce financial reports that do not balance.

---

**16** Are all checks received restrictively endorsed as soon as possible?

☐ Yes     Notes: _____

☐ No     _____

_____

_____

_____

Using a rubber stamp to restrictively endorse all checks received is a sound internal control practice. An example of a restrictive endorsement is shown in exhibit 3-1. Using this protection, any checks lost or stolen cannot be cashed. Many churches have each check endorsed by the money counters immediately after the amount is verified against the envelope.

---

**17** Is cash deposited as soon as possible after receipt?

☐ Yes     Notes: _____

☐ No     _____

_____

_____

_____

```
PAY TO THE ORDER OF
First National Bank
FOR DEPOSIT ONLY
PORTER COMMUNITY CHURCH
#946-24769
```

Exhibit 3-1   A Restrictive Endorsement

In most churches the offering is counted at the church and, within a few hours of collection, it is deposited at the bank. In other churches the offering is first deposited at the bank and then counted the next day in the bank's community service room or boardroom. These procedures have merit. Depositing funds as quickly as possible 1) lessens the risk of outright theft, 2) prevents the substitution of subsequently received receipts to cover shortages, and 3) increases the odds that the checks will be collectible. Yes, even churches encounter bad checks! Those churches waiting until Monday, Tuesday, or Wednesday to deposit Sunday's funds may be inviting trouble.

Some churches in rural areas may bank by mail. As long as only checks are being forwarded to the bank, this practice is satisfactory. But the following incident may be illuminating. A small church in the Sierra Nevada mountain range of California was more than forty miles from the nearest bank, and because church leaders did not want to leave the

Sunday offerings on the premises, they decided to bank by mail. Soon thereafter the local general store operator, who was a member of the church, offered the following plan to the treasurer. The treasurer would endorse all of the checks and turn these checks and loose currency and coins over to the merchant, who would write one check to the church for the sum total of the moneys received. The treasurer would then have to mail only one check to the bank. This practice always worked satisfactorily for the treasurer, but the merchant was later visited by the IRS for claiming a tax deduction for charitable contributions equal to the total amount of checks written to the church!

---

**18** Is all cash received deposited in the bank?

---

☐ Yes     Notes: _____

☐ No      _____

_____

_____

_____

Cash receipts should be deposited intact, that is, without being reduced by disbursements. Paying any expenses out of the available cash is a bad practice. As will be discussed later, all disbursements should be made by check or through the petty cash fund.

---

**19** Is cash safeguarded in a safe, lock box, or similar protective container when at the church?

---

☐ Yes     Notes: _____

☐ No      _____

_____

_____

_____

Cash receipts may be at the church for as little as a few hours, in the case of the Sunday offering, or as long as several days, in the case of midweek mailed-in amounts. It is imperative that all cash be protected. The combination to the safe or the keys to the lock box should not be available to accounting personnel. Remember the discussion of the separation of duties. A financial secretary, for instance, who is responsible for taking care of the accounting records and who also has access to the safe and lock box, is performing incompatible functions.

---

**20** Are collection reports given to the financial secretary or treasurer for entry into the accounting records, and a copy sent to the internal audit committee for subsequent audit purposes?

---

☐ Yes        Notes: _____

☐ No          _____

_____

_____

Collections should never be handled by people who work with the accounting records. The counting committee should deposit cash in the bank and inform the recordkeepers of their activities. The optimum system for handling collections is as follows:

The counting committee counts the offerings and prepares a collection report indicating details of currency and coins, checks included in envelopes, and checks not included in envelopes.

The counting committee prepares the bank deposit slip in triplicate and deposits the moneys in the bank. The original slip goes to the bank, one copy goes to the treasurer, and the other copy goes to the internal audit committee.

The collection report is also prepared in triplicate. The original, together with the opened envelopes, goes to the person in charge of recording contributions in the accounting records, a copy goes to the internal audit committee; another copy is retained by the counting committee.

The entire collection-handling function is shown in exhibit 3-2. Although the process may seem complex, the only difference between the suggested approach and that currently followed in many churches is that extra copies of the deposit slip and collection report are required.

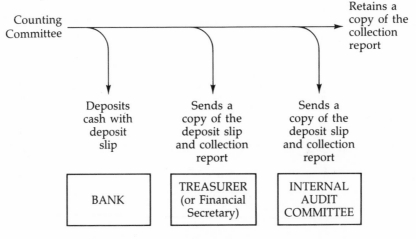

**Exhibit 3-2 Overview of Cash-Handling Procedures**

---

**21** Are incoming-mail and in-office contributions handled by people who are not responsible for the accounting records?

---

☐ Yes    Notes: _____

☐ No     _____

_____

_____

_____

It would be foolish to install internal controls for the handling of the weekly offerings, but neglect to install controls for midweek receipt of checks in the mail and in-office contributions. Yet many churches do just that, and a few have paid the price for their lack of controls. Establishing controls for incoming-mail and in-office contributions is not easy; it may involve the use of some volunteers to achieve the necessary separation of duties.

To control cash coming in through the mail, someone who does not handle the accounting records should open the mail, prepare a list of the checks received, and deposit the money in the bank. That person should retain a copy of the list of checks. The original would be given to the financial secretary or treasurer, together with a duplicate bank-deposit slip. If a substantial number of checks are involved, the church should consider more elaborate controls. They may include having two people open the mail and the forwarding of copies of receipts lists and deposit slips to the internal audit committee.

Collections may also be received in the central church office and other offices as well. Members may stop by to make a special offering or restricted gift. Parents may come by to pay the tuition for their children enrolled in the church's programs. Senior citizens may pay for any meals received. As with mail receipts, people handling the money should not handle the books. Some churches use prenumbered receipts for cash received. This practice helps prevent cash from getting "lost."

---

**22** Has the bank been instructed in writing never to cash checks payable to the church?

---

☐ Yes    Notes: _____

☐ No     _____

_____

_____

_____

It may surprise some people to learn that some bank clerks can be talked into cashing an occasional check made out to the church. The perpetrator may build rapport with the bank clerk over a long period of time, and then one day say, "The pastor asked me to cash this check for him today instead of depositing it. He's going to visit a hospitalized member in Roseville." If the bank clerk follows the request, the church has lost some money. Of course, a letter to the bank may not prevent the event from happening. It does, however, fix responsibility for the misappropriation with the bank.

---

**23** Are contribution records maintained for members?

---

☐ Yes    Notes: _____

☐ No     _____

_____

_____

_____

Keeping a record of members' contributions is a positive control, because each member can compare his or her personal records against those of the church.

---

**24** Do members receive periodic (perhaps quarterly) notices of their contributions from the internal audit committee?

---

☐ Yes          Notes: _____

☐ No            _____

_____

_____

_____

Sending members periodic notices is not only a control procedure, but also a stimulus toward fulfilling pledges. Some churches use this opportunity to remind their members of their annual pledge, the amount given thus far, and the balance of the pledge. In other churches such a comparison would be impossible, because pledges are either anonymous or are handled by a person or committee other than those responsible for recording receipts.

Regardless, periodic notices allow each member to compare his or her giving against the church's records. Errors and unusual lags in posting can be brought to the attention of the internal audit committee, which should be responsible for sending out the notices. Obviously, this process should not be handled by people responsible for the accounting records. The purpose of the procedure is to check on those involved with the books.

---

**25** Are the periodic notices of contributions sent to each member photocopied?

---

☐ Yes          Notes: _____

☐ No            _____

_____

_____

_____

Photocopying serves as an excellent internal control technique, because any irregularities, errors, and so on, are displayed to the member. Although typed notices look neater, there is no assurance that, for example, a financial secretary will not cover up a problem by typing something that is different from the information in the books. For instance, if $200 of a $500 contribution was stolen by the financial secretary, the member is likely to catch the error when the photocopied record shows a contribution of $300. But if the information is typed, nothing prevents the financial secretary from typing a notice telling the member that $500 was given, thus covering up the theft.

---

**26** Are members instructed to report to the internal audit committee any irregularities or errors in their notices of contributions?

---

☐ Yes      Notes: _____

☐ No        _____

_____

_____

_____

Many of us have received a notice from our bank telling us that the bank was being audited, our bank balance on a certain day, and to contact the CPA firm if the amount was in error.

Unlike the preceding situation, most churches do not tell members what to do if their contribution notices are incorrect. So what do most members do? They call the church office. And to whom do they talk? The person handling the accounting records. And what usually transpires? The person handling the records promises to check into the problem and send them corrected notices. If any illegal scheme was being executed, all complaints could be quickly handled by the person typing corrected notices and forwarding them to members without correcting the accounting records.

### Internal Control—Cash Disbursements

The following seventeen internal controls relate to the handling of cash disbursements in the church. The need for proper accounting controls for cash disbursements is as great as that for cash receipts.

**27** Are requisition slips prepared for anticipated disbursements that do not have standing authorization?

☐ Yes          Notes: _____

☐ No           _____

_____

_____

_____

In many churches committee chairpersons, directors, activity leaders, and others can stop by or telephone the church office to request that something be ordered. The treasurer has the obligation to make sure that the order falls within the person's budget and, if so, that it is ordered, received, paid for, and charged to the correct account. These functions are not always executed properly in many churches, because no organized system of purchasing or making payment has been established. Many churches operate with systems that are no more sophisticated than those used by individuals in their homes. Orders are placed without being documented; goods are received and paid for that were not ordered; goods are paid for twice; goods are paid for that have not been received.

The initial step in a purchasing system is the preparation of a requisition slip. Such slips can be purchased at most office supply stores. Persons authorized to make purchases prepare the requisition, indicating the item or service desired, reason for the request, estimated cost, vendor desired, and date needed. The original copy is sent to the financial secretary or treasurer, and the carbon duplicate is retained by the preparer. When the requisition slip is received, it is used to make sure that the good or service is both provided for in the budget and that the account to be charged has an adequate balance remaining. If both conditions are satisfied, the requisition is approved and a purchase order prepared. If both conditions are not met, the requisition is not approved, and the preparer informed as to the reason. Although this procedure may seem cumbersome, it has several advantages. First, it keeps people from charging goods and services to the church without approval. How many times has the church received a mysterious vendor's statement that had to be traced to a member-orderer? Second, this procedure keeps people from paying for items themselves and then presenting the receipt to the treasurer for reimbursement. Third, this procedure allows the church office to select specific vendors. Some vendors may give the church a lower price or be very dependable. The person requesting the goods and services may not be aware of this.

Many expenditures, such as those for salaries, utilities, and mortgage payments, would have a standing authorization for payment. In such cases requisition slips, purchase orders, and so on, would not be prepared.

---

**28** Are prenumbered purchase orders used for all disbursements that do not have standing authorization for payment?

---

☐ Yes       Notes: _____

☐ No        _____

_____

_____

_____

The use of purchase orders is an important internal control device for churches. Purchase orders should be used even if requisition slips are not used. Many varieties of purchase orders are available at office supply stores. Not only does the use of purchase orders provide structure and accountability for legitimate purchases, it prevents the possibility of the church being ripped off by the hordes of unscrupulous vendors who prey on churches. Knowing that churches tend to use volunteers and tend not to be as highly organized as profit-seeking businesses, some vendors will send unordered goods to churches and demand payment for the supposedly ordered merchandise. The current schemes involve maintenance supplies and photocopy supplies; who knows what will be next. The use of purchase orders will protect you from paying for unordered goods. If you receive such goods, you can write to the vendor and tell it where to pick up its goods. Without the use of purchase orders, you will always be uncertain whether the goods were really ordered.

An example of a purchase order is shown in exhibit 3-3. Note that the purchase order is prenumbered and that the vendor is specifically instructed to place the number on all invoices and shipping documents. No invoices should be paid unless and until vendors comply.

## PURCHASE ORDER

### St. Mark's Church
### 254 Main Street
### Anytown, IL 60643

No. 1019

**To**  Outdoor Furniture Co.

741 Main Street

Anytown, CA 90048

**Date** 7/22/8X

**Terms Desired** 2/10,N/30

**Ship To**  Angels Camp, Route 49, Anytown, IL 60643

**Ship Via** Truck        **Date Needed** 8/15/8X

**Please accept our order for the following:**

| Quantity | Number | Description | Price | Per | Amount |
|----------|--------|-------------|-------|-----|--------|
| 20 | T-1066 | Picnic Tables | $100.00 | Table | $2000.00 |

**Purchase order number must appear on all shipping documents and invoices.**

**Ordered By**

*Tom Smith*

Exhibit 3-3   Purchase Order

**29** Are invoices for goods and services approved by a qualified person before payment is made?

☐ Yes    Notes: _____

☐ No     _____

_____

_____

_____

The company selling the merchandise or delivering the service will send an invoice to the church for the amount involved. Often the invoice and the goods will arrive together. Before the process continues it is imperative that a qualified person approve the invoice for payment. This is best achieved by having the person who ordered the goods or services inspect what was received and sign the invoice. Only that person will know if the goods or services received are exactly what was ordered. The items can be the wrong color, size, quality, and so on. The church has no obligation to pay for anything that was not included on the purchase order.

**30** Are invoices checked for accuracy before being paid?

☐ Yes    Notes: _____

☐ No     _____

_____

_____

_____

The error rate for invoices may be as high as 3 percent to 5 percent if the vendor is not well organized or is using new personnel. But even in the best of situations, human error occurs. All invoices should be checked for accuracy. Nothing should be taken for granted, even if the invoice is computer generated. The price, calculations, and terms of sale need to be verified before payment.

**31** Is a check authorization slip prepared to support the disbursement of funds?

☐ Yes     Notes: _____

☐ No      _____

_____

_____

_____

Before a check can be written, the treasurer must be certain that all steps in the cash disbursement system have been completed. Unauthorized disbursements have a way of occurring when the system is breached. A way to monitor all aspects of the system is to prepare a check authorization slip for each disbursement. An example of such a slip is presented as exhibit 3-4. The slip has check-off spaces for the

**CHECK AUTHORIZATION**

|  | No. | ✓ |
|---|---|---|
| Requisition | 546 | ✓ |
| Purchase Order | 1019 | ✓ |
| Received |  | ✓ |
| Invoice | S-113 |  |
| Price |  | ✓ |
| Calculations |  | ✓ |
| Terms |  | ✓ |
| Approved by Receiver |  | ✓ |

Approved for Payment

*Melinda Flowers*

Exhibit 3-4 Check Authorization Slip

requisition, purchase order number, receipt of goods or services, assurance of invoice accuracy, and approval for payment.

---

**32** Are all disbursements of cash, except for minor items, made by serially numbered checks?

---

☐ Yes     Notes: _____

☐ No       _____

_____

_____

_____

Prenumbered checks are available at banks or business systems firms for churches using one-write or computer systems. Checks should be used for disbursing cash.

A summary of the cash disbursement system recommended for paying bills is presented as exhibit 3-5.

---

**33** Is a check protector used?

---

☐ Yes     Notes: _____

☐ No       _____

_____

_____

_____

A check protector is a mechanical device that embosses the amount on the check. This prevents the recipient or someone else from changing the amount of the check before depositing it at a bank. Most businesses routinely protect their checks in this manner. Used check protectors are available at a nominal cost. You could ask for a used one in the weekly church bulletin.

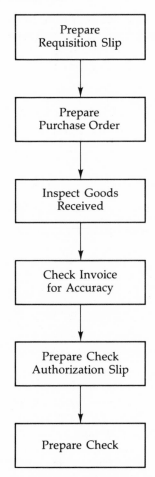

Exhibit 3-5    A Cash Disbursement System for Churches

**34** Do all check signers inspect all supporting documents before signing?

☐ Yes        Notes: _____

☐ No         _____

_____

_____

_____

Each person responsible for signing the church's checks should inspect all supporting documents before signing, regardless of who has signed before him or her. If, for example, two people must sign checks, there may be a tendency for the first person to sign without review, thinking that the second person will inspect the documents. Conversely, the second person may sign without review, relying on the first person's signature as evidence that a thorough review had taken place. It's like two baseball players letting a ball drop because each thought the other would catch it.

---

**35** **Are at least two signatures required for all checks?**

---

☐ Yes        Notes: _____

☐ No         _____

_____

_____

_____

The protection that comes from having two persons responsible for signing checks is worth the extra effort involved. Without this control one person is in charge of the cash, a topic discussed earlier. Some churches even require three signatures on checks. Many churches authorize five persons to sign checks, any two of whom will suffice for any check. This approach is wise because it considers the likelihood that some of the signers will be unavailable because of emergencies, vacations, or illnesses.

It is probably best not to have the treasurer be one of the check signers. If the treasurer signs first, implying that all supporting documents have been reviewed, few second signers will perform their duties carefully. Most will simply add their signature to the check, which of course violates the purpose of this internal control.

A final thought. What about the existence of signed blank checks in churches? Most individuals would not consider signing one of their own checks and leaving the rest blank, for fear that someone could obtain the check and insert any amount. Yet I believe that I could walk into 30 percent of all churches during the parts of the summer months when their check signers are on vacation, and find a batch of signed blank checks! This must not occur. If check signers are going on vacation, three possibilities exist. First, some bills, even salaries, can be paid early.

Second, using estimates if necessary, checks can be prepared in advance for some bills and salaries. Estimated amounts can be corrected in later periods. Check recipients will be elated to receive the bulk of their payments on time. Third, all disbursements by check can be stopped until the signers return. Creditors can be informed of the short delay; most will be understanding. Obligations to creditors must not supersede the church's obligation to protect its own assets. After all, this situation is typically of brief duration, and the creditors will get paid in full.

---

## 36 Are supporting documents canceled when checks are issued?

☐ Yes     Notes: _____

☐ No      _____

_____

_____

_____

A good practice is to cancel the supporting documents to a cash disbursement by stamping the invoice and any associated paperwork *Paid*. Many churches also indicate the date paid and the number of the check issued. Such a practice reduces the possibility that the same invoice, or a duplicate, would be paid twice. Some church treasurers complain that vendors are quick to ask for payment, but slow to respond when asked for a refund on a twice-paid bill. Also, many vendors do not have a policy of informing their customers of credit balances or of granting automatic refunds in cases of overpayment.

---

## 37 Are all voided checks marked and retained?

☐ Yes     Notes: _____

☐ No      _____

_____

_____

_____

All voided checks, whether the voiding is due to errors, ripping, or coffee damage, need to be marked *Void* with a broad felt pen and kept for reconciliation purposes. To maintain proper number sequence in the cash disbursements journal or checkbook, the check should be recorded, with a note that it was voided.

---

## 38 Is preparing a check to Cash prohibited?

☐ Yes     Notes: _____

☐ No      _____

          _____

          _____

          _____

You may regularly write checks to Cash from your personal checking account. But checks prepared in this manner do not specify what the funds were used for. The church needs to know why every disbursement occurred, so preparing checks to Cash should not be permitted.

---

## 39 Are blank, unused checks safeguarded at all times?

☐ Yes     Notes: _____

☐ No      _____

          _____

          _____

          _____

When checks are not being prepared, any blank, unused checks should be kept in a safe or lock box to prevent their theft and misuse.

**40** Are expenses always recorded in the correct accounting period?

☐ Yes     Notes: _____

☐ No      _____

_____

_____

_____

This internal control relates to the reliability of the accounting records and the informational content of financial reports. Adherence to this control means that checks would never be predated or postdated. A check would be recorded on the date written and subsequently posted to the proper account. The predating and postdating of checks hides the truth, which can affect decisions. For example, suppose a check prepared on December 22 for educational supplies is postdated and recorded on January 2 to cover a year-end budget shortage. As this expenditure will be charged to the next year's budget, church administrators will be preempted from two considerations. First, they will never get to question the efficiency of the education director, because no unfavorable variance from the budget will show. In fact, the director may be praised for staying within the budget. Further, the need for a higher budget for education will not be discussed.

Therefore if expenses are not consistently recorded in the correct period, the financial reports are unreliable and decision makers cannot do their jobs effectively.

**41** Is a petty cash fund used for minor disbursements of cash?

☐ Yes     Notes: _____

☐ No      _____

_____

_____

Another important element in the control of cash is a petty cash system. A petty cash system establishes a fund that is used to make small payments, especially those that are impractical and uneconomical to make by check. Examples of such payments include those for minor items, such as postage due, stamps, or office supplies.

A petty cash fund is created by cashing a check drawn on the church's regular checking account. The proceeds from the check are placed in a petty cash box that is controlled by a fund custodian. The custodian supervises the fund and is held accountable for any discrepancies. The fund should be adequate to cover payments for a short period—several weeks or a month.

---

**42** **Are vouchers prepared for all disbursements from the petty cash fund?**

☐ Yes     Notes: _____

☐ No      _____

_____

_____

_____

All payments from the petty cash fund should be supported with petty cash vouchers. A typical petty cash voucher is illustrated in exhibit 3-6. Each petty cash voucher indicates the date of the expenditure, individual receiving the money, purpose of the expenditure, and the amount paid. Along with various invoices and receipts, petty cash vouchers are used as evidence of disbursements. When necessary and at the end of the accounting period, the petty cash fund should be replenished. At that time the expenditures should be recorded in the accounting records.

---

**43** **Are transfers among bank accounts properly authorized?**

☐ Yes     Notes: _____

☐ No      _____

_____

_____

_____

```
┌─────────────────────────────────────────────────────────┐
│                                                           │
│                  PETTY CASH VOUCHER                       │
│                                                           │
│                                    No. _____             │
│                                                           │
│    Date _____                                  │
│                                                           │
│    Payee _____     │
│                                                           │
│    For _____     │
│                                                           │
│         _____    │
│                                                           │
│    Amount _____     │
│                                                           │
│    Charge To _____     │
│                                                           │
│    Approved By:              Received By:                 │
│                                                           │
│    _____          _____             │
│                                                           │
└─────────────────────────────────────────────────────────┘
```

Exhibit 3-6   Petty Cash Voucher

Most churches have several bank accounts. Transfers of funds between banks is typically done by check, where adequate controls may exist. But transfers of funds within a bank can be accomplished without preparing a check, without much paperwork, and possibly outside of existing internal controls. Funds may be moved from accounts with stringent requirements for disbursement to those with virtually no such requirements. Approval for all transfers should be required and documented in the accounting records.

### Internal Controls—Reconciliation Practices

Three internal control practices relating to the reconciliation of accounts are recommended. Reconciliation involves comparing two records to determine whether they agree. For example, you may have reconciled a cash register tape against the cost of each item purchased in a store to determine if you were overcharged.

**44** Are reconciliations of all bank accounts prepared monthly by a person who is not involved in writing checks?

☐ Yes      Notes: _____

☐ No        _____

_____

_____

_____

Reconciliation of bank accounts needs to be done monthly when bank statements are received. It is important that the work not be done by people who are involved in writing checks. Recall the experience discussed earlier in this chapter where the treasurer wrote fraudulent checks, covered them up in the accounting records, and destroyed the checks during the reconciling process. Such incidents can occur if treasurers who keep, prepare, and sign checks are also permitted to reconcile the bank accounts.

Bank statements should be mailed to a member of the internal audit committee or someone designated by the committee to reconcile the accounts. Monthly reconciliations should be retained for use during the yearly audit of the books.

The reconciliation of bank accounts will uncover any items that are on only the bank's books or only the church's books because of either a timing difference or an error made by the bank or the church. Common examples of timing differences follow.

Items recorded on the church books but not yet reported on the bank statement, such as:

Deposits in transit. Receipts may be recorded on the church books but not yet recorded at the bank. This situation occurs when deposits made near the end of the month are not included on the bank statement. Deposits in transit are determined by comparing deposits on the bank statement with deposits recorded on the books.

Outstanding checks. Checks may be written but not yet processed by the bank. Outstanding checks are determined by comparing checks reported on the bank statement against checks written on church records.

Items reported on the bank statement but not yet entered in the church's records, such as:

Nonsufficient funds checks. Members' checks may be returned because of lack of funds.

Bank service charges for account processing.

Interest added by the bank.

Member contributions made directly to the bank.

In addition to timing differences, errors may cause a discrepancy between the bank's recorded cash balance and the church's recorded cash balance. Bank errors may include, for example, charging the church's account for a check drawn by another bank customer, failing to record a deposit or transfer from another account, or reducing the account by an incorrect amount. Although the bank is typically larger than the church and uses the most sophisticated electronic equipment, banks make their share of mistakes. Bank statements should not be presumed to be correct until they are reviewed. Alternatively, church records could contain errors. Church errors may include, for example, incorrect addition on a deposit slip or the writing of a check for a different amount than the one recorded.

Several different types of reconciliations can be prepared. Most banks provide a reconciliation form on the back of the monthly statement. A commonly used form allows the preparer to determine the amount of cash over which the church has control at a stated date. An example of such a bank reconciliation appears in exhibit 3-7.

The reconciliation deals with those items of the church's records and the bank's records that differ between themselves. The preparer considers these items and adjusts one cash balance or the other to bring both balances into agreement. In this case First Church has an ending cash balance of $10,700 on December 31, 19XX.

---

**45** Is the petty cash fund reconciled on a surprise basis at least once a year?

☐ Yes      Notes: _____

☐ No        _____

_____

_____

**First Church**
**Bank Reconciliation**
**December 31, 19XX**

| | | |
|---|---:|---:|
| Balance per bank statement | | $10,000.00 |
| Add receipts recorded on our books but not reported on the bank statement: | | |
| December 30 deposit | | 1,500.00 |
| | | $11,500.00 |
| Deduct disbursements recorded on our books but not reported on the bank statement: | | |
| Outstanding checks— | | |
| #777 | $700.50 | |
| 778 | 42.50 | |
| 793 | 57.00 | 800.00 |
| Adjusted bank balance | | $10,700.00 |
| Balance per church books | | $ 9,400.00 |
| Add receipts reported on the bank statement but not recorded on our books: | | |
| Check deposited by Angela Rogelli to the church account | | 1,500.00 |
| | | $10,900.00 |
| Deduct disbursements reported on the bank statement but not recorded on our books: | | |
| Bank service charges | $ 10.00 | |
| Check returned for insufficient funds | 190.00 | 200.00 |
| Adjusted book balance | | $10,700.00 |

**Exhibit 3-7    Bank Reconciliation**

A member of the internal audit committee or its delegate should periodically make a surprise visit to the petty cash custodian and ask to reconcile the fund. This means that all vouchers for disbursements made from the fund would be added to the remaining cash to determine if all funds were accounted for. Therefore if vouchers totaling $43 and coins and currency of $17 were found in a fund that should have $100, the fund would be short $40. Because the custodian is responsible for the funds, some questions would need to be answered. Reconciling the petty cash fund is also a good time to see if vouchers are being prepared properly and if receipts and invoices are being saved.

**46** Are account balances in the books ever reconciled with the amounts presented in financial reports?

☐ Yes     Notes: _____

☐ No       _____

_____

_____

_____

As discussed in the first chapter, the end product of the accounting function is the preparation of financial reports for use in making decisions. If financial reports contain inaccuracies, faulty decisions could be made. The purpose of this control is to make sure that the accounting records are in agreement with the financial reports. There have been situations where embezzlement has been concealed by the embezzler preparing fictitious financial reports or where financial reports were wrong because the previous month's ending balance (the current month's beginning balance) was picked up incorrectly.

### Internal Controls—Other Assets

Four final internal controls need to be introduced and discussed. These controls relate to the safeguarding of noncash assets.

**47** Are valuables (securities, jewels, valuable documents, and so on) afforded protection in a bank safe deposit box?

☐ Yes     Notes: _____

☐ No       _____

_____

_____

_____

Valuables should be stored in a bank safe deposit box. This is so that these assets, some of which may be used in religious ceremonies, can be protected from fire, theft, accidental loss or damage, and so on. And although a bank safe deposit box does cost a few dollars per year, it affords the church much more protection than even a safe at the church. The incidence of church robberies is far greater than that of bank deposit box break-ins. People watching a bank being constructed are usually impressed with the amount of steel reinforcement in the safe deposit area.

---

**48** Are two signatures required for access to the safe deposit box?

---

☐ Yes     Notes: _____

☐ No      _____

_____

_____

As with the handling of cash, no person should be in a position to unilaterally control an asset. When only one person can get something from a bank safe deposit box, good control is violated. Therefore two signatures should be required for entry into the bank's vault. Although this may seem cumbersome for those authorized to have access to the box, visits to the bank will probably be infrequent and therefore not especially inconvenient.

---

**49** Is an updated inventory of securities, valuables, equipment, and other major noncash assets maintained?

---

☐ Yes     Notes: _____

☐ No      _____

_____

_____

An inventory of major noncash assets helps to verify the accountability for these kinds of assets, assists in determining if any assets are missing, and is valuable in case of fire or theft. All major items should be inventoried, whether in the office, sanctuary, kitchen, basement, or anywhere else. I suggest an annual inventory.

The inventory record for each item should include at least the following: cost, date of acquisition, location, and description. If items have been retired from service, traded in, or sold, that should be noted.

Few churches maintain the type of inventory suggested and would, for example, be hard pressed to file an insurance claim for a fire loss. This oversight is sometimes due to the cash-basis accounting approach used in most churches. That is, when a church using cash-basis accounting pays for a piece of equipment, it appears as an expenditure of that year. Contrast this treatment with that in a business firm, where the same piece of equipment would be set up as an asset and depreciated each month. As a consequence most churches do not monitor many of their assets after purchase. Existence and use of the asset is simply presumed.

---

**50** Are scheduled reviews made to determine if insurance coverage is adequate?

---

☐ Yes     Notes: _____

☐ No     _____

         _____

         _____

         _____

Insurance is obtained to protect the church's assets. But if no person or group is responsible for reviewing the adequacy of the coverage, loss of assets may be needlessly risked. All insurance policies should be evaluated at least every two years. Suggested new coverage can be considered as necessary. A few churches appoint an insurance committee for this purpose.

### Test Results

Now that you have reviewed all fifty internal controls, you are in a position to evaluate your church's overall system of controls. Don't fret if you failed to answer fifty questions yes; all is not hopeless. First, your church has plenty of company. Second, you now have sufficient information to make positive changes in your church.

To assist in your analysis, complete the following schedule by indicating the number of yes responses for each category of controls discussed. You will quickly be able to tell which areas need special attention. Also, if you multiply your total number of yes answers by 2, you will be able to express your test on a 100 percent basis. Thus if you answered yes for twenty-six controls, your church's score on the self-test would be 52 percent. This score would indicate that significant improvements should be made in your church's internal control system.

### Internal Controls for Churches

| Type | Number Provided | Number Yes |
|---|---|---|
| General | 9 | ____ |
| Cash Receipts | 17 | ____ |
| Cash Disbursements | 17 | ____ |
| Reconciliation | 3 | ____ |
| Other | 4 | ____ |
| | 50 | ____ |

Now review all questions to which you answered no and your accompanying notes. Indicate in the space that follows those five internal controls that should be installed as quickly as possible.

1.


2.

3.


4.


5.


Next, in the space provided, list those five internal controls that will take longer to implement but are essential to protect the church's assets.

1.


2.


3.


4.


5.


Let the preceding lists represent your short-term and long-term programs for improvement of internal controls. Be the instrument of change!

# CHAPTER 4

# Accounting Systems and Information Processing

Every church has an accounting system to process its transactions and periodically furnish information for the preparation of financial reports. Accounting systems come in all shapes and sizes. Some are simple; others are complex. Some are efficient; some are inefficient. Some conserve labor time; some waste labor time. Some have been set up by a professional accountant; others have been purchased from the office supplies section of a discount store. Some are computerized; some are manual. Some operate effectively; others have yet to reach their potential. Other than those churches that must follow denominational guidelines for processing transactions (including the accounts to use), each church uses an accounting system that is different, though perhaps only slightly, from that of other churches in the community.

In a typical church the accounting system started with the basics and developed gradually, but somewhat haphazardly, over a series of years and treasurers. Some treasurers made no alterations because they were afraid of making mistakes or were unfamiliar with accounting matters. And a few treasurers made substantial changes, some of which have yet to be understood! Therefore to a large extent the current state of a typical church's accounting system is a historical accident based on how the first set of books was set up and the personalities of its treasurers. Many church accounting systems are like a 1950 Chevrolet with a 1975 air conditioning system, a 1985 disc brake system, and a 1990 stereo system. Even with the enhancements, the most important component of this transportation system remains the vintage automobile. Perhaps this is why computers are expected to make sizable inroads into churches in the next decade. Computerization can assist churches in making a quantum leap forward in the manner in which their accounting transactions are processed.

## GENERAL OBJECTIVES OF AN ACCOUNTING SYSTEM

The general objectives of the church's accounting system are:

1. To measure and control financial activities,

2. To provide financial information to church officials, and

3. To provide financial reports to the congregation, commercial banks and other lenders, and higher-level denominational offices.

In attaining these objectives, the church should follow seven established guidelines of systems design. But as most churches are small, these guidelines need to be applied with care. First, the system should involve reasonable cost. Naturally, exactly what is reasonable depends upon the size of the church and its financial resources. Whereas a large church may be able to justify the computerization of its financial operations at a five-figure cost, a small church may have to get by with a system of journals and ledgers that are kept manually. Second, the system should be easily understood by persons working with it. Thus if the church uses a volunteer, part-time staff without accounting backgrounds to do its accounting work, the system should be a simple one. Fancier systems could be used in churches having greater accounting expertise at their disposal.

Third, the system should be efficient. Transactions should be recorded in a reasonably speedy manner, errors easily traced, and financial statement preparation the natural by-product of the system. Fourth, the system should permit the tracing of procedural steps. Posting, or transferring information from one portion of the books to another, should include an audit trail of the transaction. It should always be evident where the original transaction was recorded and where the information was subsequently posted. Thus, for example, those churches using a general ledger system should find that all entries made in the ledger are referenced to a specific page of a journal. A review of that journal would similarly reveal that all transactions have been transferred to specific numbered accounts. Fifth, the system should be able to process the vast majority of transactions in a uniform and consistent manner, yet flexible enough to handle the oddball situation. Thus the chart of accounts for churches using a general ledger should allow for the insertion of new accounts as needed within a numbering scheme that makes sense. A few churches who haven't planned their system properly find that assets, liabilities, and expenses, for instance, can be any number, rather than their assets being numbered from 100 to 199, liabilities from 200 to 299, and so on. A poorly planned system makes both recording and correcting errors more difficult. Many of those churches who entrusted their computerization to a member who was a computer hobbyist, and who may still be working on the project, understand the difficulty of handling nonroutine situations.

Sixth, the system should produce reliable data. This means that information should not be lost by the system and that any errors should surface. For example, in a general ledger system a trial balance is often used by treasurers to determine if the recording and posting process has been done correctly. If the trial balance columns fail to agree, something is in error. Perhaps when posting the payment of a $200 utilities bill from a journal, a cash account was reduced by $20 and the utilities expense account was increased by $200. This error would cause the trial balance to be out of balance by $180. Using the same rationale, some computer systems do not allow the integration of new data with existing balances until the new data is correctly entered. After all, what good is financial information if it is not reliable! Nonetheless, I have seen systems, both manual and computer, that have lost data, merged data incorrectly, or failed to signal that an error had occurred. I have also seen a church report where a difference of several thousand dollars was added to one column to make it appear equal with the total of an adjoining column!

The seventh and final systems guideline is that the financial reports emanating from the accounting system should be effective. Effective reporting will be discussed in the next chapter. Briefly, it is the ability of reports to assist users in making correct decisions about the church. If users cannot quickly glean information from financial reports because of the way in which data is organized or accounts are maintained, the reports are not effective. Thus if the church's financial affairs are recorded either through three accounts or three hundred accounts, the resultant financial reports probably will not be effective. Users want to receive some detailed information, but not too much or too little.

## BASIC TYPES OF ACCOUNTING SYSTEMS

There are two general types of accounting systems: those where processing is done manually and those where processing is computer assisted. At this time roughly 80 percent of churches use a manual system; 20 percent of churches have entered the computer age. But computer use is quickly accelerating. My discussions with church officials have revealed that about 50 percent of churches using a manual system are presently considering buying a computer to handle financial affairs. By the year 2000 probably only the smallest churches will employ a manual system to process their transactions.

## Manual Systems

There are two varieties of manual systems: write-it-several-times and one-write. As previously noted, 80 percent of churches use one of these two types of manual systems. These traditional systems are inexpensive to operate because the treasurer is likely to need little more than additional paper forms during the year. On the other hand, they can be cumbersome, confusing, frustrating, and labor wasteful if they are not properly set up.

### Write-It-Several-Times

With this manual system all transactions are initially recorded (logged in) on an appropriate form or in a journal (that is, cash receipts journal, cash disbursements journal, and so on). At the end of a specified period, perhaps a day or week, or, in some churches, whenever time permits, information initially recorded in the journal is posted throughout the system to all records that need updating because the transaction has occurred. Because several postings are necessary to process information through the system, these systems are called write-it-several-times systems. These systems are widely used by smaller churches of all denominations.

Let's follow the five-step course of a cash disbursement for those many churches using this type of system. First, a check is prepared, complete with the date, name of the payee, and amount. Second, this information is then written on the check stub: date, payee, and amount. Third, the information (date, payee, and amount) is then recorded in a cash disbursements journal that maintains a chronological record of all disbursements. Fourth, the expenditure needs to be charged to a specific account, such as maintenance, office supplies, utilities, and so on. Consequently the appropriate card or record must be located, and the information must again be entered. What information? Date, payee, and amount. And if portions of the expenditure are to be split among several accounts, the process has to be repeated for all accounts affected. Fifth, if the expenditure is for payroll, the amount earned, deductions, and amount paid need to be recorded on the employee's payroll record. With write-it-several-times systems, the same accounting information is being written over and over again. With each posting the transaction gets processed further within the system.

The handling of cash receipts in this system follows a similar pattern of multiple posting. In the church school, for instance, collections of tuition are recorded first in a cash receipts journal, then on the payor's payment record, and finally on a bank deposit slip. Some churches also provide a receipt for the paying parent. With weekly offerings member contributions are recorded in the cash receipts journal by the financial secretary or treasurer after the counting committee has submitted a collection report, offering envelopes, and duplicate deposit slip. Subsequently the financial secretary or treasurer pulls each member's record of giving to update that specific ledger.

*Problems.* There are several problems with write-it-several-times systems. These problems include the possibility of frequent errors, difficulty of system maintenance, inability to quickly generate reports needed for planning and control, and waste of human resources. Errors may occur when information is transferred from record to record. If data is posted several times within the system, each posting must be identical. For example, if a contribution of $570 is entered correctly in the cash receipts journal but recorded as $750 on the member's giving record, this error may be difficult to find in several months. Likewise, giving credit for a $100 offering to M. Rutkowski on one record and N. Rutkowski on another may take more than a few minutes to find when the church office receives a complaint about an incorrect statement. Errors in the date can cause trouble, especially for the internal audit committee. They may be trying to trace a disbursement made on 3/1 that was inadvertently dated 3/7 in the expense records. When the committee finds the error, they will be uncertain whether the error is an isolated one or the tip of the iceberg of major accounting deficiencies.

Lags may develop in the posting of information from record to record. The financial secretary or treasurer may be ill, on vacation, or busy. To many treasurers, the accounting work is secondary to banking and bill-paying. Write-it-several-times systems can eventually overwhelm these procrastinators as they get further and further behind.

The inability of write-it-several-times systems to generate speedy reports is not an indictment of these systems in specific, but of all manual systems. They are designed to process data in a certain manner and to furnish information for the preparation of certain financial reports. Special reports can be furnished only through special projects and as time permits.

The final deficiency of the write-it-several-times systems is their waste of human resources. It serves no purpose to have people copy information from one document to another. The church would benefit from a more creative and worthwhile use of its human resources. Just because the first treasurer adopted such a system, perhaps decades ago, does not mean that it should be used today. Substantial improvements in manual accounting systems have taken place in the past twenty years. Just as you would paint the exterior of the church with a spray painter, you should use a modern accounting system. To remedy most of the problems inherent in the write-it-several-times systems, churches who prefer to stay with manual recordkeeping should consider a one-write system.

### One-Write

A one-write, sometimes called pegboard, system is a recordkeeping system in which several forms for different record functions are held in alignment, so that a single writing on the top form produces the same entries on the forms beneath. This is accomplished by the use of carbons or a chemically treated, no carbon required (NCR) strip that transfers the information onto the journal or ledger below. One-write systems provide a simplified method of recording and summarizing operations having similar transactions, such as a church and its related units tend to encounter. They provide speed, simplicity, accuracy, and economy in accounting and recordkeeping. For churches, systems are available that handle cash disbursements, payroll, pledges receivable, cash receipts, and petty cash. An overview of the one-write concept for cash disbursements is pictured in exhibit 4-1. As illustrated, one writing does it all.

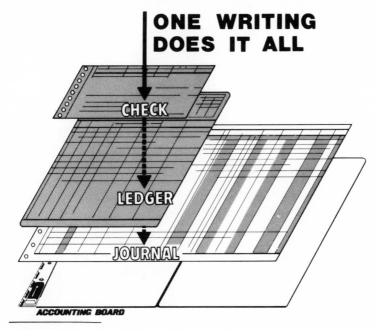

Illustration courtesy of Safeguard Business Systems

**Exhibit 4-1   The One-Write Concept for Cash Disbursements**

Within religious settings, one-write systems have been used in central offices, church schools, student organizations, parent/teacher associations, bookstores, youth organizations, missionary societies, child and family services, cemeteries, charities, hospitals, orphanages, and for special events.

In some congregations several one-write systems are spread throughout the church to capture information at the source and, in the process, spread the accounting workload. By decentralizing the recording of transactions, the financial secretary or central office is not overwhelmed with work with which they are not totally familiar. Some churches have elected to use one-write systems for cash disbursements only, including the payroll. Even churches that use computer systems to process data may use one-write systems to obtain information that is then fed into the computer. One-write systems have become more popular in churches as their advantages have become known. Yet thousands of churches use the old-fashioned write-it-several times approach for every aspect of their accounting. They could benefit immediately from one-write systems. Almost every church that has upgraded its system to a one-write has been pleased.

There are two key elements to the one-write system. There is the pegboard, which provides a hard writing surface beneath the forms and a pegged strip with locking device to hold forms in their proper places. The boards are no longer actually made of pegboard, but have evolved into thin stainless steel or aluminum surfaces covered with vinyl or other durable material. Pegboards come in many colors, so that church offices using several systems can easily tell them apart.

Then there are the forms. Unlike the forms used in the write-it-several-times systems, which can be purchased at office supply firms, the forms used in a one-write system are purchased from a business systems dealer. They are designed to fit together to allow the user to accomplish several different functions with a single writing. The forms are precision printed, punched, and trimmed to allow for perfect registration when placed on top of each other on the pegboard in the proper writing position. With a one-write system, therefore, the church is purchasing paper that has been organized into a system by business systems specialists.

Three examples of one-write systems are presented as exhibits 4-2, 4-3, and 4-4. The systems illustrated are general, off-the-shelf types of systems available to churches as well as other businesses and nonprofit organizations. Many churches using one-write systems have designed customized systems for their specific needs.

Exhibit 4-2 is an illustration of a combination payroll and disbursements system. This system is used to pay both employees and bills. It has five components. First, the checks, which are printed for the church

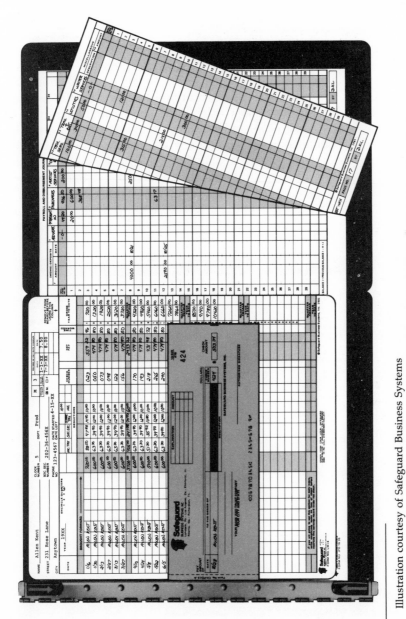

Illustration courtesy of Safeguard Business Systems

Exhibit 4-2   One-Write Combination Payroll and Disbursements System

by the business systems company, are consecutively numbered, which is a basic internal control procedure. Second, a duplicate check can be written, which can serve as the employee's pay statement or a voucher stapled to paid invoices. Third, there's the earnings ledger, which is placed beneath the check and duplicate, to keep information on each employee's earnings. Fourth, underneath the earnings ledger there's a journal, which folds out to provide columns for the distribution of the expenditures to accounts. In a one-write system, each column is an account, with the balance forward entered at the top and the ending balance at the bottom of the page. Fifth, placing the completed check in a window envelope eliminates addressing, yet another timesaver.

Most one-write disbursement systems are designed to allow the loading of the pegboard with a shingled batch of twenty-five or so checks; checks do not have to be inserted individually. Further, most systems have proofing instructions printed on each page to permit users to make certain that, for example, the total of all disbursements allocated to the individual account columns equals the dollar amount of checks

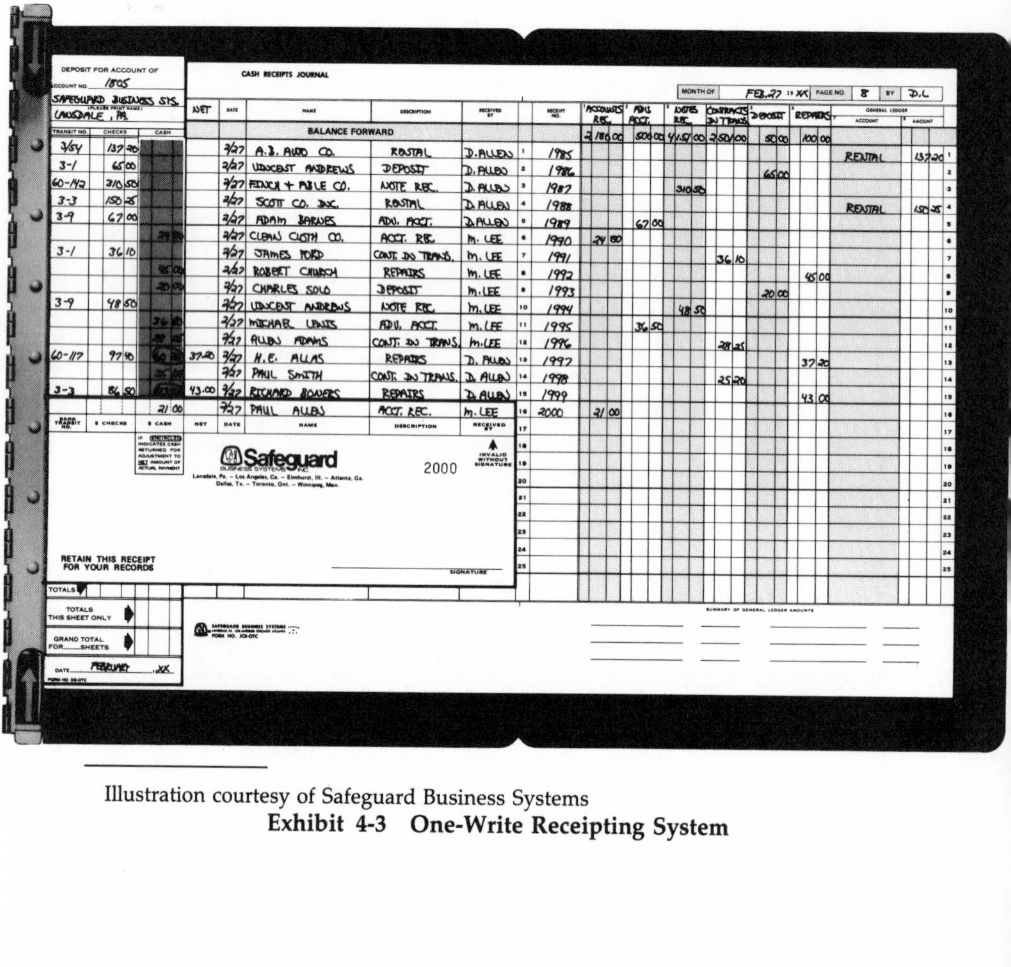

Illustration courtesy of Safeguard Business Systems
**Exhibit 4-3   One-Write Receipting System**

written, or that the current cash balance is equal to the beginning cash balance plus deposits and minus cash disbursed.

Exhibit 4-3 is an example of a receipting system that is used by some church schools for handling cash receipts. The system shown is composed of a receipt slip (sometimes with duplicate), bank deposit slip, and cash receipts journal. As the receipt slip is being prepared, the receipt is simultaneously recorded on the bank deposit slip and cash receipts journal. A family ledger card could also be used in this system to further expedite the processing of individual cash receipts.

Exhibit 4-4 illustrates the application of one-write systems to the general office petty cash fund. The need for a cash control system to handle small disbursements was discussed in chapter 3.

*Advantages.* One-write systems have several advantages over other systems, both manual and computer. Pegboard systems are inexpensive, easy to use and understand, labor saving, efficient, and, of great importance, eliminate both posting errors and lags. Errors in arithmetic can still occur, but if the controls built into most systems are

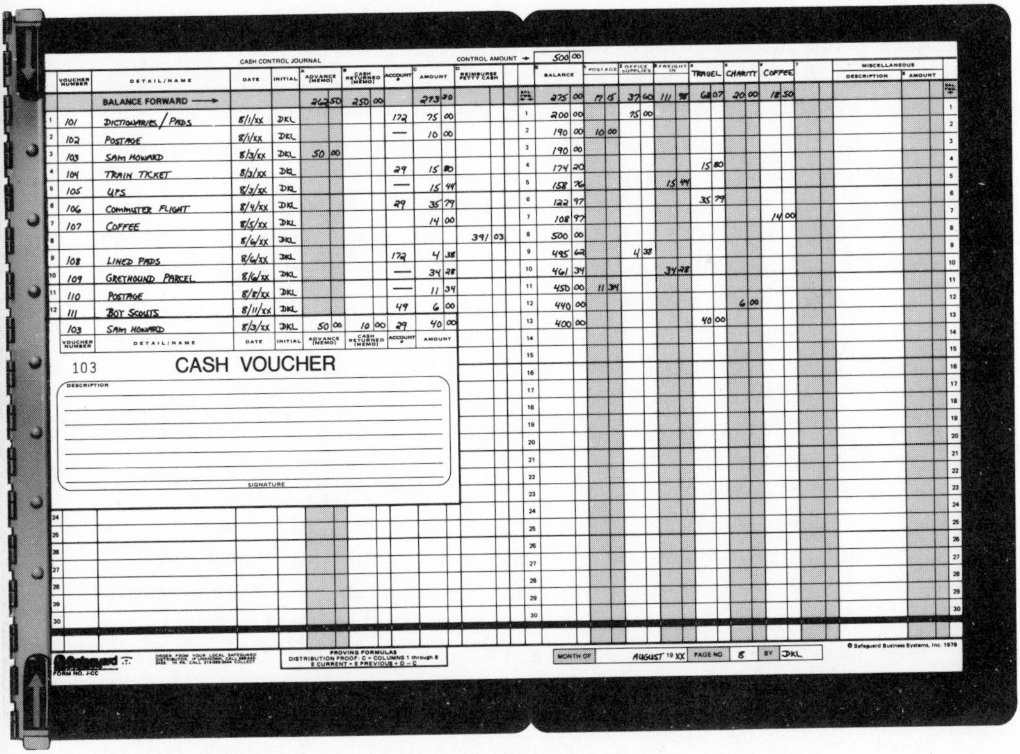

CASH CONTROL JOURNAL — CONTROL AMOUNT → 500.00

| | Voucher Number | Detail/Name | Date | Initial | A Advance (Memo) | B Cash Returned (Memo) | Account # | C Amount | D Reimburse Petty Cash | | E Balance | 1 Postage | 2 Office Supplies | 3 Freight In | 4 Travel | 5 Charity | 6 Coffee | 7 | Miscellaneous Description | 8 Amount |
|---|---|---|---|---|---|---|---|---|---|---|---|---|---|---|---|---|---|---|---|---|
| | | BALANCE FORWARD → | | | 262.50 | 250.00 | | 273.30 | | Bal. Fwd. | 275.00 | 17.15 | 37.60 | 111.98 | 68.07 | 20.00 | 18.50 | | | |
| 1 | 101 | Dictionaries / Pads | 8/1/xx | DKL | | | 172 | 75.00 | | 1 | 200.00 | | 75.00 | | | | | | | |
| 2 | 102 | Postage | 8/1/xx | DKL | | | — | 10.00 | | 2 | 190.00 | 10.00 | | | | | | | | |
| 3 | 103 | Sam Howard | 8/3/xx | DKL | 50.00 | | | | | 3 | 190.00 | | | | | | | | | |
| 4 | 104 | Train Ticket | 8/3/xx | DKL | | | 29 | 15.80 | | 4 | 174.20 | | | | 15.80 | | | | | |
| 5 | 105 | UPS | 8/3/xx | DKL | | | — | 15.44 | | 5 | 158.76 | | | 15.44 | | | | | | |
| 6 | 106 | Commuter Flight | 8/4/xx | DKL | | | 29 | 35.79 | | 6 | 122.97 | | | | 35.79 | | | | | |
| 7 | 107 | Coffee | 8/5/xx | DKL | | | | 14.00 | | 7 | 108.97 | | | | | | 14.00 | | | |
| 8 | | | 8/6/xx | DKL | | | | | 391.03 | 8 | 500.00 | | | | | | | | | |
| 9 | 108 | Lined Pads | 8/6/xx | DKL | | | 172 | 4.38 | | 9 | 495.62 | | 4.38 | | | | | | | |
| 10 | 109 | Greyhound Parcel | 8/6/xx | DKL | | | — | 34.28 | | 10 | 461.34 | | | 34.28 | | | | | | |
| 11 | 110 | Postage | 8/8/xx | DKL | | | — | 11.34 | | 11 | 450.00 | 11.34 | | | | | | | | |
| 12 | 111 | Boy Scouts | 8/11/xx | DKL | | | 49 | 6.00 | | 12 | 440.00 | | | | | 6.00 | | | | |
| | 103 | Sam Howard | 8/3/xx | DKL | 50.00 | 10.00 | 29 | 40.00 | | 13 | 400.00 | | | | 40.00 | | | | | |

103 CASH VOUCHER

DESCRIPTION

SIGNATURE

PROVING FORMULAS
DISTRIBUTION PROOF: C = COLUMNS 1 through 8
E CURRENT = E PREVIOUS + D − C

MONTH OF AUGUST 19 XX PAGE NO 8 BY DKL

© Safeguard Business Systems, Inc. 1979

FORM NO. J-CC

Illustration courtesy of Safeguard Business Systems

**Exhibit 4-4 One-Write Petty Cash System**

used, those errors can be easily traced and corrected. Posting errors where figures have been reversed are impossible, because all relevant documents are processed simultaneously. Records will be either all correct or all incorrect. The instantaneous nature of information processing also eliminates lags due to vacations, illnesses, procrastination, and so on.

*Problems.* Negative comments on one-write pegboard systems have been few. Some churches have found that although pegboard systems processed information beautifully, the system failed to provide them with sufficient financial information. A one-write system will not prepare financial statements or special reports the way a computer system will. Additionally, some churches have noted that their growth has outstripped the processing capacity of their one-write system. This can occur because a one-write system, after all, is manual and paper-oriented. Unless pegboards can be placed at the different points where cash is received, disbursed, or controlled, these churches may be candidates for computers. A final negative comment is that a fine point pen and some pressure are necessary for figures entered into the system to be legible on all forms. But few financial secretaries and treasurers have ever found this more than a minor concern.

*How to Buy.* If you would like to step up from your write-it-several-times system to a one-write system for all or a part of your church's financial affairs, several steps need to be taken. Initially, you need to locate local vendors. Ask accountants, other churches, and merchants to recommend the names of several vendors. If that fails, look up Business Forms and Systems in the telephone directory. There are several national suppliers of one-write systems that distribute their products through local office supply firms or distributors. Next, get together with several vendors and have each showcase its products and services. Ask to see what each vendor is doing for other churches in the community and for similar-sized churches in your denomination. Most vendors maintain a library of forms at their national headquarters. They will be glad to share them with you. Differences exist between systems and vendors, and these need to be considered fully. Some differences may be the types of systems and options available, reputation in the community, color of paper used, cost, ability to customize, and ability to service its accounts. In regard to the last aspect, some companies have customer service representatives who teach newly hired financial secretaries or new elected treasurers how to use the system free of charge; others have no such service. Also, some vendors periodically visit the church to obtain reorders of checks, receipts, ledger cards, and journals; others simply wait for your telephone call. After you have selected the vendor, your first order for supplies and materials should be small. You will need time to adjust to the system and think of ways that the forms can be improved. Beware of a vendor who suggests that your initial order should be ten million of anything in order to get the best price. The salesperson is thinking more of his or her commission than of you. At the start buy in small quantities, even if the cost is a penny or two higher per form. Order larger quantities of supplies only after you are certain that each form used in the system is exactly what you want. And if a general form is unsuitable, have customized forms designed for your church. The slight extra cost is worth it.

## Computer Systems

Given the growing use of computers, it is inevitable that computers will become significant in church accounting. For several years churches have lagged behind businesses and much of the nonprofit sector in embracing the computer. Reasons for this include the small size of many churches, their frequent use of part-time volunteers to process information, the cost of equipment, and a computer fear common to many people. Computer fear is quickly dissipating as computers have become more familiar and better understood in our society. Discussions that used to focus on "if we should computerize" are now focusing on "when we should computerize." Because of this greater acceptance and the steadily decreasing cost of using computers, I expect to witness a boom in church computers during the next ten years. By the year 2000 probably only the smallest congregations will be without a computer.

But as some churches have already found out, there's a big difference between purchasing a computer and having an effective computer system. Those people who believe that a computer will solve their every problem usually forget that a computer is simply a tool, like an automobile. Without a qualified operator and a plan to get from point A to point B, an automobile may not do you much good. In fact, you may be better off walking to your destination. Turning a computer into an effective processing system also takes a qualified operator and thorough planning. The best computer installations have occurred in churches that had operated successfully with manual systems. The horror stories usually come from churches that expected the computer to bail them out of trouble. The computer is not a panacea for the problems of a poorly operated church.

Churches turn to computers for many reasons. A few of the reasons are the church's inability to 1) improve membership communications, 2) increase membership participation, 3) increase the productivity of paid employees and volunteers, 4) get a better handle on financial affairs, 5) establish discipline in the handling of financial matters and set up internal controls that cannot be easily violated, 6) obtain comprehensive and timely reports, 7) obtain special, one-time reports as needed, and 8) employ the computer in nontraditional areas, such as music, youth education, and pastoral support. Because of the variety of different reasons churches have for computerization, computers are found in a variety of roles within churches. Some of these applications are:

Stewardship

> Lists of contributors
> Weekly contribution lists
> Contribution breakdown analysis
> Monthly giving analysis
> Member contribution reports
> Pledge to contribution analysis by member
> Summary pledge to contribution analysis for the congregation
> Statement of contributions to members
> Bank deposit slips
> Restricted gifts report
> Pledge cards

Membership

> Family directories
> Membership rosters
> Activities/interests/talents
> Religious education participation
> Baptism/confirmation status reports
> Child/youth data reports
> Prospective member reports
> Visitor records
> Participation reports
> Attendance reports for church and Sunday school
> Absentee reports
> Mailing lists
> Birthday/anniversary lists
> Labels/cards
> Third class bulk mail preparation

Finance and Accounting

> Chart of accounts
> General ledger report
> Transactions summary
> Payroll
> Accounts payable/vendor lists
> Accounts receivable: tuition, rentals, billables

Cash receipts journal
Cash payments journal (check register)
Budgeting and projection reports
Monthly financial statements
Property inventory
Fund accounting
Pension reports
Loan reports
Investment reports
Drive reports: building, capital fund, and so on

General Office

Word processing: weekly bulletin, letters, and so on
Typesetting selector
Calendar: scheduling of church events

Music

Library management
Music selection
Recordkeeping of use, cost, and so on

Religious Education

Bible study
Games and quizzes for elementary education

Pastors

Sermon preparation
Newsletter preparation

### Planning for a Computer System

Planning is vital to a successful implementation of computers. Nothing is easy in this area of administration, but the hard work of good planning will pay dividends. Poor planning, on the other hand, has resulted in, among other things, selecting computers that were either too small or too large, choosing vendors who were on the brink of bankruptcy, purchasing unseen software that proved to be inadequate, having a member develop a software program that never worked properly, encountering conversion traumas, and getting shortchanged because of an oral contract. With computers, it is safe to say that *you get what you plan for.*

The first step in the computer selection process is the appointment of a computer committee, computer task force, or advisory committee on computers. The role of this committee is to determine whether the church should use a computer, study available products and make recommendations to the administrative board, and, of great importance, supervise the installation of the computer system. The committee should be composed of five to ten members. Contrary to what you may have guessed, it is not wise to have the committee dominated by "computer people." Such individuals are biased in favor of computers regardless of their viability; they may have strong feelings toward certain computers, vendors, computer languages, and so on; and they often use their expertise and jargon to control the committee. The committee should be composed of a cross section of individuals, including some with computer, accounting, and business interests and some with no computer background. The committee should be balanced between staff and laypersons and should include the church treasurer. The financial secretary may also be on the committee. The pastor should be an ex officio member of the committee. The broad base of needs and opinions within the church should be considered when assembling the committee.

After the committee is organized, the next step is for its members to become educated about computers. The education may be provided at an evening meeting by a "computer person" on the committee, another church member informed about computers, or a local computer representative. The education may also come from having members read a book about selecting a computer or, specifically, about selecting a church computer. These books are available at many religious bookstores. Whatever method of education is used, members will need to understand what common computer terms mean, terms such as hardware, software, interface, documentation, K, floppy disks, disk drives, hard disk, dot matrix, letter quality, terminals, operating systems, on-line, and turnkey systems. At this juncture the education should be general. No specific products should be reviewed or vendor presentations permitted.

The third step involves conducting a survey of needs as they are perceived by the church's clergy, administration, and program leaders. This is to identify all areas and functions that would benefit from the use of a computer. Therefore the needs analysis should not be restricted to a review of accounting, financial reporting, and other administrative activities. The committee conducting the review of needs should seek the opinions of all who could conceivably enhance their work or programs through the computer, from education to evangelism. One large church in San Antonio, Texas, conducted a needs survey before obtaining their computer and, quite to their surprise, found that they could use thirty-six computer terminals spread around the church and adjacent buildings. Rather than purchasing a small business computer just to handle the accounting and financial reporting functions, they decided to purchase a much larger unit that had the capacity to process the workload of thirty-six remote terminals.

In conducting the needs survey, the committee cannot help but review those activities being done manually, for these are the activities that surface as prime prospects for computerized assistance. In a sense, then, the committee performs a systems review of the church as a prelude to selecting a computer. This systems review has important benefits. The church's computer committee may determine that the church really does not need a computer. It may only need to become more efficient by changing personnel, establishing better controls, or using advanced manual systems, such as a one-write accounting system in place of the write-it-several-times approach. And if computerization is deemed necessary, the committee is more likely to recommend products that can be integrated easily into church operations. The committee is better able to make these kinds of decisions, because they have become more informed about various church affairs.

The next step in the selection process is to develop a timetable for the decisions. Six months to one year may be prudent. Without a timetable the committee could get bogged down for years or might feel rushed to decide. Both extremes are fraught with danger. Given the recommended composition of the committee, members will need several months to feel comfortable about their work.

The fifth step involves the selection of the computer products. The main choice involves selecting between using a service bureau and purchasing a computer. If the in-house option is chosen, the committee must select the computer programs (software), computer (hardware), and number and location of terminals, printers, and so on. A detailed review of the search process is in the next section, including the recommendations to search out companies that have proven track records of serving churches, obtain references for all companies, visit existing installations, and review the capabilities of all computer systems carefully.

The sixth step is to recommend specific computer products to the administrative board, together with those contractual terms that the church should specify in its contract with a vendor. If the committee has done its job correctly, no one should be able to ask questions concerning the recommendation that cannot be answered by the committee. Likewise, committees who are less than thorough in their search can be embarrassed when presenting their report.

The final step is to assist the church in installing the computer. What better resource to guide the church into the computer age than the group who knows how the church operates manually, determined that a computer would help, witnessed the recommended hardware and software in action, and has already built rapport with the vendor? The computer committee should not be disbanded until the computer is working exactly as intended. Churches that allow the committee members to go their separate ways after the committee has made its recommendations have a higher probability of experiencing a chaotic conversion to the computer and a lower probability of achieving the efficiency that was promised.

The responsibilities of the computer committee are illustrated in exhibit 4-5. The circular approach is used to emphasize that the committee's role does not end until the computer has been installed and the church's needs are satisfied.

### Computer Selection: Service Bureau or In-House Computer?

The church has two choices when it decides to computerize. It can buy services from a service bureau, which owns and operates computers and offers computer services to organizations. Or it can purchase a computer of its own. When computers were larger and more expensive, churches tended to use computer service bureaus. As computers have

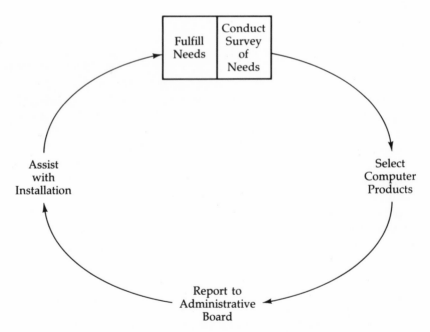

**Exhibit 4-5   Responsibilities of the Computer Committee**

become less bulky and more affordable, as more inexpensive software has become available, and as computers have become more accepted by the average person, churches have preferred the in-house option. Further, this trend is likely to continue, as probably 90 percent of those churches currently considering a computer are contemplating ownership. But there are churches that could benefit from a computer service bureau, so both options will be explored here.

### Computer Service Bureaus

The service bureau option should be considered by churches that desire to upgrade their manual system to a computer system, but are either too small to purchase an in-house computer or fearful of the problems that outright ownership may incur. Some churches in the latter category find that using a service bureau for a few years is a good intermediate step between their old manual system and the full-fledged in-house computer that they ultimately plan to purchase. Using a service bureau gives them time to learn about both computers and their own needs before they buy a computer. On the other hand, a service bureau may not have computer programs to handle the stewardship, membership, and financial aspects of church administration, let alone applications in religious education, music, and so on. Thus churches using service bureaus may be forced to continue to use their manual system in some areas.

In evaluating service bureaus five factors must be considered—the vendor, conversion, input, output, and cost.

*The Vendor.* The short history of firms who offer data processing to churches has been a checkered one. In the 1970s it seemed as if everyone was in the business—moonlighting engineers, accountants, computer programmers, businesses with excess computer time, computer companies of all types, and even banks. The results were less than satisfactory for many churches. Service was often sporadic, promises were not kept, reports were more appropriate for profit-seeking businesses, and firms went bankrupt or discontinued the services to churches because of their failure to attract a sufficient number of churches to make a profit. This often left churches in uncertain and chaotic conditions. Imagine how distressed you would feel if, after spending several months converting your manual accounting system to one used by the service bureau's computer and after relegating your old set of books to the cellar, you suddenly found out that the computer firm had closed up! In fact, most firms or individuals who have entered the field have left it. Lack of capital, lack of management, and lack of expertise in either churches or computers are big reasons for failure. On the other hand, in some areas of the country, well-managed service bureaus specializing in church processing have grown by offering excellent services. In fact, some churches have been receiving services from the same computer service bureau for the past decade. Thus because of the large variability of quality among providers, it is critical that you get to know as much about the vendor as you can. Ten questions to ask are:

1. How large is the firm in terms of sales, number of offices, and number of employees?

2. What percentage of sales is derived from church data processing services?

3. How many years has it served churches?

4. How many churches are currently using its services?

5. Will it provide you with a full list of its church clients in your area to serve as references? If the firm refuses to give you a complete list so you can select those churches to contact, you should refuse to continue the dialogue.

6. Has the firm been successful? Review a copy of its financial statements. If the firm refuses to share this information with you and it is a corporation, you can obtain its latest financial statements from the secretary of state of its state of incorporation for a nominal fee. If everything else fails, ask for a bank reference.

7. During your visit to vendor offices, assess the quality of management, condition of the office, and the general tone at the computer center. Does the staff appear organized, confident, and capable?

8. How many employees does it have who are available to serve you to correct errors and train any new personnel at the church?

9. Does the service contract have any provisions that bother you or that are not clear? If so, have the vendor reword the contract or change it to suit your particular needs. You should have the church lawyer review the contract as a precautionary move.

10. Is the firm planning to change the existing program in the near future? Some of the changes are probably intended to correct problems.

*Conversion.* Installing a computer system requires a partnership of the church staff and the service bureau. The church must be sure that church people working with the computer are not fearful of computers or of losing control of their niche. Otherwise the project may be doomed. Further, the church must make sure that records are accurate and currently posted by church personnel. It serves no purpose to transfer errors to a computer. On its part, the computer service bureau should provide a complete and understandable operating manual, a training program for those who will provide data to the computer, a commitment to effect the conversion within a reasonable period, and a follow-up system to handle postconversion questions and problems quickly.

Generally stated, installation problems have a direct relationship to the extent of computerization. Those systems that physically receive a batch of information from the church to process involve less complicated installation procedures than on-line systems that enable church personnel to update records automatically in the service bureau's computer.

Ten questions to ask about the conversion plan are:

1. What is the vendor's commitment to conversion? The real question is who is going to get the existing stewardship, membership, and financial information ready to enter in the computer—the church staff or the service bureau staff? Some churches hasten the conversion time by starting with a service bureau on the first of the year or month and not computerizing old information.

2. Does the installation procedure seem planned and orderly in light of the church's personnel and the time of year?

3. Does the church staff have major responsibilities for the installation? Is anyone likely to feel abused?

4. Does the vendor impose a numbering or filing system that is different from the one currently used?

5. How long will conversion take? Review the conversion schedule.

6. Will the present system and the proposed computer system operate simultaneously for a few months to work out any bugs in the new system? If not, does that make you apprehensive? If they will, is there any charge for the computer service during this testing phase?

7. How are the church staff and others trained to use the vendor's computer data processing system?

8. Does the vendor provide an operating manual to assist the office staff and any newly hired people?

9. Is the operating manual easily understood?

10. What were the major installation problems for other churches using the system? Ask the churches.

*Input.* Simplicity is the key to the successful transmission of information from the church to the service bureau's computer. If paper forms are to be filled out, writing should be minimal and the number of input forms few. Beware of firms that have a special form for this and a special form for that, and, of course, several different batch transmittal forms to use when sending the special forms to the firm. Simplicity is also vital if data is first entered on a computer terminal and subsequently sent to the computer over telephone lines. Data must be easily entered and easily corrected. Once inaccurate data is merged with existing records, it may prove troublesome to correct.

Ten questions to ask in this area are:

1. Is the input procedure clearly understood?

2. Is the input procedure acceptable to those staff members who must work with the computer on a daily basis? For instance, some churches use a service bureau hundreds of miles away and mail or bus their information for processing. This situation leaves the financial secretary or treasurer at the mercy of the turnaround time, which could be more than a week. Faced with sending away the fresh data and being a guardian of the stale data, the financial secretary or treasurer is apt to manually process the data before sending it off, just in case up-to-date reports are required. In this instance the distant computer serves no function except to check on the accuracy of the financial secretary or treasurer's work. Probably the computer is not needed. Such a financial secretary or treasurer, however, may benefit significantly from an on-line service bureau option.

3. Are input documents or procedures designed specifically for churches?

4. Are input documents or procedures few in number and easy to understand?

5. Does any input document or procedure have or require irrelevant or confusing computer codes?

6. Does the system have any safeguards to prevent errors from being entered into the computer?

7. How are the errors spotted by the computer system?

8. How are errors corrected? Is the vendor readily available to help correct errors?

9. What security precautions are taken with regard to entering false data or obtaining confidential information?

10. What are the biggest input problems for churches using the system? Would these problems be likely to occur in your church?

*Output.* The extent and quality of reports and information provided by computer service bureaus varies significantly. Some computer systems retard productivity by severely limiting the reports that can be produced. Just because data is computerized does not mean that the computer can respond to all inquiries for information. The computer needs to be properly programmed to do anything. To use a baseball analogy, some service bureaus can do nothing more than provide information on runs, hits, and errors. Others can provide information on the number of ground balls hit to the second baseman by game, by day of the week, and by hat size of the batter!

Ten questions to ask concerning the output are:

1. What is the extent of output from the system? Obtain this information in detail.

2. Do the reports and other output provided satisfy your needs?

3. Is the output you will use internally within the church well organized and easy to understand?

4. Is the output you will distribute to members *very* well organized and *very* easy to understand?

5. If the reports are not exactly what you need, is the vendor willing and able to modify its program without undue cost?

6. When are reports and other output available? How are they delivered to the church?

7. When are hard copies (printed copies) available? Could this pose a potential problem?

8. Can some information that is immediately needed be obtained? If so, how?

9. What special inquiries and reports can the system furnish?

10. What are the system's report limitations for churches that use it? How have they coped with the deficiencies? Are you prepared to do the same?

*Cost.* With a service bureau the main cost is the charge for monthly computer processing. Most firms have a graduated fee basis, with cost per member or per transaction inversely related to the size of the church. Thus smaller rural churches may find this computer option much less economical than their big city counterparts. Some service bureaus also charge installation fees and miscellaneous fees for certain reports or services. Cost comparisons must be done with care, because some firms appear inexpensive yet wind up being costly because they charge for every conceivable service. On the other hand, some firms that initially appear expensive are really competitively priced, as a hefty monthly service fee is counterbalanced with a host of free reports and services. Whichever firm is selected, a contract should be prepared that permits the church to discontinue the computer service within a month or two should problems develop.

Probably at least one member of the computer committee will continually bring up the cost of computers. The scenario usually starts with a What does it cost? question and develops into a That's a lot of money observation. Remind those individuals that the goal of making business decisions in not to minimize cost. Tell them that if that were the goal, we would close up the church and avoid all of the costs of operation! Would it really be optimal to close the church? Of course not. Our mission, therefore, in the context of church operations, is to make sure that in all decisions the benefits exceed the costs to the highest extent possible. This means that computers will not be viable until the dollar value placed on the benefits exceeds the cost of computerization. (I recognize the difficulty of valuing many of the benefits, but the process should not be sidestepped just because it's not easy.) Further, the committee may be perfectly reasonable in recommending the use of a $1-per-month-per-member service bureau that provides superlative comprehensive reports and good local service over a firm that charges 30 cents per month per member for elementary reports and that operates by mail from American Samoa!

In reviewing the costs of a service bureau, the following ten questions should be asked:

1. How is the monthly service fee for processing determined? Calculate the church's projected monthly fee. If it is not easily calculable in advance, imagine doing this every month.

2. Does the firm charge for installation? If so, how is this fee determined?

3. What other fees are likely? Obtain a schedule of fees.

4. Are there extra charges for correcting errors that result from mistakes made by the church staff?

5. If equipment is involved, are there charges for special electrical wiring, maintenance, or insurance?

6. Are there any hidden costs? This is a good question to ask present users of the system.

7. How are fee disputes handled?

8. Is there a cap on future increases in fees?

9. Are costs in line with what present system users expected? Has the vendor ever surprised them with extra or unexplained charges? (Again, ask other users.)

10. Does the vendor know if any of the quoted charges could be reduced? There may be some ways to reduce fees and still have the computer provide an acceptable (not optimal) level of service. This question may be germane to those churches where the costs appear prohibitive.

### In-House Computers

As noted earlier, most churches that think about computer data processing consider the purchase of their own computer system. Selecting a computer system is much more involved and distinctly different from purchasing a television or telephone. All televisions show the same channels. All telephones can receive the same long-distance telephone call, regardless of whose service was used to transmit the call. A computer, on the other hand, works through programs specifically designed for that model. Thus software designed for an IBM PC computer will not usually work on an Apple computer. Similarly, programs written for an Apple II computer may not necessarily work on the Apple IIe computer. Further, the different church programs written for an IBM PC computer, for example, are not necessarily equal in quality or capability. Each software program embodies only what its designer included. Contemplating the combination of many different kinds of software programs and many brands of computers, which all purport to do similar things, could provide some uneasy moments for the computer committee.

The committee will find that some vendors specialize in software; other vendors specialize in hardware. Yet other vendors will put together a combination of available software and hardware. Other firms offer a turnkey, or complete church computing system, which they have designed. Whichever direction is taken by the committee, all vendors must be thoroughly checked out. Several vendors have exited from the scene, and as this business matures, several more are likely to leave as well. The committee should deal only with vendors who are likely to survive.

Before we begin to discuss in earnest the procedures for selecting an in-house computer, three frequently encountered, troublesome computer topics must be addressed. The first involves the situation where a member donates a computer to the church, for both the church's use in its accounting and for the tax deduction that it provides the donor. Odds are that the computer is either obsolete or defective. I have heard of few situations where the donated computer was state of the art and brand spanking new. Even if it is new, however, the computer committee should not give up its quest to locate the best computer system for the church. Acceptable church programs may not be available to operate with the donated computer. In fact, there are computers for which I have been unable to find any church-related financial software at all. Also, the donated equipment may not suit the needs of the users—the keyboard may be awkward, the computer may be too small or too large, the monitor screen may be hard to read, its capacity may be too limited, and so on. Don't settle; select. If the donated computer is not adequate, it can be sold or perhaps relegated to meet a specialized and more limited need in the church school, in music, or as the pastor's word processor. I am amazed at the number of churches that receive a donated computer and naively take it for granted that their computer selection problems have ended.

The second topic involves the situation where a member volunteers to write the program for the new church computer. Although I commend such members for their heroism, programming for the church's needs is an extremely difficult task. For every church that has gone this route successfully, there are ten churches that have yet to implement computers because the program is still being worked on and worked on and worked on. There are endless bugs to remove, things to add, and things to check. Also, there is no security net in case the volunteer member becomes ill, gets transferred to another community, or simply quits. Documentation of the programs is rarely adequate in case the job has to be completed by another person. Church officials are reluctant to complain about the problems and delay. After all, the job is being done for free. Nonetheless, the church may be wasting yet greater valuable resources for every month that passes without adequate computer data processing. A motto from the business world may be appropriate here: Don't hire someone that you can't fire.

The third topic involves whether the church should have customized software designed or purchase packaged software. With customized software, programs are designed and written to meet your specific needs. The advantage is obvious; you can get exactly what you want. This should allow you to reduce considerably any changes in your operations caused by the computer. Success hinges on the ability of the programmer to understand your needs thoroughly and the efficiency and effectiveness of the program. Although this approach can produce optimum results, it can also produce little. Computer programmers are not licensed, need no certificate to practice their trade, and, based on my experience, vary dramatically in their capabilities. With packaged, off-the-shelf software, the church purchases a tested and proven product. There is no doubt that it works! Further, it is usually much less expensive than customized software and generally easier to implement too. But a packaged program forces you to provide data in a prescribed manner and may not match up exactly with your needs. Consequently you may have to forgo some computer benefits when employing off-the-shelf products. In weighing the pros and cons of the two approaches and the risks involved, I recommend that all but the largest of churches should consider only packaged programs written specifically for churches. I think it's preferable to get 80 percent of your needs met at a lower price than to risk getting only 40 percent of your needs met at a higher price. Large churches and those with very special circumstances may need to design their own software because of their multiple or special activities.

*Selection Process.* The initial step is to select the best software. Contrary to what you may have heard, hardware should never be purchased before software. In other words, the computer itself is secondary to the programs that will operate the computer. If you buy the computer first, you're buying backward. In this phase of the computer committee's work, members must locate those software programs most able to fulfill the church's requirements as determined by the survey of needs. Computer sales representatives, computer magazines, advertisements in periodicals serving church administrators, other churches, and libraries are good sources for leads. Demonstrations of programs should be arranged through the systems developer or local retailers who sell the program. Some of these demonstrations will be free; some will involve the purchase of a demonstration disk for a small fee. Visits to churches already using the software are highly recommended. If possible, all committee members should attend all demonstrations. The demonstrations prevent you from buying blindly.

After the software has been selected, the committee will have to select compatible hardware. In some cases selecting hardware is easy, either because the software can operate only on a particular computer or because the software vendor's recommendations and reasoning are so compelling. On the other hand, the committee may have several hardware possibilities. Some software can operate on several different models of a line of computers and on lower priced computers, called clones, which are supposedly compatible with more well-known computers. But compatibility does not necessarily mean 100 percent compatibility; it sometimes means 90 percent compatibility. Caveat emptor.

Similar decisions have to be made on the other pieces of hardware too, such as the terminal and printer. In some cases the committee may decide to purchase hardware from one company or vendor. In other cases almost every piece of hardware being considered may be manufactured by a different company or sold by a different vendor. As with selecting software, use free demonstrations to your advantage. Don't buy anything without seeing it operate first.

The final step in the process is to assist in the development of contractual terms that protect the interests of the church. If something's not in writing, you're not apt to get it. Remember that the glib salesperson will be your best friend until a problem develops. At that point you'll be asked to refer to the contract to determine responsibility. If the contract was written by the vendor and signed without thorough review, the church will lose.

The selection process for an in-house computer is depicted in exhibit 4-6.

As can be seen from this discussion, the computer committee must study certain critical areas when considering an in-house computer. Four areas to investigate are 1) software and software support, 2) hardware and hardware support, 3) cost, and 4) contract. The following one hundred questions need to be asked by members of the computer committee. The list is not intended to be exhaustive, because the number of questions that could be asked is almost endless. But when answered they should provide a firm underpinning for the decision. Successful installations occur in churches that know why they want a computer and exactly what they plan to use it for. Unsuccessful

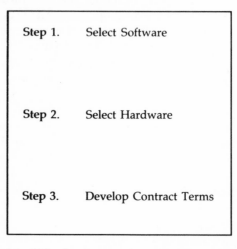

|  |  |
|---|---|
| **Step 1.** | Select Software |
| **Step 2.** | Select Hardware |
| **Step 3.** | Develop Contract Terms |

**Exhibit 4-6  Selection Process for an In-House Computer**

installations occur when the opposite is true. The value of organization and planning should be evident.

*Software and Software Support.* The following list of thirty-six questions relates to the selection of computer software and the support of the software's capabilities.

1. Who designed the software? (Some programs are designed by individuals working at home; others by large, nationally recognized companies. You want to determine who is standing behind the software.)

2. Is the designer financially viable? (Your program may need to be changed or updated because of, for instance, changes in income tax regulations relating to payroll. You want to be reasonably certain that your software designer will still be in business.)

3. How many years has the program been available?

4. Is the program written expressly for churches? Your size of church? Your denomination?

5. How many churches are currently using the software?

6. Are the users satisfied with the program? Obtain a list of users and contact several.

7. Can you see a demonstration of the program locally?

8. Is the program easy to use (i.e. menu-driven)?

9. Are there help screens to assist the operator?

10. Does the program have other special features to assist the operator?

11. Does the software come with an operating manual?

12. Would the operating manual be understood by a new staff member or volunteer who had never worked on a computer or in a church?

13. Does the software vendor provide support—short term and long term—in correcting errors, answering questions, completing updates, and so on?

14. Is there an 800 or local telephone number to call when the manual is not sufficient?

15. Are there training, instructions, or lessons available to provide for systems education in small doses? (Reading any manual tends to be a chore.)

16. Is the training or lessons available locally?

17. What warranties are available?

18. Is a backup program available?

19. What happens if the software becomes damaged?

20. Can the software be damaged by operator error?

21. Does the program require a great deal of inputting or duplication of effort that would increase the chances of error?

22. Does the program fulfill your needs (membership, stewardship, financial, word processing, and so on)?

23. Does the program work fast enough? (Some are slow or have long pauses.)

24. Are data being entered validated in any way before merger?

25. Has the system been human engineered to reduce keystrokes?

26. Does the system respond quickly to routine inquiries?

27. Does the system provide an audit trail in the financial areas?

28. Does the vendor supply a list of internal controls that are built into the system?

29. Does the system have adequate security features?

30. Does the program enable linkage between church applications? (With proper linkage the recording of contributions in the pledge or stewardship records can automatically be transferred to the financial records without rekeying. Also, address changes made in one record can be simultaneously made in all other records. Linkage eliminates duplication.)

31. Can the program be modified? By whom?

32. What does any modification cost?

33. What agreements are voided if someone other than the vendor modifies or troubleshoots the program?

34. Are updates of the program automatically sent and billed to the church?

35. Are training, instructions, or lessons provided along with new program releases?

36. Are all reports and processed information well organized and easy to follow? Can you customize the program, if necessary?

*Hardware and Hardware Support.* The following group of questions concerns the selection and support of hardware.

37. Are the manufacturers of the computer, disk drives, terminal, printer, and so on, financially viable and readily accessible? (Silicon Valley in California has many empty buildings that just a few years ago housed high-tech computer firms. It's hard to get support from a company that no longer exists or is in Hong Kong.)

38. Does the equipment have the capabilities the church will need in three to five years? (Buying dead-end equipment is a common problem. The printer needs to be fast enough. The computer needs to have a sufficient capacity and speed. Any peripherals need to be state of the art.)

39. Does the hardware use the latest technology, relative to the church's expected needs?

40. Does the hardware have a record of reliability? Is the reliability information objective or provided by the vendor's salesperson?

41. Can the hardware be expanded or modified if needed?

42. Does the system use a hard disk?

43. Does the processor use an operating system, such as MS-DOS, PC-DOS, or OS/2, which will support both the software selected and other possible applications?

44. Does the system allow for simultaneous use of several terminals?

45. What size diskettes are used? (The 5 1/4-inch floppy disk is most popular at this writing. But the 3 1/2-inch diskette is much more durable and state-of-the art.)

46. Are all of the components 100 percent compatible? If so, will the vendor note that fact in the contract?

47. Is the hardware easy to use?

48. Are manuals available for the hardware?

49. Are the manuals easy to read and understand?

50. Is the video display terminal the right size, shape, and screen color?

51. How does the keyboard feel? Does it have a ten-key pad or various function keys to simplify operation?

52. Does the printer provide dot matrix printing, letter quality printing, or a combination of these?

53. Is the printer's speed adequate?

54. Will the printer handle the forms, reports, and labels that you need to print?

55. Can the printer produce different sized letters and fonts for special purposes? Boldface? Underlining?

56. Does any equipment have special temperature, humidity, or electrical requirements?

57. Does the hardware vendor provide postinstallation support? How? Does it provide a telephone number to call?

58. Is a hardware maintenance contract available? If service is required, does the technician come to the church or do you take the equipment to the technician?

59. Are spare parts locally available?

60. What happens if a vendor-dealer or manufacturer goes bankrupt? (Run through the worst case scenario.)

61. Are computer technicians locally available? What is the cost?

62. Are loaners provided if necessary?

63. Where are the nearest factory repair centers?

64. Are computer materials and supplies locally available? Diskettes, paper, labels, forms, and so on, should be available at a local business supply company, but ask around anyway.

*Cost.* Following is a list of sixteen key questions related to cost.

65. What are the initial costs for each item of hardware if purchased individually or the system if purchased as a whole? (Don't forget to include all peripheral devices, cables, connectors, and so on.)

66. What is the cost of all software—both the systems software and the applications software?

67. What is the cost of the start-up stock of supplies?

68. Are there any costs for site modifications?

69. Are there any installation costs, including costs for new electrical lines, humidity/temperature controls, and telephone lines?

70. Are there any costs for personnel training?

71. What is the cost of converting the existing files, forms, and procedures to the new computer system?

72. What is the cost of maintenance contracts—for both hardware and software?

73. Will there be a cost for insurance on the system?

74. What is the estimated cost of using parallel systems (using both old and new systems if the new one has to be debugged)?

75. If you purchase the computer under an installment contract, what will be the effective annual interest rate and the total of interest charges?

76. Is leasing or a lease-purchase arrangement possible? (Some churches may have needs but little cash. If so, consider having a member buy the system and lease it to the church.)

77. What are the legal costs for contract inspection?

78. Will you need a computer consultant to assist you to select, install, and implement the computer system? If so, what will this cost?

79. Has the committee evaluated the benefits of a computer in dollars and cents as compared with the total costs of a computer in dollars and cents? (All too often committees wind up comparing a narrative list of things that the computer will do for them with the dollars and cents the computer will cost. But just as the costs are quantified, so should the benefits be quantified. How long will it take the church to recover its investment in a computer system?)

80. Should the committee recommend that special donations be solicited to finance the entire computer system or parts of it? Or should the committee perhaps recommend that several members buy the system selected by the committee and donate it to the church?

*Contracts.* The importance of contracts varies with the situation. If the committee decides to purchase readily available hardware and off-the-shelf software from a computer store and put the system together themselves, there may be no contract. There still would be, nevertheless, product warranties for all items purchased. If, however, the committee decides to purchase a turnkey system from a single vendor or desires a customized system, a good contract written to protect the church is prudent. The following twenty questions relate to contracts.

81. Does the contract cover the hardware and software? (Determine if the vendor stands behind what it is selling and places all representations or warranties of any kind in the contract. Further, make sure that the fine print does not get the vendor off the hook. It's amazing what can be in the fine print.)

82. Does the contract cover training procedures?

83. Does the vendor have any liability to the church for deficiencies of the system, defects in the system, interruption of service, or any consequential damage arising out of the use of the system?

84. Can the vendor assign the contract to another party? If so, can the church reject the assignee?

85. Are the installation procedures and responsibilities specified?

86. Is there a specific timetable for installation?

87. Are damages awarded for a delay in installation or for not meeting the performance specifications?

88. Is there a cancellation clause to protect the church if the vendor does not perform according to the contract?

89. Are the full purchase price, deposit, and payment terms clearly noted?

90. Does the contract specify the level of continuing support and any costs for it?

91. Does the contract specify the speed with which repairs will be made? (It took two months to have my personal printer fixed!)

92. Does the contract say what happens in the event of a dispute? Does it go to arbitration? Will the church receive liquidation damages if breach of contract has occurred?

93. Has anything been promised verbally that is not written in the contract? If so, put it in writing.

94. If compatibility has been promised, is it specified in the contract?

95. If modularity (the ability of your system to be expanded) has been promised, is it specified in the contract?

96. If backup availability has been promised, is it in the contract?

97. Performance is critical to the successful use of computers, so does the contract specify the expected level of performance? If not, why? Is it clear when the church accepts the system as being fully installed?

98. If the vendor goes out of business or merges with another firm, is it clear what happens to the contract and all items covered by the contract?

99. Has the contractual phase of the process been carried out in haste by the committee, perhaps hurried by the vendor's sense of

urgency? Why is there a hurry? Does the vendor critically need this sale? (Regardless of what the salesperson says, the price of computers has consistently gone down. Churches that have waited until now to purchase their computers will get much more for their money than their counterparts who purchased just a few years ago.)

100. Has the contract been thoroughly reviewed by the church attorney? If not, why not?

Several examples of computer-prepared documents for churches are presented in exhibits 4-7 through 4-10. Exhibit 4-7 shows a parish income and expense statement. Note the comparison of budgeted expectations with actual results, both for the month and for the year to date. Exhibit 4-8 is an example of multifont typesetting, which can be cost effective in printing orders of worship, church bulletins, invitations, certificates, newsletters, and awards.

Exhibit 4-9 is a stewardship statement of account that can be sent to each donor periodically to advise him or her of his or her pledge and amount given in aggregate and by fund. Exhibit 4-10 is a monthly income and expense report for a nursery school, a department of a church. With computers it is as easy to get departmental and program reports as it is to get a complete report, such as that shown in exhibit 4-7.

*Electronic Spreadsheets.* The electronic spreadsheet is a recent addition to the arsenal of software programs available to church accountants. Electronic spreadsheets (that is, worksheets) configure the memory of a computer to resemble an accountant's columnar pad, but a pad that is much larger than could be printed on a piece of paper. For instance, a popular spreadsheet at the time of this writing has more than 2000 rows and 250 columns. This vast working area is used to perform mathematical operations (for example, the addition of data in column six to that in column seven, with the result stored in column eight) and to format various schedules and reports.

Some churches use an electronic spreadsheet program to assist them in their annual budgeting operations, where the process may go several rounds and may involve many changes and refinements. Budgeting with a spreadsheet requires that users enter mathematical formulas in the computer. The formulas express the financial relationships of the church. They show, for example, that the ending cash balance is equal to the beginning cash balance, plus contributions and minus expenditures. Once the formulas are developed, spreadsheets allow administrators to perform "what if" testing. A treasurer can study the financial impact of changes in specified budget variables. For example, the impact of a 10 percent decrease in peak month contributions on summer month cash balances can be reviewed in seconds. Likewise, the impact of salary

## Your Church/Parish Name Goes Here

| ACCOUNT TITLE | Current Month | | | Year to Date | | | ANNUAL BUDGET | % |
|---|---|---|---|---|---|---|---|---|
| | ACTUAL | BUDGET | % VAR | ACTUAL | BUDGET | % VAR | | |
| * * * * * OPERATING ACCOUNTS * * * * * | | | | | | | | |
| I-N-C-O-M-E  R-E-C-E-I-P-T-S | | | | | | | | |
| PLATE OFFERINGS | | | | | | | | |
| 175101 Sunday Plate Offerings | 1,475.09 | 3,021 | −51.2 | 4,484.94 | 6,042 | −25.8 | 36,400 | 12.3 |
| 175102 Miscellaneous Plate Offerings | 511.86 | 208 | 146.1 | 971.73 | 415 | 134.2 | 2,500 | 38.9 |
| PLEDGE PAYMENTS | | | | | | | | |
| 175201 Previous Year's Pledge Payments | 714.27 | 7,000 | −89.8 | 7,766.93 | 14,000 | −44.5 | 28,000 | 27.7 |
| 175202 Current Year's Pledge Payments | 10,466.37 | 18,675 | −44.0 | 32,036.24 | 37,350 | −14.2 | 225,000 | 14.2 |
| CONTRIBUTIONS FROM PARISH ORGANIZATIONS | | | | | | | | |
| 175301 Faith Bible Class | 73.73 | 208 | −64.6 | 230.17 | 415 | −44.5 | 2,500 | 9.2 |
| 175302 Girls Missionary Group | 54.18 | 91 | −40.5 | 210.40 | 183 | 15.0 | 1,100 | 19.1 |
| 175303 Annual Bazaar | 0.00 | | | 0.00 | | | 9,000 | 0.0 |
| OTHER INCOME | | | | | | | | |
| 175400 Contributions from Diocese | 2,517.19 | 4,150 | −39.3 | 6,667.19 | 8,300 | −19.7 | 50,000 | 13.3 |
| 175500 Investment and Endowment Income | 0.00 | | | 19,500.00 | 19,500 | 0.0 | 78,000 | 25.0 |
| 175501 Gain/Loss on Sale of Investments | 2,896.45 | 5,750 | −49.6 | 2,896.45 | 5,750 | −49.6 | 23,000 | 12.6 |
| 175600 Contrib. & Legacies - Undesig. | 563.84 | 1,245 | −54.7 | 1,853.38 | 2,490 | −25.6 | 15,000 | 12.4 |
| 175601 Miscellaneous Income | 2,048.78 | 98 | ***** | 2,154.76 | 195 | ***** | 1,176 | 183.2 |
| 175602 Discounts Earned | 0.00 | | | 0.00 | | | | |
| T-O-T-A-L INCOME | 21,321.76 | 40,446 | −47.3 | 78,772.19 | 94,640 | −16.8 | 471,676 | 16.7 |

E-X-P-E-N-D-I-T-U-R-E-S

| | | | | | | | | |
|---|---:|---:|---:|---:|---:|---:|---:|---:|
| **DIOCESAN EXPENSES** | | | | | | | | |
| 186400 Diocesan Assessments | 122.54 | 415 | −70.5 | 621.06 | 830 | −25.2 | 5,000 | 12.4 |
| 186401 Diocesan and General Church Prog | 2,894.91 | 2,307 | 25.5 | 5,202.36 | 4,615 | 12.7 | 27,800 | 18.7 |
| 186600 Other Purposes Outside Parish | 138.12 | 208 | −33.6 | 463.90 | 415 | 11.8 | 2,500 | 18.6 |
| TOTAL DIOCESAN EXPENSES | 3,155.57 | 2,930 | 7.7 | 6,287.32 | 5,860 | 7.3 | 35,300 | 17.8 |
| | | | | | | | | |
| **SALARIES AND BENEFITS** | | | | | | | | |
| 186701 Salaries - Clergy & Assisting Cl | 4,666.00 | 8,051 | −42.0 | 12,717.69 | 16,102 | −21.0 | 97,000 | 13.1 |
| 186702 Salaries - Sexton, Janitors, Eng | 2,617.00 | 2,263 | 14.6 | 4,871.96 | 4,565 | 6.7 | 27,500 | 17.7 |
| 186703 Salaries - Organist, Music Dir | 312.50 | 996 | −68.6 | 1,308.50 | 1,992 | −34.3 | 12,000 | 10.9 |
| 186704 Salaries - Parish Secretaries | 1,152.00 | 2,117 | −45.6 | 3,418.54 | 4,233 | −19.2 | 25,500 | 13.4 |
| 186705 Salaries - Other | 931.25 | 664 | 40.2 | 1,252.65 | 1,328 | −5.7 | 8,000 | 15.7 |
| 186706 Salaries - Taxes Expense | 319.38 | | | 319.38 | | | 3,542 | 9.0 |
| 186707 Pension Premiums (Clergy Only) | 235.41 | | 0.0 | 425.41 | 1,900 | −77.6 | 9,500 | 4.5 |
| 186708 Other Insurance & Benefits | 464.80 | 465 | −26.6 | 940.01 | 930 | 1.1 | 5,600 | 16.8 |
| TOTAL SALARIES AND BENEFITS | 10,698.34 | 14,576 | | 25,254.14 | 31,050 | −18.7 | 188,642 | 13.4 |

Presented by the courtesy of Membership Services, Inc., Irving, Texas.

**Exhibit 4-7  Parish Income and Expense Statement**

# Trinity United Church

## DALLAS, TEXAS

## THE ORDER OF WORSHIP

### Sunday, May 15, 1985

Organ Prelude      **'Overture in G Major'**      Tchaikovsky
**

Call to Worship:      **'Psalm 150'**      Franck
The Sanctuary Choir

The Invocation      Rev. Frank Clarke
**

Hymn No. 4 **PRAISE TO THE LORD, THE ALMIGHTY**
Stanzas 1, 2, and 5

The Scripture Lesson      Isaiah 54:1–12
**

Meditation and The Prayer of Intercession
**

Hymn No. 243     **O JESUS, I HAVE PROMISED**
Stanzas 2 and 4

The Morning Offering
Offertory:    **'How Lovely Is Thy Dwelling Place'**    Beethoven
Mrs. Elizabeth Arden, Flutist

Soloist:      **'O Lord, Most Holy'**      Franck
Dean Wilder, Tenor

The Sermon:    *"A Man For All Seasons"* Dr. J. M. Frost

Hymn No. 400     **'Something For Thee'**

The Benediction
Choral Response:    "For Thine Is The Kingdom"

** Ushers may seat worshipers

---

Prepared using the Order of Worship Typesetter, Membership Services, Inc., Irving, Texas.

### Exhibit 4-8    Church Typesetter

```
                    First Community Church
                    Print Steward Statement
                         June 13, 1988

          Name of Giver
          Address

Previous Year            0.00                              2,220.00
Total Given Ytd     1,110.00

Fund                          Receipts
------------------------------------------------------------------
    1 Building Fund                        Pledge:       600.00
      01/11/1988                 50.00
      02/08/1988                 50.00
      03/14/1988                 50.00
      05/09/1988                100.00
      06/13/1988                 50.00
      Total Transactions        300.00    Total Ytd      300.00
------------------------------------------------------------------
    2 General Fund                         Pledge:     1,020.00
      01/11/1088                 85.00
      02/08/1988                 85.00
      03/14/1988                 85.00
      04/11/1988                 85.00
      05/09/1988                 85.00
      06/13/1988                 85.00
      Total Transactions        510.00    Total Ytd      510.00
------------------------------------------------------------------
    3 Missions Fund                        Pledge:       600.00
      01/11/1988                 50.00
      02/08/1988                 50.00
      03/14/1988                 50.00
      05/09/1988                100.00
      06/13/1988                 50.00
      Total Transactions        300.00    Total Ytd      300.00
------------------------------------------------------------------
```

Prepared using the LOGOS II Church Management System (Version 5.0), copyright 1989 by Lowell Brown Enterprises, Ventura, California.

**Exhibit 4-9   Stewardship Statement of Account**

increases, program overexpenditures, or changes in church school enrollment on cash balances can be quickly assessed. If paper, pencils, and a calculator were the only tools at hand, performing the required computations would take hours. And even then, some administrators might not be satisfied with the results and might request a recalculation using slightly different assumptions. With the spreadsheet, data or formula changes are entered into the computer by depressing a few keys; electronics does the rest. Newly generated reports are produced in a matter of seconds.

Although spreadsheet programs are most applicable to budgeting operations, a few church treasurers are using them to handle their routine stewardship and financial/accounting matters as well. Therefore rather than relying on either customized or off-the-shelf church software, these treasurers have set up their financial records within the confines of the spreadsheet.

ROMAR FD DEMO General Fund
198X FISCAL YEAR
MONTHLY INCOME AND EXPENSE
Nursery School

| | - Feb 1, 198X to DATE - ACTUAL | - Feb 1, 198X to DATE - BUDGET | -- Jan 1, 198X to DATE -- ACTUAL | -- Jan 1, 198X to DATE -- BUDGET | - YEARLY BUDGET - REMAINING | % |
|---|---|---|---|---|---|---|
| INCOME | | | | | | |
| Nursery School Income | | | | | | |
| 4110.02-Nursery School Offerings | 268.00 V | 2,000.00 | 2,962.37 | 4,000.00 | 2,962.37- | 92 |
| 4120.02-Nursery School Tuition | 74.69 V | | 1,849.69 V | | 22,150.31 | 80 |
| | $342.69 V | $2,000.00 | $4,812.06 | $4,000.00 | $19,187.94 | 80 |
| PERSONNEL | | | | | | |
| Other Personnel | | | | | | |
| 5210.02-Nursery School Salaries | 63.00 | 3,000.00 | 1,563.00 | 6,000.00 | 34,437.00 | 96 |
| Employer's Payroll Taxes | | | | | | |
| 5920.02-Employer's FICA - Nursery Sch. | 0.00 | 50.00 | 12.87 | 100.00 | 587.13 | 98 |
| -TOTAL-PERSONNEL | $63.00 | $3,050.00 | $1,575.87 | $6,100.00 | $35,024.13 | 96 |
| BUILDING & MAINTENANCE | | | | | | |
| Electricity | | | | | | |
| 6130.02-Nursery School Electric | 57.00 | 100.00 | 109.30 | 200.00 | 1,090.70 | 91 |
| Telephone | | | | | | |
| 6170.02-Nursery School Telephone | 91.37 > | 50.00 | 73.87 | 100.00 | 526.13 | 88 |
| -TOTAL-BUILDING & MAINTENANCE | $148.37 | $150.00 | $183.17 | $300.00 | $1,616.83 | 90 |
| EQUIPMENT & SUPPLIES | | | | | | |
| Educational Materials | | | | | | |
| 7020.02-Nursery School Supplies | 0.00 | 1,000.00 | 75.00 | 2,000.00 | 11,925.00 | 99 |
| TOTAL INCOME | $342.69 | | $4,812.06 | | | |
| TOTAL EXPENSES | $211.37 | | $1,834.04 | | | |
| INCOME - EXPENSES | $131.32 | | $2,978.02 | | | |

Presented through the courtesy of Romar Systems, Elkhart, Indiana.
Exhibit 4-10  Church Nursery School—Monthly Income and Expense Report

# APPENDIX A:
# ALTERNATIVE ACCOUNTING SYSTEMS

Chapter 4 dealt with accounting systems and information processing at a managerial level. The presentation was a general, broad-brush, and critical-thinking approach, which was relevant to all readers, regardless of their accounting expertise or the accounting system used in their church. Perhaps you became convinced that there was a need for a computer in your church or, at a minimum, that your church needed a more efficient manual system. If I had instead discussed accounting systems on a microlevel by detailing a particular processing system and particular accounts, such as fund balance, contingency fund, and board-designated fund, many readers would have had difficulty relating the discussion to their church, where the books would have been different and the accounts would have had different names. After all, each church is unique, with its own locale, membership, and religious and financial leadership. Even in those denominations that advocate uniform accounting among their churches (and that possibly publish an accounting reference handbook), many treasurers routinely make exceptions for local conditions. As a consequence, each church's accounting system, including the books and accounts used, is customized over time.

But, even though each church has a unique set of accounting records, four general varieties of church accounting systems can be identified. The system varieties are as follows:

1. Checkbook system

2. Twin-journal system

3. One-fund, general ledger system

4. Fund-accounting system

Each of these varieties of systems is briefly reviewed in this appendix.

### Checkbook System

In very small congregations a checkbook may constitute the accounting system. Weekly contributions and other cash receipts are entered as additions to the cash balance. Checks written are entered as deductions from the cash balance. In this system the checkbook, with information noted on the check stubs or check register, is the entire accounting system and forms the basis for information contained in financial reports. Besides the checkbook no formal accounting record, such as a journal or ledger, exists. No accounts are used. Files, however, are maintained, containing bills paid and bank deposit slips, as well as records of individual member giving and payroll for income tax purposes.

Using a checkbook system, financial reports are prepared by 1) categorizing cash income by type, from information noted in the checkbook or kept in the files, and 2) categorizing cash expenditures by type (that is, utilities, salaries, maintenance, supplies, and so on). A large worksheet is sometimes used to help prepare financial reports. Classifying expenditures is made easier if the treasurer indicates the reason for the disbursement on each check. The annual financial report, providing aggregate information on income and expenditures, is prepared by adding together the amounts on monthly reports. Special reports are rarely prepared.

The checkbook system may work satisfactorily for very small churches. After all, you probably use the same system to handle your own personal financial affairs and to derive your current cash balance. But if the number of transactions that need processing is increased or if many different types of reports need to be prepared, the checkbook system quickly becomes inefficient. Further, the checkbook system, being a single-entry system, does not contain a built-in safeguard of checks and balances to help detect errors in the recording process. This is a major flaw of the system.

### Twin-Journal System

The twin-journal system involves the use of two journals, a cash receipts journal and a cash disbursements journal, to record and report cash transactions. Small churches that find the checkbook system of monitoring cash inadequate for their needs may find this system more acceptable. As with the checkbook system, no formal accounts are employed, but files of bills paid and bank deposit slips are kept, and records of individual giving and payroll are maintained.

All cash inflows, whether from regular weekly offerings, special gifts, tuition, investments, or any other source, are recorded in the appropriately labeled column of a cash receipts journal when received. A summary entry can be made for all moneys collected at a Sunday service rather than each contribution being listed separately. Cash received via the mail or during the week is recorded on the day received. To capture all income transactions, the journal must be designed with a sufficient number of columns to handle the various sources of church income. A miscellaneous column is often used for minor cash receipts received from diverse sources. The system facilitates the preparation of monthly reports of cash receipts, because only a totaling of columns is necessary.

And if year-to-date column totals are maintained each month, the addition of the previous month's activity to the preceding eleven-month total will produce the annual amounts of cash received. Additionally, by classifying income according to source when it is received, timely information can be provided to system users before formal reports are issued. For example, a comparison may be made between the monthly budget for offerings and the offerings for the first two Sundays of the month to assess progress toward meeting the monthly goal. If contributions are lagging, steps can be taken to stimulate member giving.

On the expenditure side, all cash disbursements are recorded individually in the appropriate column of the cash disbursements journal. Each category of church expenditure has a separate column. A miscellaneous column can be provided for nonroutine expenditures not having a separate column. Information on each cash payment can come from a checkbook stub, check register, or paid invoice. Use of a one-write system can permit the check register and the cash disbursements journal to be prepared simultaneously. (Review exhibit 4-2 for an example of a combination payroll and disbursements system.) As with church income, the classification of expenditures by type at the time of disbursement facilitates the preparation of monthly and annual financial reports, comparisons with budgeted amounts, and the availability of information on an as-needed basis.

| CASH RECEIPTS JOURNAL | | | | | | P. 10 |
|---|---|---|---|---|---|---|
| Date | Total | Offerings | Special Offerings | Gifts and Bequests | Tuition | Misc. |
| Beg. Bal | $75,000 | $60,000 | $5,000 | $5,000 | $3,000 | $2,000 |
| October 7 | 2,000 | 2,000 | | | | |
| 14 | 2,250 | 1,900 | 350 | | | |
| 21 | 2,750 | 2,000 | | 750 | | |
| 28 | 3,000 | 2,000 | 500 | | 500 | |
| 30 | 50 | | | | | 50 |
| End. Bal. | $85,050 | $67,900 | $5,850 | $5,750 | $3,500 | $2,050 |

## CASH DISBURSEMENTS JOURNAL

| Date | Check Number | Payee | Total | Salaries | Grounds | Debt Retirement | Equipment | School Expenses | Misc. |
|------|--------------|-------|-------|----------|---------|-----------------|-----------|-----------------|-------|
| Beg. Bal. | | | $70,000 | $40,000 | $10,000 | $9,000 | $7,000 | $3,000 | $1,000 |
| Oct. 1 | 570 | Henke | 1,500 | 1,500 | | | | | |
| 3 | 571 | Craft | 500 | | 500 | | | | |
| 4 | 572 | Bank | 1,000 | | | 1,000 | | | |
| 5 | 573 | Ace Co. | 100 | | | | 100 | | |
| ⌇ | ⌇ | ⌇ | ⌇ | ⌇ | ⌇ | ⌇ | ⌇ | ⌇ | ⌇ |
| 30 | 600 | Lynn | 700 | | | | | 700 | |
| End. Bal. | | | $84,000 | $49,000 | $11,000 | $10,000 | $8,000 | $3,900 | $2,100 |

**Your Church**
**Statement of Cash Receipts and Disbursements**
**for the Month Ended October 31, 19XX**

| | October | YTD |
|---|---------|-----|
| Beg. Cash Balance | $ 5,000 | $0 |
| **Receipts** | | |
| Weekly offerings | $ 7,900 | $67,900 |
| Special offerings | 850 | 5,850 |
| Gifts & bequests | 750 | 5,750 |
| Tuition | 500 | 3,500 |
| Miscellaneous | 50 | 2,050 |
| | $10,050 | $85,050 |
| **Disbursements** | | |
| Salaries | $ 9,000 | $49,000 |
| Grounds | 1,000 | 11,000 |
| Debt retirement | 1,000 | 10,000 |
| Equipment | 1,000 | 8,000 |
| School expenses | 900 | 3,900 |
| Miscellaneous | 1,100 | 2,100 |
| | $14,000 | $84,000 |
| End. Cash Balance, Oct. 31 | $1,050 | $ 1,050 |

**Exhibit A-1   Twin-Journal System and Cash Report**

Like the checkbook system, the twin-journal system also is a single-entry system and has no mechanism for detecting errors in the recording process. If all items of cash inflow and outflow have been recorded properly in one of the two journals, however, the resultant financial report explains the change in the cash balance from the beginning of the period to the end of the period. The amount of cash can be verified when a bank reconciliation is prepared (see chapter 3). A simplified example of a twin-journal system and resultant cash report is presented in exhibit A-1.

## One-Fund, General Ledger System

The one-fund, general ledger system is a system commonly used by churches of all sizes except the smallest. Its foundation is the double-entry bookkeeping system developed for and used by business enterprises and taught in high school bookkeeping courses and college accounting courses. In fact, when originally installed, one-fund, general ledger systems were adaptations of business systems that church treasurers and CPAs had worked with in their nonchurch activities.

With this approach the church is presumed to be operating its many programs and activities from a single pool of capital. The level of the pool is constantly changing because of the inflow and outflow of cash. The accounting records and reports the activities of the pool for a period. Unlike businesses, however, churches receive amounts restricted by the donor. To recognize these restrictions, such amounts in the pool of capital are labeled restricted. Thus the single pool of church capital is divided into the portion that is restricted and the portion that is unrestricted. The restricted portion may be composed of several funds, each fund perhaps having a particular restriction. The unrestricted portion is often called the general fund.

The tools of accounting needed to process transactions and summarize financial activity in the one-fund, general ledger system are accounts, the chart of accounts, debits and credits, journals, and a trial balance. Following is a brief explanation of these tools.

Accounts. The records that are kept for each individual asset, liability, fund, source of income, and type of expense are known as accounts. In most churches the recordkeeping for each account is normally performed on a separate piece of paper, where increases and decreases that result from transactions are recorded. All the accounts taken together compose the church's general ledger. Essentially the general ledger is a book that contains separate listings for each account that appears on the church's financial statements.

Chart of accounts. The chart of accounts is a detailed listing of the church's accounts, along with associated account numbers. For example, assets (cash—checking, cash—savings, furniture, equipment, buildings, land, and so on) may have numbers in the 100s. Liabilities (mortgage payable, taxes payable, and so on) may have numbers in the 200s. Equity balances (fund balance for total, unrestricted church equity and specifically named funds from restricted giving, such as the organ fund or the building fund) may have numbers in the 300s. Unrestricted income sources for the year (contributions, gifts, interest earned, and so on) may have numbers in the 400s. Expenses to be paid from the year's unrestricted giving (salaries, utilities, maintenance, office, and so on) may have numbers in the 500s. Each church using this system has its own numbering scheme. Thus the chart of accounts provides the basis for the organization of the general ledger.

Debits and Credits. Debits and credits are used to increase and decrease account balances. Certain accounts are debited to record an increase; that is, entries are made on the debit (left) side or in the debit column. These accounts, in turn, are credited to reduce their balance; that is, entries are made on the credit (right) side or in the credit column. To keep the books balanced, the opposite rule is used with other accounts, namely, increases are recorded by credits and decreases are recorded by debits. Exhibit A-2 summarizes the debit/credit rules used in church accounting.

Journals. Journals, sometimes called books of original entry, serve as the starting point into the church's accounting system for transactions. Journals bring order into the recording

| Account Type | Normal Balance | To Increase | To Decrease |
|---|---|---|---|
| Assets | Debit | Debit | Credit |
| Liabilities | Credit | Credit | Debit |
| Equity (fund bal.) | Credit | Credit | Debit |
| Revenues | Credit | Credit | Debit |
| Expenses | Debit | Debit | Credit |

Exhibit A-2   Debit/Credit Rules of Church Accounting

process by summarizing a transaction in one location. The journals used in the one-fund, general ledger system are the cash receipts journal, used to record cash receipts, the cash disbursements journal, used to record cash payments, and the general journal. The general journal is used to record 1) transactions that are not appropriate to the two cash journals, 2) transfers between accounts, and 3) entries to correct, adjust, and close the accounting records.

Trial balance. A trial balance is a listing of the ledger accounts, along with dollar balances, prepared after the transactions are recorded. It is used to determine whether the accounting records are in balance. If the accounting records are correct, church financial statements can be prepared and distributed. This check for internal consistency is a feature of double-entry bookkeeping.

The sequence of the church accountant's work in the one-fund, general ledger system follows prescribed steps. Each step is explained briefly. Readers who desire a more thorough review of the tools just discussed, the steps, or the elements of double-entry bookkeeping should consult a bookkeeping or accounting textbook.

Step 1. Record Transactions in a Journal
Cash receipts are recorded in the cash receipts journal. Cash payments are recorded in the cash disbursements journal. All other transactions, transfers, and so on, are recorded in the general journal. Examples of a cash receipts journal and a cash disbursements journal were shown in exhibit A-1. Because the one-fund, general ledger system uses accounts, column headings in the two cash journals will indicate appropriate account numbers. A general journal entry to illustrate a transfer from the organ fund to the building fund follows.

### General Journal

| | | | |
|---|---|---|---|
| Feb. 8 | Organ fund—acct. 307 | 2,000 | |
| | Building fund—acct. 309 | | 2,000 |
| | To transfer restricted contributions to the building fund | | |

This transfer did not involve the shifting of cash. The church cash account was not involved; it will be affected only when the building is paid for. What occurred was that a donor of $2,000 to the organ fund decided that the money would be better used in the building fund.

Restricted moneys must be spent according to the instructions of the donor. Separate accounts in the accounting records does not mean that separate bank accounts must be maintained for every different restricted gift. A church could conceivably handle the financial affairs of several hundred restricted gifts, as well as unrestricted amounts, in a single bank account.

Step 2. Post (Transfer) Journal Entries to Ledger Accounts in the General Ledger

In the posting process account balances will increase or decrease, depending on the transaction. For example, the cash account will increase when the church receives cash and will decrease when cash is disbursed. At the conclusion of posting from the cash receipts journal and the cash disbursements journal, the cash account—checking may appear as follows:

**Cash Account—checking**    #101

| Date | Explanation | Debit | Credit | Balance |
|------|-------------|-------|--------|---------|
| Feb. 28 28 | Total receipts Total payments | 9,000 | 9,500 | 14,000 23,000 13,500 |

Posting should be done using column totals taken from the cash receipts and cash disbursements journals. Significant time can be saved each month by using appropriate totals.

Similarly, the building fund account may appear as follows after the posting of the transfer from the organ fund as recorded in the general journal.

**Building Fund**    #309

| Date | Explanation | Debit | Credit | Balance |
|------|-------------|-------|--------|---------|
| Feb. 8 | Transfer | | 2,000 | 4,000 6,000 |

Step 3. Prepare a Trial Balance

After all transactions have been posted to general ledger accounts, a trial balance is prepared to ensure that the posting has been done correctly and the accounting records have internal consistency. The trial balance is prepared by listing the ending balances in all general ledger accounts. If the totals of account balances agree, the church accountant can be reasonably certain that the books are free from error and that financial reports can be prepared. An illustration of a trial balance is presented in exhibit A-3.

Step 4. Prepare Church Financial Statements
The church treasurer who uses the one-fund, general ledger approach is in a position to prepare several financial statements at the end of each month. First, the treasurer could prepare a balance sheet, which presents the church's assets, liabilities, and equity. But because this statement does not typically answer the questions that most administrators and members ask (that is, How is the church doing?), its preparation is optional. The second financial statement is a statement of revenues and expenditures, with actual results often compared against

### First Church
### Trial Balance
### February 28, 19XX

|  |  | Debit | Credit |
|---|---|---|---|
| #101 | Cash—checking | $13,500 |  |
| 102 | Cash—savings | 9,000 |  |
| 110 | Furniture | 4,000 |  |
| 120 | Equipment | 7,000 |  |
| 130 | Buildings | 48,000 |  |
| 140 | Land | 20,000 |  |
| 201 | Mortgage payable |  | $41,000 |
| 301 | Fund balance— |  |  |
|  | unrestricted |  | 49,000 |
| 309 | Building fund |  | 6,000 |
| 311 | Scholarship fund |  | 4,000 |
| 401 | Contributions |  | 12,000 |
| 402 | Gifts |  | 2,000 |
| 414 | Miscellaneous income |  | 1,000 |
| 501 | Salaries expense | 7,000 |  |
| 502 | Office expense | 4,000 |  |
| 503 | Maintenance expense | 1,000 |  |
| 504 | Utilities expense | 1,000 |  |
| 514 | Miscellaneous expense | 500 |  |
|  |  | $115,000 | $115,000 |

Exhibit A-3   Trial Balance

year-to-date amounts as well as the budget. The third financial report is the statement of changes in fund balances, which provides a detailed analysis of increases and decreases to all equity balances for the period covered by the statement. Abbreviated examples of these statements, using the data contained in the trial balance, are presented in exhibit A-4.

Step 5. Close the Books

The revenue and expenditure accounts (those numbered in the 400s and 500s at First Church) are called temporary accounts by accountants, because they accumulate data over a period and are then closed at the end of that period. In the case of First Church, data was accumulated in three revenue accounts and five expenditure accounts for a month. At the end of a period, perhaps a month, the temporary accounts must be closed to enable them to receive fresh data for the next accounting period. Such accounts are reduced to zero via the closing process. The entry necessary to close these accounts for the First Church would be made in the general journal.

### General Journal

| | | | |
|---|---|---:|---:|
| Feb. 28 | Contributions | 12,000 | |
| | Gifts | 2,000 | |
| | Miscellaneous income | 1,000 | |
| |   Salaries expense | | 7,000 |
| |   Office expense | | 4,000 |
| |   Maintenance expense | | 1,000 |
| |   Utilities expense | | 1,000 |
| |   Miscellaneous expenses | | 500 |
| |   Fund balance | | 1,500 |
| | To close temporary accounts and transfer the excess of revenues over expenditures to the fund balance. | | |

## Fund-Accounting System

Larger churches (or those that turn to a CPA for advice) often use the fund-accounting system for keeping the books. The fund-accounting method is used by local municipalities and other governmental organizations to control their operations. Because of its unique features applicable to not-for-profit organizations, fund accounting is also used extensively by volunteer health and welfare organizations, hospitals, and colleges.

The foundation of fund accounting is that resources made available to the entity are typically restricted. That is, their use may be limited to

## First Church
## Statement of Revenues and Expenditures
## for the Month Ended February 28, 19XX

**Revenues**

| | | |
|---|---:|---:|
| Contributions | $12,000 | |
| Gifts | 2,000 | |
| Miscellaneous income | 1,000 | $15,000 |

**Expenditures**

| | | |
|---|---:|---:|
| Salaries expense | $7,000 | |
| Office expense | 4,000 | |
| Maintenance expense | 1,000 | |
| Utilities expense | 1,000 | |
| Miscellaneous expenses | 500 | 13,500 |
| Excess of revenues over expenditures | | $ 1,500 |

## First Church
## Statement of Changes in Fund Balances
## for the Month Ended February 28, 19XX

| | Beg. Bal. | Increase | Decrease | Trans. | End Bal. |
|---|---:|---:|---:|---:|---:|
| Unrestricted | $49,000 | $15,000 | $13,500 | | $50,500 |
| Organ fund | 2,000 | | | $(2,000) | — |
| Building fund | 4,000 | | | 2,000 | 6,000 |
| Scholarship fund | 4,000 | | | | 4,000 |
| Total fund balances | | | | | $60,500 |

## First Church
## Balance Sheet
## February 28, 19XX

**Assets**

| | |
|---|---:|
| Cash—checking | $13,500 |
| Cash—savings | 9,000 |
| Furniture | 4,000 |
| Equipment | 7,000 |
| Buildings | 48,000 |
| Land | 20,000 |
| | $101,500 |

**Liabilities**

| | |
|---|---:|
| Mortgage payable | $41,000 |

**Equity**

| | | |
|---|---:|---:|
| Fund Balance—unrestricted | | |
| Beginning balance | $49,000 | |
| Increase for month | 1,500 | 50,500** |
| Building fund | | 6,000 |
| Scholarship Fund | | 4,000 |
| | | $101,500 |

**Note: Fund balance represents the amount of unrestricted equity, or assets minus liabilities and restricted funds, that the membership has invested in the church. At the end of February, fund balance totals $50,500.

## Exhibit A-4  Financial Statements

specific purposes or activities. Within a church people may give moneys to purchase a new organ, repave the parking lot, put on a new roof, build a parsonage, or add a wing to the church. Because the church must be able to show that the funds were spent as directed, the receipt of restricted funds is accompanied by a significant accountability obligation. Further, even when unrestricted funds are received by the church via weekly offerings, there is a presumption by givers that those funds will be used to pay church expenses. To some extent, therefore, even unrestricted funds have conditions attached. Additionally, the administrative board may designate that a certain amount of unrestricted funds received be used in a specific way, such as for new choir robes, a new van, or a computer. Although the board may change its mind about how to use the funds (and often does), the internal restrictions placed on these amounts also creates accountability obligations. To control earmarked resources and to ensure compliance with both external or internal restrictions, separate funds are created.

Each fund is an independent fiscal and accounting entity with a self-balancing set of accounts established to carry out specific activities or attain certain objectives, in accordance with its special restrictions and limitations. Each fund, therefore, 1) is separate and distinct from all other funds, 2) has its own set of numbered accounts, and 3) has its own set of financial statements.

A church using a fund-accounting system may have scores of different funds. For example, if a member contributed $1,000 toward the installation of railings on a set of stairs, a new fund would have to be created for that restricted gift if a fund did not already exist. From an operational point of view, this would mean establishing separate accounts in the general ledger for the new fund, for any interest earned on the moneys before they were spent, and for bills paid from fund assets. Whenever financial reports are prepared, it means reporting on the status of the fund both over a period of time (via a statement of revenues and expenditures and a statement of changes in fund balances) and on the date of reporting (via a balance sheet). The multiplicity of different funds being accounted for separately can make the general ledger large and unwieldy and periodic financial reports long and incomprehensible. For example, although General Motors, a multibillion dollar organization, can report its financial affairs to stockholders in a five-page report (excluding footnotes), a church with a $200,000 budget using fund accounting and reporting on each fund separately may have a one hundred-page report! The extensiveness of financial reports with fund accounting is a key obstacle to more widespread use. Users read church financial statements to learn how the church is doing; the reports tell them, fund by fund. It's like asking a member of the U.S. Forest Service the condition of the American forests and getting a tree-by-tree analysis as an answer! Possibly the saying, "You can't see the forest for the trees" can be attributed to a fund-accounting user.

Congregations who employ fund accounting typically have several different types of funds. A brief review of each type of fund follows.

The fund used to pay operating expenses, utilities, salaries, supplies, and so on, is called the general fund. The source of moneys for this fund is unrestricted weekly offerings and other unrestricted gifts made by members. It is almost always the most important fund within the church, as the majority of transactions are recorded in general fund accounts.

A second type of fund is a restricted fund. Restricted funds are used to handle donor gifts for special items or events, such as the organ, the altar, a memorial, a scholarship, or a special service. Because the variety of restricted gifts is endless, some churches use one umbrella fund to handle all restricted gifts. In that way the number of different funds can be dramatically reduced. But the treasurer must still keep track of each individual restricted gift to make certain that the moneys are disbursed according to the wishes of the donor. Alternatively, some churches create a separate fund for each restricted gift received.

A third type of fund is a property, plant, and equipment fund. This fund is sometimes called a plant fund or a fixed assets fund. The fund is sometimes used, especially in large churches, to record the cost of property, plant, and equipment invested in church facilities. The cost of additions are added to this fund; disposals are subtracted from this fund. Cash funds provided to the church for building improvements can be placed in this fund. Another approach is to record the building improvement contributions in a fund called restricted fund—building improvements until the improvements are complete. At that point an interfund transfer is made from the restricted fund—building improvements to the property, plant, and equipment fund. Those churches maintaining a property, plant, and equipment fund believe it important to know both the resources committed to facilities and equipment and the annual depreciation on such assets. (Depreciation accounting is discussed in the appendix to chapter 5.) Suffice it to say that the full cost of church programs cannot be calculated without considering depreciation of plant assets.

A fourth type of fund is the board-designated fund. These amounts are carved out of the unrestricted general fund and set aside by the administrative board for special purposes. By cubbyholing some of the general fund, the board reduces the amount of unrestricted funds available for other church programs and expenses. Just as these funds can be created by the board, they can be eliminated by the board or part of their balance can be moved to another fund.

It is also possible to have several other types of funds. There can be endowment funds for gifts received where the donor has indicated that the principal of the gift is to remain intact and only the interest can be spent. There can be trust and agency funds for assets held by the church in a trustee capacity for individuals, organizations, or a higher church unit. Examples are pensions held for pastors and church personnel and special offerings taken for missionary work. The possibility for an internal service fund exists in large churches to account for goods and services provided by one church department or program to other departments or programs of the same church. Last, certain segments of church operations, such as a high school, cafeteria, thrift shop, recreational facility, and so on, may be operated in a manner similar to private business enterprises. The intent of the church may be to cover all costs of this activity, including depreciation, through user charges. Such segments may use enterprise funds to account for their operations.

To recapitulate, churches employing a fund-accounting system typically have several different types of funds besides the general fund. Further, a church may have many individual funds within a particular type of fund, such as for restricted funds and for board-designated funds. Accounting for many different funds may be a headache for the treasurer; reporting on each fund may be overwhelming for the reader.

Churches using a fund-accounting system use the same tools of accounting and follow the same steps as in the previously discussed one-fund, general ledger system. But because several different funds are involved, each with its own self-balancing set of accounts, there are many more accounts in the general ledger in a fund-accounting system. For instance, there may be a cash account for every fund that exists, as opposed to one cash account for the entire church. Fund-accounting computer software is available and should be considered by churches using a fund-accounting system.

Examples of the financial statements of the general fund, the flower fund (restricted), and the endowment fund of a church using a fund-accounting approach is shown in exhibit A-5. Observe that 1) a statement of revenues and expenditures (and, if necessary, transfers) and 2) a balance sheet are prepared for each fund. Unlike the financial statement in exhibit A-4, no overall financial statements are prepared for Second Church. Each fund is reported on separately.

Some users of fund-accounting statements become confused when they try to assess what really took place. So some churches report only the activities of the general fund on a monthly basis. Other funds, where less activity is likely to take place and where restrictions exist, are reported on quarterly, semiannually, or annually. In this way readers can focus on the receipt and use of unrestricted moneys. Alternatively, some churches prepare one summary statement of the activities of all funds. Each fund is summarized in a single column, with revenues, expenditures, transfers, and beginning and ending fund balances noted.

**Second Church**
**General Fund**
**Statement of Revenues, Expenditures, and Transfers for the Month**
**Ended March 31, 19XX**

**Revenues**

| | | |
|---|---|---|
| Contributions | $11,000 | |
| Investment interest | 1,000 | $12,000 |

**Expenditures**

| | | |
|---|---|---|
| Salaries | $ 4,000 | |
| Maintenance | 2,000 | |
| Supplies | 1,000 | |
| Utilities | 1,000 | 8,000 |
| | | $ 4,000 |
| Excess of revenue over expenditures | | |
| Fund balance, February 28 | $ 2,000 | |

**Transfers**

| | | |
|---|---|---|
| Organ fund | (2,000) | |
| Roofing fund | ( 500) | (500) |
| Fund balance, March 31 | | $ 3,500 |

**Second Church**
**General Fund**
**Balance Sheet**
**March 31, 19XX**

**Assets**

| | |
|---|---|
| Cash | $ 3,500 |

**Fund balance**  $ 3,500

**Second Church**
**Flower Fund**
**Statement of Revenues and Expenditures for the Month**
**Ended March 31, 19XX**

**Revenues**

| | |
|---|---|
| Contributions | $100 |

**Expenditures**

| | |
|---|---|
| Altar flowers | 105 |
| Excess of expenditures over revenues | $     5 |
| Fund balance, February 28 | 60 |
| Fund balance, March 31 | $   55 |

**Second Church**
**Flower Fund**
**Balance Sheet**
**March 31, 19XX**

**Assets**

| | |
|---|---|
| Cash | $    55 |

**Fund balance**  $    55

**Second Church**
**Endowment Fund**
**Statement of Revenues, Expenditures, and Transfers for the Month**
**Ended March 31, 19XX**

**Revenues**

| | | |
|---|---:|---:|
| Contributions | $ 500 | |
| Investment interest | 100 | |
| Investment dividends | 150 | |
| Gain on the sale of securities | 3,000 | $ 3,750 |
| **Expenditures** | | |
| Administrative costs | | 300 |
| Excess of revenues over expenditures | | $ 3,450 |
| Fund balance, February 28 | | 10,000 |
| Transfer to the pastor's education fund | | (2,000) |
| Fund balance, March 31 | | $11,450 |

**Second Church**
**Endowment Fund**
**Balance Sheet**
**March 31, 19XX**

**Assets**

| | | |
|---|---:|---:|
| Cash | $ 800 | |
| Bonds | 4,000 | |
| Common stocks | 6,650 | $11,450 |
| **Fund balance** | | $11,450 |

Exhibit A-5   Examples of Financial Statements from a
Fund-Accounting System

Restricted funds and board-designated funds are grouped in one column for purposes of presentation. A final column labeled Total of All Funds provides aggregate data on all revenues received, expenditures made, and so on. By showing the activity of all funds in a single statement, one of the biggest objections to fund accounting is overcome. Nonetheless, accounting purists would call such grouping dangerous and potentially misleading, because church moneys received have different levels of restriction.

Fund accounting is a specialized accounting topic within the field of governmental and nonprofit accounting. Entire books have been written on the subject. Those treasurers working with a fund-accounting system or thinking of installing a fund-accounting system may find such a book useful.

# CHAPTER 5

# *Financial Reporting*

Church financial statements are the real products of the accounting process. Time-consuming budgeting and tedious, accurate processing of transactions through an accounting system are not ends in themselves. They are done to make sure that the church financial reports can be used for planning, control, and decision making. You don't budget for the sake of budgeting or process data for the sake of accounting. You do this preparatory work to ensure that users of church financial reports receive information relevant to their needs. Without well-prepared financial reports, church administrators may misunderstand the financial data and make incorrect decisions. New programs may be approved, raises may be given, and debt may be incurred—all in error. Many treasurers attend meetings where their financial reports are being distributed, just to prevent such errors from occurring. Further, many churches fail to receive the full support of their membership, because the financial reports distributed to the congregation are unintelligible to the average member. Statements such as, Why do they have to make these financial statements so difficult to understand? and What good are financial statements if no one understands them? are common. Frustrated members can't help but hold back their support. Because they can't rely on the financial statements to assess the financial condition of the church, they must rely on someone else's interpretation. And if they do not trust that person, they will always have doubts. I remember a commercial that alleged that the best milk came from contented cows. Applied here, full support comes from contented members, that is, members who understand the financial reports.

## COMMUNICATION

The key to financial reporting by the church treasurer is to remember that reports are issued to communicate information. Communication is the process of sending information and receiving a response. For communication to be effective, a channel must be established between the sender and the receiver through which a message is sent and a response is received. An appropriate response indicates both that the message was clear and that the receiver understood the message. Breakdowns in communication occur if the sender fails to send a clear message, the receiver fails to understand the message, or both problems occur. In most churches the failure of the financial reports to communicate can be attributed to problems with both the sender (the treasurer) and the receivers (the finance committee, administrative board, or membership).

In regard to the treasurer's situation, first, there's the problem of tradition. If certain financial reports have been issued monthly for eons, most treasurers are reluctant to change the reporting format. After all, they may hold the position for only a year and not feel sufficiently confident to second guess their predecessors. Second, there's the problem of knowledge. Many church treasurers who are pressed into service do not have an accounting background. Thus although they hear receiver complaints, they don't know what to do about them. Third, some receivers do not complain, because if they are too critical of the financial reports, they may wind up being next year's treasurer. Thus receiver complaints are often muted or hidden. Fourth, a treasurer may often have a misplaced emphasis. He or she may spend countless hours processing every transaction through four hundred different accounts and subaccounts, balancing the books to the penny. This person feels that the treasurer's role is to process data, not communicate financial information, and that the role of the receiver is to check on his or her work. This attitude results in financial reports that are voluminous and complex—but correct. The financial statements are presented the same way a proud artist shows a piece of art.

There are also problems on the receiving end. Members of the administrative board or finance committee, for example, may be selected because they can help the church face the financial challenges of the year ahead. Some are astute businesspeople. Yet these people can become unnerved quickly when they read the church's financial reports if they are not familiar with church accounting. They may be accustomed to the accrual basis of accounting; the church probably uses the cash basis. They may never have seen fund accounting, transfers between funds, pledges, or noncash contributions in their business setting. This lack of expertise in nonprofit accounting may render the financial reports less useful than they would otherwise be. Stated differently, the message may not be fully received.

Members of the general congregation have the same kind of problem. But here the problem is magnified, because many members have not previously received and digested financial information. Few are trained in finance and accounting. Many abhor statistics, numbers, and mathematics. The sender has to take special measures to make sure the communication is as simple as possible. Without forethought, the channel can get overloaded and the message will not get through. An example may be helpful.

Let's say that you want to take your very young son/grandson/ nephew to the store and treat him to a candy bar. To give him a choice, you take him to a large discount drugstore that carries many different kinds of sweets, and you accompany him to the appropriate aisle. You give him instructions to select a candy bar while you pick up a few things in another section of the store. Five minutes later you return with your shopping completed, only to find that the youngster has not yet selected a candy bar. You again instruct the child to make a selection while you go to pick up one more item that you just remembered. Ten minutes later, after selecting the one last item and chatting with a friend, you return to the candy section expecting the child to be waiting impatiently for you. Instead the child stands in front of the different bins of candy assessing the various kinds, shapes, sizes, flavors, and colors available. At this point you may press the issue and force the child to make a choice. Even then, however, he will not be quick to do so and may resort to some sort of game to make the selection. Some adults get mad at the child for being so tentative. Other adults pretend that they're going home, expecting the child to make a speedy choice and follow them to the checkstand. Sometimes this ploy backfires on the adult who happens to be in a quick line, and he or she has to get out of line to go fetch the child.

What's happened here? Should you feel angered? Of course not. You have inflicted a case of information overload on the poor child by taking him to a store that has too many choices. The child's brain is confused by all of the data on the various candy bars and, in computerese, is in a loop. It would have been better if you had taken the child to a small store that stocked only three or four kinds of candy bars. The child could make a choice in minutes.

This story is relevant to church financial reporting. Whereas a child might stand in front of the candy bins all day, an adult faced with an information overload might say, Why do they have to make these financial statements so difficult to understand? or What good are financial statements if no one understands them? Sound familiar?

Research conducted at a large northwestern university in the early

1970s studied people's capacities to process financial information. Although the studies were limited, they did point out that people are unable to simultaneously process and understand many different financial variables. If, for example, your monthly financial report lists 1) five types of revenues and total revenues, 2) ten types of expenditures and total expenditures, 3) the excess of cash revenues over expenditures or vice versa, and 4) the beginning and ending cash balance, there is already a total of twenty bits of financial information. If budgeted expectations are presented side by side with the actual amounts, the number of bits of information increases to forty. If the statement also includes year-to-date columns, both actual and budgeted, you now have eighty bits of financial data to comprehend. Even without budgeted data, the situation can get out of hand. Exhibit 5-1 presents an actual church financial statement given to me several years ago by Erol, a church treasurer. Parts of some account names have been removed to avoid denominational references. Note the clutter, due to an overwhelming number of items, numbers for each line, and reporting in pennies! Just eliminating the number for each line would make the statement appear less formidable. The statement has over 250 bits of information if you count the data, headings, line numbers, account names, and monetary amounts. Further, some of the monetary amounts are negative; these should be processed differently than positive amounts. An untrained person cannot digest the report, ask intelligent questions, and make correct decisions based upon this report.

To summarize, faulty communication can be caused by both senders and receivers of messages. What can be done about it? One option is to educate the receivers. As an educator myself, I'd love it. It would be the equivalent of Congress passing the Accounting Professors Full Employment Act! But that's not the most efficient alternative. The easiest and most direct avenue is to have church treasurers, the senders, refine their products to allow their receivers to use the reports. In providing effective accounting, your aim is to satisfy the requirements of users.

## PRINCIPLES OF FINANCIAL REPORTING

The effectiveness of planning, controlling, and decision making depends largely on the ability of the financial reports to help people make correct decisions. As we have discussed, this includes not only the receipt of data, but also an understanding of the message. And, as in the business world, there is no standard set of reports that is equally effective for every church. Reports must be tailored to the personalities, circumstances, and business acumen of the users in each church. The content, design, and manner of presentation of reports are all important factors in communication. One church may rely on a certain technique; another church within the same denomination may rely on another technique. Nonetheless, there are five key principles of reporting that transcend all organizations. Where applicable, these principles should be used for reports of financial information, whether for dissemination to the membership or for internal use by church managers. Not all principles apply to every report. A review of these principles should provide you with a wealth of ideas for modification of your own reports.

1. **Responsibility Reporting Should Be Used.**
   Responsibility reporting is based on the organizational structure of the church. For example, the church may have centers, departments, committees, or programs for worship, missions, buildings and grounds, education, youth, administration, music, kitchen, and so on. The thrust of responsibility accounting is that reporting is done by specific area rather than by aggregate. Thus, for example, salaries and wages are spread out among the various centers rather than just the grand total being reported as an expense. Also, centers that produce both revenue and costs, such as schools, show a matching of these items. With responsibility reporting users can better assess the performance of individual centers and, in the process, of their administration.

2. **Exception Reporting Should be Used.**
   Financial report users should be directed to the out-of-the-ordinary performance. If performance is generally as expected, then valuable energy and time is not wasted looking at acceptable, expected results. Some treasurers accomplish this by preparing a percentage variance when actual and budgeted data is presented side by side. For example, if actual contributions are shown as $226,221 and expected contributions are $229,845, a shortfall of 1.6 percent is indicated. Thus users do not have to calculate the difference of $3,624 and ponder whether that is a material amount. They are advised that the difference is 1.6 percent of budget, which by any standard can be chalked up as an estimation error. But if actual contributions are $188,473 and budgeted contributions are $229,845, the shortfall is 18 percent, which is major and should be written in red or in capitals.

3. **Summarized Reporting Should Be Used.**
   The kind of information needed by the membership is not the same as that needed by the finance committee. The finance committee keeps a close eye on all church activities. It needs

## Financial Statement - November 30, 19X2

| | Balance 12-31-X1 | Transfers to Accounts | Income | Disbursements | Balance 11-30-X2 |
|---|---|---|---|---|---|
| 1. HOME OPERATING | (4,447.31) | (173,123.05) | 164,685.82 | | (12,884.54) |
| 2. Salaries & Wages | | 134,728.39 | | 134,728.39 | |
| 3. Pension & Health | | 12,114.12 | | 12,114.12 | |
| 4. Janitor Supplies | | 996.24 | | 996.24 | |
| 5. Church Supplies | | 1,098.00 | | 1,098.00 | |
| 6. Office Supplies | | 3,273.27 | 270.00 | 3,543.27 | |
| 7. Utilities | | 10,302.96 | 59.15 | 10,362.11 | |
| 8. Conferences & Conventions | | 2,850.83 | 333.68 | 3,184.51 | |
| 9. Church Publications | | 1,027.32 | 41.50 | 1,068.82 | |
| 10. Insurance | 400.00 | 3,551.10 | | 3,551.10 | 400.00 |
| 11. Continuing Education | | 400.00 | | 400.00 | |
| 12. Board of Youth Ministry | | 1,015.15 | 340.00 | 1,355.15 | |
| 13. Welfare | | 407.98 | 230.00 | 637.98 | |
| 14. Scholarships Paid | | 200.00 | | 200.00 | |
| 15. Vacation Bible School | | 228.84 | 246.97 | 475.81 | |
| 16. Community Relations | | 286.90 | 30.00 | 316.90 | |
| 17. 1% of H-O to Church College | | 1,271.09 | | 1,271.09 | |
| 18. Total Home Operating | | | 166,237.12 | 175,303.49 | |
| 19. RADIO BROADCAST | 488.80 | | 4,240.50 | 4,118.76 | 610.54 |
| 20. BROADCAST EQUIPMENT | 53.68 | | | 16.67 | 37.01 |
| 21. SUNDAY SCHOOL | 429.17 | | 1,090.19 | 1,370.75 | 148.61 |
| 22. REPAIRS | 3,662.16 | | 4,471.87 | 6,434.39 | 1,699.64 |
| 23. DEBT & CAPITAL IMPROVEMENT | 2,877.70 | (280.00)* | 5,101.93 | 2,500.00 | 5,199.63 |
| 24. SCHOOL BOOKS & SUPPLIES | 552.98 | | 6,426.00 | 5,602.41 | 1,376.57 |
| 25. PERFORMING ARTISTS | 72.29 | | | | 72.29 |
| 26. CHOIR MUSIC | 90.41 | | | 90.41 | |
| 27. CHURCH LIBRARY | 50.00 | | | 27.50 | 22.50 |
| 28. NON-BUDGET ITEMS | | | 1,903.50 | 1,893.02 | 10.48 |
| 29. Hymnal Fund | (16.49) | | 301.40 | 230.50 | 54.41 |

| # | Account | | | | | |
|---|---------|---|---|---|---|---|
| 30. | VAN FUND | 1,289.31 | | | | 1,627.92 |
| 31. | OFFICE EQUIPMENT | 243.40 | 123.36 | 700.28 | 485.03 | (414.60) |
| 32. | WORD PROCESSOR | | | 2,012.00 | 2,670.00 | 748.85 |
| 33. | MEMORIAL | 325.00 | | 3,350.00 | 2,601.15 | 62.95 |
| 34. | STUDENT TUITION AID | 100.00 | | 4,111.98 | 262.05 | 3,284.48 |
| 35. | INSURANCE REPAYMENT | | (472.50) | 3,940.00 | 455.00 | 1,567.98 |
| 36. | REFORMATION SUNDAY | | | 525.50 | 2,372.02 | 304.28 |
| 37. | Total Local Accounts | | | 204,412.27 | 221.22 | |
| | | | | | 206,654.37 | |
| 38. | DISTRICT   $21,792.62 | | | | | |
| 39. | World Missions | | | 11,267.75 | 11,267.75 | |
| 40. | Mission Festival | | | 8,244.00 | 8,244.00 | |
| 41. | "In His Service" | | | 395.00 | 395.00 | |
| 42. | Church Extension Fund | | | 820.80 | 820.80 | |
| 43. | The Hour | | | 309.00 | 613.28 | (304.28) |
| 44. | Good Samaritan Home | | | 186.00 | 186.00 | |
| 45. | Braille Workers, Inc. | | | 123.00 | 123.00 | |
| 46. | Foundation | | | 59.00 | 59.00 | |
| 47. | University | | | 7.00 | 7.00 | |
| 48. | Bible Translators | | | 24.02 | 24.02 | |
| 49. | School for the Deaf | | | 4.00 | 4.00 | |
| 50. | World Relief/World Hunger | | | 249.05 | 249.05 | |
| 51. | Women's Missionary League | | | 20.00 | 20.00 | |
| 52. | Armed Forces Commission | | | 49.00 | 49.00 | |
| 53. | Christmas Offering | | | 35.00 | | 35.00 |
| 54. | TOTALS | 6,171.10 | | 226,204.89 | 228,716.27 | |

---

* Interest in forbearance transferred to Home Operating Account 12-3-X2

EROL, Treasurer

**Exhibit 5-1   Sample Financial Statement**

details, sometimes pages of them. The general members do
not keep a close eye on anything. They just want to know if
the church can pay its bills. Summarized data is all they need.
Generally speaking, as you move up the organizational ladder,
the focus should become more summarized, because the scope
of responsibility has broadened. Hence, one church financial
statement cannot serve the needs of all constituents. Different
audiences need different reports. Not only are perspectives
different, but, as discussed earlier, so are capabilities. Using
the organization chart from chapter 1, the most detailed
financial report should be provided to members of the finance
committee; less detailed information should be provided to the
administrative board; and yet less detail should be provided to
the congregation.

4. **Comparative Reporting Should Be Used.**
   Often absolute financial figures mean nothing. A report that
   says that weekly offerings were $20,000 doesn't impart any
   real information. Data must be compared with something to
   be valuable; compared with a budget, with last week's
   offering, with last year's offering for the same week, and so
   on. The reader must be able to grasp quickly how the actual
   results compare with some yardstick. Guiding users through
   the data by showing relationships is important. For example, a
   deviation from expected contributions may not be brought to
   the attention of readers properly if the treasurer merely shows
   weekly offerings in one column and year-to-date offerings in a
   second column, with no reference to budgeted expectations.
   Comparative reporting means two amounts are compared, not
   that two columns are merely presented side by side.

5. **Interpretive Reporting Should Be Used.**
   Interpretive reporting means adding meaningful comments to
   figures to help readers digest the information. Few church
   treasurers employ this technique. Instead many treasurers feel
   compelled to show up at every meeting where the financial
   report is discussed, in order to explain it. But if a few
   sentences of explanation were added at the bottom, the report
   might be able to stand alone. Commentary might indicate
   significant variances from the budget and, when known, the
   reasons for the variances. Interpretive reporting could be
   helpful to those persons unable or unwilling to read financial
   reports.

### Other Factors in Financial Reporting

The five principles of financial reporting just discussed are basic to a good financial reporting system. In addition, several others factors can assist the reader to understand the message.

1. **Reports Should Be Accurate.**
   Nothing discredits a report more than for a reader to find an inaccuracy, no matter how small. When an error is found, it jeopardizes the credibility of all the other figures on the report, the accounting system that processed data into information, and the treasurer, who failed to find the error. Church financial reports must be proofed before they are distributed. Many public accounting firms proof their financial reports three times before they issue them!

2. **Reports Should Be Simple and Clear.**
   "Busy" statements, such as the one in exhibit 5-1, should be avoided. Information should be arranged so that the reader can secure the essential facts in a reasonable period of time and with a minimum of effort. When necessary, lay terms can be substituted for accounting terms. Similarly, accounts that puzzle readers month after month can be renamed for financial reporting purposes only. After all, if people are continually asking what the quasi-endowment fund is, maybe it would be best to call this fund a board-designated fund on the financial report and to indicate the reason it was created by the administrative board. There's no accounting rule that says that accounts cannot be renamed or grouped creatively for purposes of communication.

3. **Information Should Be Presented Meaningfully.**
   Financial data must be displayed in a logical format. The preparer must, in a sense, take the reader by the hand and march him or her through the report. Thus you might show revenues as a group with an appropriate total before you present expenditures. You might treat expenditures in a similar manner. Alternatively, when a flow concept, as for cash, is presented, you might start with the beginning balance, add inflows, and subtract outflows to derive the ending balance. Logical as this presentation may seem, many users of church financial reports have to grapple with information that is organized in another manner, such as by account number. Erol's report, in exhibit 5-1, organizes items

into home operating, local, and district accounts. This method
of organization is good, but within each category items appear
to be listed by account number. I infer this because items with
large and small monetary amounts are intermingled.

4. **Pennies and Insignificant Amounts Should Be Eliminated.**
Again, the role of financial reporting is to help users plan,
control, and make decisions. It is not the role of users to check
up on the treasurer's work. Therefore there's little purpose in
carrying out amounts to pennies; whole dollar reporting
should be followed. Round amounts up to the nearest whole
dollar if they are more than fifty cents; round down if they are
less. If, when arriving at the dollar total, the amount is one
dollar different than the correct dollar total, use the correct
figure, follow it with an asterisk, and state in a footnote that
the difference is due to rounding. If Erol had eliminated
pennies in exhibit 5-1, his report would be ten spaces shorter
and appear less complicated. Further, insignificant amounts,
such as any account with a beginning and ending balance and
transactions of less than one hundred dollars can be grouped
in one account, called, for example, miscellaneous district
account. By doing this Erol would save more than ten lines on
his statement. Thus it is possible for an account to appear in
one month's financial report and not reappear until something
significant has again occurred. Few treasurers thin out their
reports to make them look less cluttered. Try it; your readers
will like it.

5. **The Costs of Report Preparation Should Be Considered.**
All reports have costs. Churches using a computer service
bureau may pay for each regular report or run prepared, plus
pay a surcharge for special reports. With other churches the
costs involve preparer time. Whether a preparer gets paid for
services or is a volunteer, the church uses resources in the
preparation of the report. As discussed extensively in chapter
2, human resources are as important to the church as cash
resources. Given that all reports cost, the church should have
only those reports prepared where the benefits of preparation
exceed the costs of preparation. There is agreement within
church circles that the benefits of preparing monthly financial
reports and an annual financial report exceed the costs,
because these provide congregations with the raw materials
necessary to plan, control, and make decisions. Put
differently, these reports are a natural process in the
accounting process. Likewise, the benefits of completing

reports for the higher denominational authority and Internal Revenue Service are seen as greater than the costs of their preparation. But the same rationale does not apply to other reports requested by boards, committees, or members. These groups or individuals may not think in terms of costs. They may think that information is free, and all you have to do is look it up in the file. To illustrate this naïveté, I heard of a church member who walked into the church office and asked the secretary where she kept the statistics, as if they were in one drawer! It is your responsibility to inform those persons asking for special information or special reports how long it will take you or the staff to compile the report, and if hourly wages are involved, how much it will cost the church. Informed of the costs, the requesting group or party is then in a position to assess the costs to the church against the benefits they expect the church to receive from the report. If they expect the church to have a net benefit, they will ask you to go ahead and have the report prepared. But you will be surprised how many people, when informed of the costs to the church, will drop their request. We can assume from this that the benefits to the church were marginal and/or the information desired was for personal purposes. You can't waste your time on these kinds of projects. So when someone asks you for information that is not readily available, let them know the cost. You will save some time, and the church will conserve its resources.

6. **Reports Should Be Timely.**
   A report is like a fish; the older the information, the less useful it is. If reports are to be used for every monthly meeting of the finance committee or administrative board, they should be available for the meeting. Excuses such as "The financial secretary was ill," "The computer was broken," or "I went on vacation" are not legitimate excuses. In fact, some church administrators have told me that even death is not a legitimate excuse! For a group to meet without financial information may not only be a waste of their time but may imply that they can proceed without reports. It's a bad precedent. An ancillary problem relates to the timeliness of information within the report. It serves no purpose to furnish anyone a June 30 financial report in mid-July that includes all transactions up to April 15. A June 30 report should include the result of all activity up to that date. When processing lags develop, financial reports, like fish, begin to give off an odor.

I've seen programs overspend their annual budgets because spending ran several months ahead of the reports. Think of the dire consequences to the nation's banking system if withdrawals from savings accounts were recorded two months after funds were withdrawn! To prevent such an occurrence, banks record withdrawals immediately. Churches too should process transactions through their accounting systems as quickly as possible.

By employing the preceding principles and factors you will help make your financial presentations more useful to users. With each improvement the message will get clearer, because the channel of communication will get stronger.

## DIFFERENT AUDIENCES, DIFFERENT REPORTS

As noted earlier, there are several different audiences for church financial statements, each with its own capacity to understand and need for information. First, there's the general membership. Members use financial statements to help them reach certain conclusions on the status of the church. For example, if the church is doing well financially, members will generally place more confidence in the abilities of the church's leadership. They are more apt to attend church activities, handle jobs for the church, and give for special needs. Further, knowing that the church is financially strong takes pressure off individual members for financial support. When the opposite financial condition exists, membership confidence and support may be lacking. You may hear a lot of grumbling. Members may be torn between giving money to help the church survive and withholding their money from the group who has mismanaged it. Uncertainty causes confusion; confusion causes anger. As in sports, people like to be associated with a winner. Thus knowing how the church is doing and if the church can pay its bills are pivotal to the membership.

A second audience is composed of the finance committee, administrative board, program leaders, pastors, and, in large churches, full-time church administrators. These groups need detailed information to both manage current operations and plan for the future. As a consequence the financial statements provided to these groups should be much more extensive than those provided to the general membership. And if the church retains a certified public accountant to conduct a yearly audit, the financial statements must be prepared according to generally accepted accounting principles.

The third audience for church financial statements is composed of banks that have loaned the church funds, trustees who are responsible for the repayment of capital to bondholders (those who hold church bonds issued to finance church expansion or modernization), the Internal Revenue Service, and the church's higher denominational authority. Each of these users will specify the form and content of the financial statements that satisfy its needs.

The presence of different audiences means that several different financial reports will have to be prepared to cover the same period. Thus there is no such thing as "the" church financial report. Those church treasurers who attempt to appease all users with a single report have their priorities mixed up. A treasurer's goal should not be to minimize the time spent in report preparation, but to maximize the usefulness of reports in helping people to make correct decisions. Thus just as General Motors produces hundreds of different kinds of cars for different markets, effective church treasurers produce several different financial reports for different audiences.

### Reports to the General Membership

As noted, members need summary information presented to them in the simplest form possible. Spare them the details; spare them the jargon. This means that the monthly, quarterly, and annual financial reports to members need not be comprehensive or lengthy. A few sentences of narrative interpretation will make the reports more useful. Your goal is to develop a one-page monthly report. Be careful, though; Erol wrote a one-page report, and it's confusing. One page, therefore, does not mean a commitment to reduce the print size and completely fill up an 8½-×-11 piece of paper. It means evaluating the needs of your members and the financial activities of the church. It means presenting only the important facts and comparative relationships. It means leaving plenty of white space. The annual report too must be well thought out. A one-page overview of activities and, in a few churches, the traditional list of individual contributors, name by name, should suffice. You may add a note that a more detailed presentation of financial affairs has been prepared for the finance committee or administrative board and is available at the church office. Having a few members request copies is far better than overwhelming all members.

Most of the church financial reports intended for the general membership that I have seen do not "pass the test" outlined in this chapter. In fact, many churches seem to share the same dilemma. It seems as though church treasurers in the 1950s were so confident that their general purpose reports were perfect that they printed 10,000 copies of the forms and stored them in the church basement for future use. Each month since then, the treasurer has gone down to the basement, taken one copy from the pile, and filled in the numbers. Based on my calculations, many churches have more than 9,500 copies left to use! And, of course, each month that a report is prepared and issued, members ask, "Why do they have to make these financial statements so difficult to understand?" and "What good is a financial statement if no one understands it?" My suggestion for report preparers who have fallen into this trap is to first go down into the basement, gather up the unused forms, and sell them to a used-paper dealer. In that way your church can get some benefit from the forms, and some trees will be saved too. Second, you need to design a new, one-page report. You may find it helpful to determine what other churches are doing, within your denomination and outside of it. Your streamlined easy-to-understand, one-page report may be the biggest legacy you'll leave the church. You may have to experiment for several months, using different terminologies, formats, and accounts. Let the congregation know what you are doing. Insert a paragraph in the Sunday church bulletin that notes that you are experimenting with alternative ways of presenting the church's financial information in order to improve its understandability. Point out that several different approaches will be tried for the next several months and that comments are welcome.

One final word about reports to the membership. It concerns the whereabouts of the cash in the church's cash accounts and investments. Many churches have checking accounts, which may be interest bearing, or passbook savings accounts or certificates of deposit with long maturities. Some churches also have investments in the form of stocks, bonds, or real estate. In monthly financial reports to the general membership, it is unwise to be specific about the exact location of these assets. It is necessary only to present the balances of each category in their broadest terms. For example, to state that the church has cash of $14,500 consisting of $1,000 in a checking account, $3,500 in savings accounts, and $10,000 in a certificate of deposit is sufficient. Some churches are much more specific and present something like the following in their financial reports:

| | | |
|---|---:|---:|
| Checking account, Eastern National Bank, | | |
| noninterest bearing | | $ 1,000 |
| Savings accounts | | |
| Southern State Bank, 5½ percent | $2,000 | |
| Northern Trust Bank, 6 percent | 1,500 | 3,500 |
| Six-month certificate of deposit | | |
| Western Hills Bank of Commerce | | |
| 7 percent, matures 4/15/XX | | 10,000 |
| | | $14,500 |

But although this method is informative, mentioning banks, maturity dates, and interest rates, is dangerous. The danger comes from members using the information to second-guess those within the church empowered to make financial commitments. For example, there's the question of banks. Given the preceding information, a member is likely to note that Troy Townsend, a member of the church, has just been appointed assistant vice president of the Bank of Timbuktu and recommends that you move all of the church's funds to his bank. Yet the recommending member probably does not know anything of the financial condition of the bank, whether it is federally or state insured, or even whether Troy would personally look after the church's funds. Troy may be in charge of processing boat loans!

Then there's the maturity of the certificate of deposit. It's easy to be critical of the church's six-month maturity, when it's obvious to some that a longer maturity usually commands a higher interest. Then again, if the church had a longer maturity, some people would comment that a six-month maturity would have been far superior, because interest rates were expected to rise.

Finally, and most important, there's the interest rate debate. Given the current interest rates, the church in the example does not appear to be earning an especially high yield on its investments. Yet even if the church were earning 16 percent or 26 percent on its funds, some member would point out that he or she knew of a higher-yielding investment for the church. No matter what the church was earning on its funds, some members would indicate that it was unwise for the church not to be earning a higher return.

In summary, the second-guessing related to which banks, maturities, and interest rates the church has committed to can destroy overall confidence in the investment decision makers. Those members making offhand comments typically do not have all of the facts and have never had the fiduciary responsibility of managing the church's assets.

The goal of the church's investment decision makers, whether treasurer, finance committee, or administrative board, is not to maximize the return on its money. If that were the case, they would make risky investments. The goal of the decision makers is to protect the church's capital and, in the process, earn some interest or receive some dividends. The key is *not to lose the money*. What most second-guessing members fail to realize is that in finance there is a tradeoff between risk and return. That is, those who are willing to take the biggest risks get the greatest return, and those unwilling to take risks get the lowest return. This tradeoff between risk and return is illustrated in exhibit 5-2.

I trust that the investment decision makers reach their conclusions about the safety of banks, the trend in interest rates, and the risks inherent in each investment in a prudent manner. If their wisdom is continually criticized and if they eventually yield to pressure, the church may be headed for trouble. Some churches have suffered large losses in

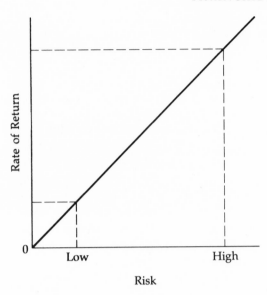

**Exhibit 5-2   The Investment Tradeoff**

search of a higher rate of return. Can your church handle the risk? If not, don't foster the second-guessing by providing ammunition in the financial report. Keeping the presentation general in monthly financial reports implies that it's someone else's responsibility to work out the investment details.

Annual reports, however, should be more specific, providing full details and possibly even the average rate of return earned on cash assets in the twelve-month period. In churches that elect officers and appoint committees annually, it is useful to know how the outgoing group has managed the funds. This information can provide a benchmark for the incoming group as well as provide information to those who may seek to hold an office or serve on a committee. Thus if all excess cash funds were kept in a noninterest-bearing checking account, I would want to become involved in obtaining some interest earnings for the church. Likewise, if the church were financing the building of vacation condominiums in Peru, I would not hesitate to become one of the investment decision makers and voice my disapproval.

Several examples of one-page monthly financial reports to the general membership are presented in exhibits 5-3 through 5-6. Please review these exhibits. You may get some ideas for improvements in your own financial reporting.

| | |
|---|---:|
| Given in April | $ 8,090 |
| Expenditures in April | 13,290 |
| Deficit for the month | 5,200 |
| Cash balance, April 30 | 15,750 |
| Commitments for May | 6,500 |

The cash balance of $15,750 on April 30 is approximately $6,000 lower than the expected balance at this date. This is due to the unplanned payment of $6,100 made in April to repair the damage caused by the flood of early March. Other contributions and expenditures were as expected.

Exhibit 5-3    One-Page Financial Report

## Reports to Management

Financial reports are also needed by church management—the finance committee, the administrative board, church administrators, program leaders, the pastor, and so on. As noted, financial reports prepared for this group need to be more extensive and detailed than reports provided to the general membership. Pay particular attention to the principles and factors of sound financial reporting. Thus heeding the responsibility reporting concept, the chairperson of the Christian education program will receive only the financial details for his or her operation. All other financial data is irrelevant to that program. On the other hand, those responsible for or needing to know about all church activities will receive a more complete financial report. Remember, different audiences mean different reports. Following the principle of exception reporting, direct the attention of internal users to those areas that vary significantly from expectations, whether good or bad. Further, present data in comparative form, provide summarized data when appropriate to gain a perspective, and include interpretive comments.

As with reports to the general membership, you have to rethink your goals in reporting financial information to internal users. If there have been complaints about understandability, new forms should be developed. A period of experimentation may be necessary before both you and the users settle on a particular format and contents. If no one is asking for information that the reports do not contain, it could be that the reports are too extensive. To use a sports analogy, you may be giving everyone a play-by-play presentation of a football game when all they want is the score by quarters. An overly lengthy report can cause confusion among users, while driving up the divorce rate for preparers.

| | Actual | Budget |
|---|---|---|
| **Revenues** | | |
| Weekly offerings | $10,000 | $ 9,800 |
| Restricted donations | 6,000 | 5,000 |
| School tuition | 8,000 | 8,000 |
| Interest on savings | 400 | 500 |
| Other | 500 | 550 |
| Total revenues | $24,900 | $23,850 |
| **Expenditures** | | |
| Pastor's salary | $ 2,000 | $ 2,000 |
| Pastor's allowances | 750 | 800 |
| Office salaries | 1,200 | 1,400 |
| Utilities | 400 | 250 |
| School expenses | 8,500 | 7,800 |
| Mortgage payment | 1,000 | 1,000 |
| Purchase of computer | 3,000 | 3,000 |
| Payout of restricted donations | 4,900 | 4,900 |
| Other | 470 | 600 |
| Total expenditures | $22,220 | $21,750 |
| Excess of revenues over expenditures | $ 2,680 | $ 2,100 |
| Cash balance, beginning of month | 32,000 | |
| Cash balance, end of month | $34,680 | |
| **Cash composition** | | |
| Checking account, petty cash | $ 3,280 | |
| Savings accounts | 6,400 | |
| Certificate of deposit | 25,000 | |
| | $34,680* | |

---

* Restricted donations yet to be disbursed total $12,100. Board-designated restrictions of cash total an additional $5,000. The remainder is unrestricted.

| **Restricted donations** | | |
|---|---|---|
| Beginning balance of restricted gifts | | $11,000 |
| Restricted donations received | | |
| For new bus | $ 5,000 | |
| For computer programs | 1,000 | 6,000 |
| | | $17,000 |
| Restricted donations paid out | | |
| Paid for kitchen equipment | $   900 | |
| Paid to world missions | 4,000 | 4,900 |
| Ending balance of restricted gifts | | $12,100 |

**Exhibit 5-4   One-Page Financial Report**

|                                                          | Actual     | Budget     |
|----------------------------------------------------------|-----------:|-----------:|
| Unrestricted revenues                                    | $12,000    | $11,000    |
|                                                          |            |            |
| Unrestricted disbursements                               |            |            |
|   Salaries                                     | (3,000)    | (3,000)    |
|   Administration                               | (4,000)    | (3,500)    |
|   School expenses                              | (3,500)    | (4,000)    |
|                                                          |            |            |
| Excess (or deficiency) of unrestricted revenues over unrestricted disbursements | $ 1,500 | $    500 |
|                                                          |            |            |
| Restricted revenues                                      |            |            |
|   Foreign missions                             | $ 1,000    | $ 3,000    |
|   New van                                      | 20,000     | 20,000     |
|                                                          | $21,000    | $23,000    |
|                                                          |            |            |
| Restricted disbursements                                 |            |            |
|   Purchased new van                            | (20,000)   | (20,000)   |
|                                                          |            |            |
| Excess of restricted revenues over restricted disbursements | $ 1,000 | $ 3,000 |
|                                                          |            |            |
| Total excess (or deficiency) of revenues over disbursements | $ 2,500 | $ 3,500 |
|                                                          |            |            |
| Add beginning cash balance                               | 20,000     |            |
|                                                          |            |            |
| Ending cash balance                                      | $22,500    |            |

Analysis of Ending Cash Balance

| | |
|---|---:|
| Undisbursed, restricted amounts | $ 7,000 |
| Needed to pay existing bills | 5,000 |
| Unrestricted, uncommitted cash | 10,500 |
| | |
| Ending cash balance | $22,500 |

Author's note: Year-to-date columns could be added to this report if desired.

Exhibit 5-5   One-Page Financial Report

Some treasurers prepare a monthly financial report that is more than twenty pages long! If you believe that your reports are too detailed, leave out a page and wait for the response. If people don't complain it means that they didn't really use the information that you have omitted. I recommended this approach to a Texas church treasurer who was faced with the task of preparing a sixteen-page financial report each month. Leaving off one page each month, she got down to twelve pages before someone said, "What's going on here?" After she stated the problem, the board agreed that much of the data had been of marginal use. They suggested that the treasurer prepare a four-page monthly

|  |  | Unrestricted | Restricted | Total |
|---|---|---|---|---|
| Beg. bal. | June, 19XX | $4,000 | $2,000 | $6,000 |
| Receipts | June, 19XX | 3,500 | 1,000 | 4,500 |
| Disbursements | June, 19XX | (3,200) | (1,500) | (4,700) |
| End. bal. | June, 19XX | $4,300 | $1,500 | $5,800 |

| | Total |
|---|---|
| Savings accounts | $5,000 |
| + Checking account | 800 |
| = End. bal. | $5,800 |

| | Month | |
|---|---|---|
| | Actual | Budgeted |
| Total unrestricted receipts | $3,500 | $4,000 |
| Program/dept. disbursements | | |
| Fellowship | $ 750 | $ 500 |
| Stewardship | 250 | 100 |
| Education | 500 | 800 |
| Worship | 500 | 500 |
| Buildings and grounds | 100 | 1,000 |
| Outreach | -0- | 100 |
| Evangelism | 100 | 100 |
| Administration | 1,000 | 1,000 |
| Total disbursements | $3,200 | $4,100 |
| Net increase or decrease | $ 300 | ($ 100) |
| Total restricted receipts | $1,000 | $1,000 |
| For computer | $ 400 | $ -0- |
| For altar flowers | 100 | -0- |
| For church college | 500 | 1,000 |
| Restricted disbursements | | |
| Paid to church college | $1,500 | $1,500 |
| Net increase or decrease | ($ 500) | ($ 500) |

Author's note: Year-to-date columns could be added to this report if desired.

**Exhibit 5-6   One-Page Financial Report**

report and a sixteen-page annual report. An example of a four-page financial report to church management is presented in exhibit 5-7.

Your experimentation can lead to improved financial reporting if you 1) recognize how your various user groups obtain information from the reports, and 2) help them with their analysis. For example, it has been my experience that most members want to know the current cash balance. Therefore all of the one-page financial reports presented in the preceding section contained this information. For the same reason, all reports for members presented information on member giving and expenditures. Members of the finance committee or administrative board may ask for different kinds of information and, in their minds or on scratch paper, may calculate certain relationships. You may find, for instance, that some committee members are mentally relating the current cash balance to next month's bills. Thus a cash balance of $25,000 will cover $5,000 of liabilities five times. They may then compare this coverage against those of preceding months or years to judge whether the church is becoming more or less solvent. If this is the case, why not calculate the relationship (sometimes called a ratio) for the group? Alternatively, if the group is not using the reports to their fullest, maybe you can encourage better use by calculating some of these relationships. Naturally these relationships should be studied over a long period of time, possibly several years. Conclusions based on one month's results could be erroneous. Some other relationships that may have relevance to your church are:

Unrestricted Cash Received Related to Total Cash Received
     This ratio shows whether the church is receiving sufficient unrestricted cash to pay its general expenses. Although the

**Exhibit 5-7  Four-Page Financial Report to Church Management**

**Summary Page**

|  | Current Month | Year 19X2 To Date | Year 19X2 Budget |
|---|---|---|---|
| **Receipts** | | | |
| Pledged contributions | $32,818 | $210,190 | $600,000 |
| Nonpledged gifts | 1,209 | 9,371 | 15,000 |
| Restricted | 2,000 | 6,431 | 5,000 |
| Other | 2,336 | 49,824 | 75,000 |
| Total | $38,363 | $275,816 | $695,000 |
| | | | |
| **Disbursements** | | | |
| Administration | $ 5,722 | $ 38,082 | $ 76,475 |
| Property | 16,997 | 118,045 | 218,600 |
| Local programs | 20,041 | 113,460 | 229,925 |
| Missions | 2,304 | 11,635 | 85,000 |
| Total | $45,064 | $281,222 | $610,000 |

| **Analysis of cash** | |
|---|---|
| Checking account balances | $ 1,987 |
| Money market account | 32,802 |
| Certificate of deposit | 15,000 |
| Total cash | $49,789 |

## Disbursements Analysis

|  | Current Month | Year 19X2 to Date | Year 19X2 Budget |
|---|---|---|---|
| **ADMINISTRATION** | | | |
| **Administration and finance** | | | |
| Secretarial salaries | $ 3,031 | $ 18,377 | $ 36,800 |
| Stationery and printing | 282 | 2,352 | 4,500 |
| Supplies and Miscellaneous expenses | 136 | 1,837 | 2,100 |
| Postage | 385 | 2,022 | 4,400 |
| Telephone | 310 | 2,443 | 3,800 |
| Annual pledge campaign | | | 600 |
|  | $ 4,144 | $ 27,031 | $ 52,200 |
| **Miscellaneous** | | | |
| Payroll taxes | $ 656 | $ 3,966 | $ 9,075 |
| Kitchen manager | 250 | 1,500 | 3,000 |
| Kitchen manager auto expenses | 75 | 450 | 900 |
| Church nursery | 597 | 4,275 | 8,000 |
| Conference—lay delegates | | 450 | 600 |
|  | $ 1,578 | $ 10,641 | $ 21,575 |
| **Contingencies** | | | |
| General contingencies | | $ 410 | $ 2,700 |
| Total administration | $ 5,722 | $ 38,082 | $ 76,475 |
| **PROPERTY** | | | |
| **Church plant** | | | |
| Note to bank | $ 5,160 | $ 30,960 | $ 61,920 |
| Murray note | | 2,500 | 6,250 |
| Atherton note | 2,499 | 17,288 | 30,000 |
| Security system | | 270 | 800 |
| Normal maintenance | 617 | 2,825 | 4,000 |
| Capital maintenance | 2,041 | 15,104 | 10,000 |
| Salaries—superintendent | 416 | 2,500 | 5,000 |
| Auto expenses | 55 | 330 | 660 |
| Custodial salaries | 1,386 | 8,544 | 16,640 |
| Maid salary | 994 | 5,813 | 11,400 |
| Laundry | 167 | 786 | 1,130 |
| Utilities: electric | 2,640 | 14,683 | 30,000 |
| gas | 65 | 3,736 | 6,000 |
| water | | 717 | 1,000 |
| Insurance | | 5,249 | 14,000 |
|  | $16,040 | $111,305 | $198,800 |
| **Parsonages** | | | |
| Wildwood utilities | $ 135 | $ 928 | $ 2,700 |
| Lockewood utilities | 139 | 972 | 2,400 |
| Peavey housing and utilities | 683 | 4,100 | 8,200 |
| Parsonage maintenance | | 740 | 6,500 |
|  | $ 957 | $ 6,740 | $ 19,800 |
| Total property | $16,997 | $118,045 | $218,600 |

**LOCAL PROGRAMS AND MINISTRIES**
**Ministerial and professional supervision**

| | | | |
|---|---|---|---|
| District superintendent | $ 610 | $ 3,659 | $ 6,098 |
| Denominational fund | 126 | 754 | 1,256 |
| Pension fund—A | 1,327 | 7,963 | 13,271 |
| Pension program—ministers | 1,741 | 7,540 | 15,070 |
| Staff salaries | 8,958 | 53,675 | 113,100 |
| Staff travel | 1,918 | 7,789 | 17,400 |
| Medical insurance | 527 | 3,762 | 9,205 |
| Professional education | 671 | 1,515 | 1,800 |
| | $15,878 | $ 86,657 | $177,200 |

**Christian education**

| | | | |
|---|---|---|---|
| Literature and audiovisual | $ 1,296 | $ 2,730 | $ 4,600 |
| Supplies and equipment | | 40 | 900 |
| Leadership education | 41 | 135 | 600 |
| Children's ministries | 368 | 610 | 1,400 |
| Youth ministries | 94 | 481 | 2,150 |
| Young adult ministries | | 135 | 250 |
| Adult ministries | 55 | 198 | 400 |
| Sports ministries | | 225 | 400 |
| Library | | 30 | 100 |
| | $ 1,854 | $ 4,584 | $ 10,800 |

**Worship**

| | | | |
|---|---|---|---|
| Organists' salaries | $ 650 | $ 3,900 | 7,800 |
| Music and choral supplies | 310 | 1,145 | 2,000 |
| Training and conference | | 260 | 450 |
| Worship materials | 44 | 744 | 600 |
| Guest musicians | | 200 | 1,200 |
| Cleaning—choir robes | | | 275 |
| Music maintenance | | 1,315 | 7,800 |
| Youth choir tour | | | 1,000 |
| Concert series | | 500 | 500 |
| Altar guild | | | 100 |
| | $ 1,004 | $ 8,064 | $ 21,725 |

**Membership and evangelism**

| | | | |
|---|---|---|---|
| Literature | | $ 372 | $ 2,000 |
| Radio broadcast | $ 465 | 3,534 | 4,800 |
| Revival | | | 1,000 |
| Special activities | 190 | 789 | 1,000 |
| Promotion | 650 | 9,261 | 10,000 |
| Bible study | | 189 | 250 |
| | $ 1,305 | $ 14,145 | $ 19,050 |

**Stewardship**

| | | |
|---|---|---|
| Job bank | | $ 200 |
| Wills and estate planning | | 250 |
| Stewardship education | | 100 |
| | | $ 550 |

**Council on ministries programs**

| | | | |
|---|---|---|---|
| Council activities | | $ 10 | $ 600 |
| Total local programs/ministries | $20,041 | $113,460 | $229,925 |

**MISSION OUTREACH**
**Apportionments**

| | | | |
|---|---:|---:|---:|
| World service | | | $ 10,482 |
| Conference fund | | | 8,779 |
| Jurisdictional fund | | | 984 |
| Interdenominational co-op | | | 283 |
| Conference of churches | $ 221 | $ 442 | 2,375 |
| Special ministerial | 29 | 58 | 294 |
| Church colleges | | 750 | 4,515 |
| Campus ministries | 568 | 1,636 | 5,677 |
| Black colleges | | 650 | 2,137 |
| Ministerial education | | 500 | 4,485 |
| Lodi assembly | | | 1,223 |
| Homes for the elderly | | | 979 |
| Missional priorities | | | 1,234 |
| Progress fund | 783 | 2,316 | 7,831 |
| District missions | 690 | 2,070 | 6,900 |
| | $ 2,291 | $ 8,422 | $ 58,178 |

**Advance specials**

| | | | |
|---|---:|---:|---:|
| Commision on missions | $ 13 | $ 213 | $ 8,422 |
| World specials | | | 6,000 |
| Central America work | | 400 | 2,250 |
| Alcohol and drug education | | 200 | 200 |
| Mission home | | | 2,000 |
| Seacrest Plaza home | | 1,100 | 2,750 |
| Soup kitchen | | 1,200 | 2,000 |
| Peters Convalescent Center | | | 2,000 |
| Society of St. Blaine | | 100 | 1,200 |
| | $ 13 | $ 3,213 | $ 26,822 |
| Total mission outreach | $ 2,304 | $ 11,635 | $ 85,000 |
| Grand total | $45,064 | $281,222 | $610,000 |

church may be receiving increasing amounts of cash, much of it may be restricted.

Total Spending Related to Unrestricted Cash Received

This ratio may show whether the church is living within its means. Thus a ratio of less than 100 percent each month would indicate that the church is saving money. A ratio of more than 100 percent would indicate that savings are being depleted and, eventually, loans may have to be sought. Data for some months may be distorted because of some large expenditures, such as those for large equipment or a motor vehicle.

Cash Applied to Debt Reduction Related to Unrestricted Cash Received

This ratio demonstrates management's commitment to debt reduction. If there is no prepayment penalty, mortgage debt and other debt is often reduced as excess funds become available. Significant savings in interest payments may result.

Total Giving Related to Total Pledges

By relating giving to pledges, you can assess whether the church has the active support of its members.

One final word about financial reporting to management. A few times each year you may be asked to prepare a special report for an individual, possibly a member of a committee, necessitating a search through the accounting system. Unless you want this special inquiry to become part of your monthly routine for the entire committee, present the information privately. Individual requests merit individual reports. Committee requests merit committee reports. In either case, be sure to point out the costs of report preparation.

## Reports to Others

Periodically you will have to prepare financial reports for other users, such as trustees, the higher denominational authority, the Internal Revenue Service, or, if funds have been borrowed, perhaps a bank. These users typically are quite specific about the financial information they want and the format they want you to use. Banks, for example, may ask to see financial statements that have been either audited or reviewed by a certified public accountant. Bankers are accustomed to reading financial reports that are prepared in accordance with generally accepted accounting principles (see appendix B) and that have been attested to by an independent accounting professional. This requirement may exist for each year that the funds are owed.

The Internal Revenue Service (IRS) provides free forms for your reports to it. Thus, for example, if your church is subject to taxation on unrelated business income, you would need to file the appropriate form. The IRS seems to have a form for almost every possible event. The church's external accountant can greatly assist the church in complying with any federal, state, and city income tax regulations.

The higher denominational authority usually requires churches to submit monthly, quarterly, or annual financial reports. Usually the church treasurer is provided with copies or examples of the forms and expense accounts to use and definitions of terms. For example, *plate offerings* may be defined as "loose offerings that are unrestricted or undesignated. These are to include all offerings at Easter, Christmas, and so on, if made for general purposes." Likewise, *pledge payments* may "include all amounts placed in regular pledge offering envelopes even from persons making no pledge, whether moneys are intended for general operating purposes or designated by the donor." Note the specificity needed to answer treasurers' questions in advance and to foster the preparation of uniform reports. Such uniformity is necessary for higher church authorities to assess the financial condition and progress of groups of churches within its jurisdiction. Without uniformity, information from different churches might not be comparable. It could be like trying to compare apples and oranges.

Because each user has specific needs, preparing financial reports for others can take considerable time and be costly. In an attempt to cut the costs of report preparation, some churches organize their accounting system so that, for instance, the report for the higher denominational office can be prepared quickly. This is satisfactory if the system can then be used to prepare reports that are equally useful to the general membership and church managers. Often, however, this is not the case, and the church loses more resources by having members and management make decisions without relevant information. Unless your church is required to use particular accounts, forms, and formats internally, I suggest that you not let the reporting needs of others dictate what you do internally.

Reporting the financial results of church operations is the end product of the budgeting and accounting process. It should not be an afterthought that results in a mishmash of unprocessed and poorly organized data. It should be well planned and artfully executed.

## APPENDIX B:
## GENERALLY ACCEPTED ACCOUNTING PRINCIPLES
## FOR CHURCHES

In 1978 the American Institute of Certified Public Accountants (AICPA) issued a "Statement of Position on Accounting Principles and Reporting Practices for Certain Nonprofit Organizations." The accounting principles and reporting practices covered in the AICPA statement are intended for many different types of nonprofit organizations, including religious organizations, that prepare financial statements in accordance with generally accepted accounting principles (GAAP)—that is, those financial statements that may be audited by an independent certified public accountant. Churches that prepare their financial statements on some other basis of accounting, such as the cash basis, may continue to do so. Some churches may conclude that 1) the costs of adopting these principles and practice are prohibitive, 2) an audit of the financial statements is unnecessary, and 3) non-GAAP accounting principles and reporting practices serve their needs adequately. But these churches, of course, cannot describe their statements as being in accordance with GAAP.

A summary of the AICPA's most important accounting principles and reporting practices for certain nonprofit entities, including churches, is presented in the following pages. You might get a few ideas that can be put to immediate use, even if an annual audit is not being considered. You can also assess how the accounting principles and reporting practices used within your church compare with those currently espoused by the accounting profession.

### Accrual Basis Accounting

The most important accounting principle in the AICPA statement is the requirement that accrual basis accounting be used for financial reporting. This does not mean that the accounting records must be maintained on the accrual basis. Church treasurers and financial secretaries may find it practical to keep books on the cash basis. Personally or with the assistance of their external accountant, they may prepare end-of-period journal entries to convert the records and financial reports to the accrual basis of accounting.

Perhaps a word or two about the difference between the cash basis and accrual basis of accounting would be useful. Using the cash basis of accounting, revenues are recognized on the books in the period of receipt, and expenses are recognized in the period of payment. Thus revenues and expenses are triggered when cash is received or paid. For example, suppose that in August a church received $4,000 in offerings (assume that the church did not take pledges); $2,000 for September's tuition at the church school, which had been closed all summer; and $600 in interest on a six-month certificate of deposit, which matured on the last day of the month. For this church monthly revenues would be $6,600 on the cash basis. Similarly, if the church paid out $4,000 for August salaries, $1,000 for the preceding month's utilities, and a $2,000 deposit on travel expenses to the denominational convention, monthly expenses would be $7,000 on the cash basis. Taken together, the church's financial report would indicate that cash expenses exceeded cash revenues by $400 ($7,000 − $6,600) for the month.

Under the accrual basis of accounting, revenues are recognized on the books when the amounts are earned. Expenses are recognized when the costs incurred in producing revenue are incurred. Thus expenses of a church should be entered in the financial report in the same period that the revenues they helped to produce are entered. Following the accrual basis of accounting, the church in the preceding paragraph would have revenue of $4,100, the total of the $4,000 of offerings and $100 of interest earned during August. The tuition moneys received would be considered a liability until the end of September, by which time the moneys would all be earned. It would appear on the church's end-of-September financial report as revenue, because it was earned in that month. Similarly, $500 of the $600 interest received on the certificate of deposit would have been earned in preceding months and would be considered interest receivable at the beginning of August. Only the interest earned during the month would be entered for August. On the expenditure side, accrual based expenses would total $4,000 for services received from employees during the month. The amount paid for the preceding month's utilities would not be an expense of August but of July, when the services were received. The church would merely be paying off an accounts payable in August. The amount paid in advance for the convention would be a prepaid asset. It would become an expense in the month that the convention was held and the travel services were consumed. Using accrual accounting the church would indicate revenues over expenses of $100 ($4,100 − $4,000). Thus the cash basis of accounting would indicate a shortfall of $400, and the accrual basis would indicate a positive $100 for the month. Such differences are common and can be much more dramatic.

Cash basis accounting is criticized as not being in accord with economic reality. The receipt and disbursement of cash do not adequately measure financial activity within a given period of time. For this reason the AICPA mandated the use of accrual basis accounting for financial reports.

### Fund Accounting

The AICPA statement indicates that fund accounting (discussed in appendix A) should be used for reporting purposes when it is necessary to disclose the nature and amount of resources that have been restricted by persons external to the church. Emphasis, however, is to be placed on the clarity and usefulness of the financial information rather than on the use of fund accounting per se. So adherence to fund accounting for reporting purposes, with its lengthy fund-by-fund disclosure, which readers often find confusing and complicated, is secondary to the appropriateness and quality of the disclosure. Thus those churches that use a fund accounting system do not have to report their financial results fund by fund. Meaningful fund groupings, which might combine funds into only unrestricted and restricted columns or expendable and nonexpendable columns might be appropriate in many instances. Expendable funds would include amounts available for current operations, whether restricted or unrestricted. Nonexpendable funds would include amounts not available for current operations, either because of donor restrictions or because of their nature (such as the donation of a used computer).

### Required Financial Statements

The AICPA statement requires that three basic financial statements be prepared:

1. A balance sheet, showing assets, liabilities, and fund balances of the entity at the end-of-period date. Organizations who have both restricted and unrestricted funds (this is most churches) should classify their assets and liabilities as either current or long term in nature, unless the fund classifications themselves adequately disclose such information.

2. A statement of activity for the period. This statement could be titled with any number of different names, such as the statement of income and expenses or statement of revenues, expenses, and changes in fund balances.

3. A statement of cash flows for the period. This statement reveals the cash flows from operating, investing, and financing activities.

Footnotes to the financial statements may be necessary to provide a complete disclosure of economic activity.


### Required Financial Disclosures

The AICPA statement, although indicating that three financial statements are required, does not prescribe the format for the financial statements. A church may select the format most appropriate for its use. Regardless of format, however, there are some required financial disclosures, as follows:

1. The fund balance section of the balance sheet should disclose the a) total amount of unrestricted fund balances, b) total amount of the major types of restricted fund balances, and c) total amount of fund balance invested in fixed assets.

2. The statement of activity should a) disclose operating income and expenses separate from legally restricted, nonexpendable or capital-type gifts and income, b) disclose the principal sources of restricted revenue, c) disclose the total of all unrestricted revenue and support, and d) clearly label the excess of operating income over expenses before and after the addition of legally restricted, nonexpendable or capital-type gifts and income.

## Nonexpendable or Capital-Type Gifts and Income

The AICPA statement indicates that legally restricted, nonexpendable or capital-type gifts and income are to be reported separately from amounts received that can be currently spent. Two common types of nonexpendable gifts are those for endowments and those for purchases of fixed assets. Similarly, any investment income and capital gains that have been specifically restricted for nonexpendable purposes would also be reported separately. But board-designated amounts should not be considered nonexpendable.

## Current Restricted Gifts and Grants

Current restricted gifts are amounts received and earmarked for a specific current or operating purpose. Restricted gifts, including those made to acquire fixed (plant) assets, should be recorded as deferred income on the balance sheet until the church has spent the money in the way the donor specified. After the money has been spent, these gifts would be reflected as income in the statement of activity. Thus when funds are received, the cash account increases, as does an appropriately named deferred income account, which is a liability. The liability exists because the church has the obligation to honor the donor's request in spending the money. When the money is spent, two entries are needed. First, the deferred income account is reduced, and income is recognized in an income account. Second, an expense is recorded for the expenditure, together with a reduction in the cash account.

The church has no obligation to use the donor's funds specifically, only to meet the legal restriction. For example, assume that a member gives a $1,000 gift specifically restricted for an office computer. Assume further that later in the year the church spends $4,000 of its unrestricted funds to purchase a computer. According to the AICPA statement the restriction has been met, and the $1,000 restricted gift should be reflected as income in the period.

Grants, which may be received by churches connected with colleges and universities, are to be handled in the same manner as current restricted gifts. That is, grants received before expenditures are made should be placed on the balance sheet as deferred income and remain as liabilities until the terms of the grant are met. If, however, the grant comes without any restrictions, it may be recorded as revenue when received.

## Pledges

According to the AICPA statement, pledges that a church could legally enforce should be recorded as pledges receivable on the balance sheet, net of an allowance for the estimated amount that is not expected to be collected. Although few churches attempt to legally enforce collections, most can estimate fairly accurately the percentage that will not be collected. This accounting treatment is in accordance with the accrual basis of accounting and recognizes that pledges represent an asset of the organization. In fact, many banks accept pledges as collateral for a loan. Many church treasurers have difficulty accepting this position, because their church would never think about initiating legal action to collect. But it is the

> legal right to enforce collection that is important in recording the item and not necessarily the non-profit organization's ability or willingness to take legal action. . . . Churches that do not want to record pledges may have donors sign a card indicating their right to withdraw their pledge at any time. Being unenforceable, the pledge need not be recorded.[1]

The recognition of pledges in the statement of activity is another matter. The AICPA statement holds that if the donor has not specified the period in which he or she intends a pledge to be used, that pledge is not considered income until the year that it is paid. Until that year the pledge is to be reflected as deferred income on the balance sheet.

### Donated and Contributed Services

The AICPA statement establishes criteria for recording the monetary value of services contributed by volunteers. Because the program services of churches are principally intended for the benefit of church members, almost all churches would be prohibited from placing a value on donated and contributed services or considering them revenue. Donations of assets, however, such as securities, furniture, and so on, would be recorded at their fair market value on the date of donation.

Although the AICPA statement precludes the valuation of donated and contributed services by most churches in financial statements prepared in accordance with GAAP, nothing prevents churches from valuing such resources in budgets, internal monthly or quarterly financial reports, or financial statements prepared on a non-GAAP basis. Thus the discussion of donated services in chapter 2 remains relevant, and the methodology recommended should be followed by churches that have many volunteers.

---

[1] Terry L. Arndt and Richard W. Jones, "Closing the GAAP in Church Accounting," *Management Accounting*, v. 64 August 1982, 27.

## Fixed Assets and Depreciation

Many churches have invested large amounts of money in assets used to provide religious services and programs over many accounting periods. Assets with long lives acquired for use in church operations include land, buildings, vehicles, office equipment, computers, musical equipment, furniture, and fixtures. Such assets are sometimes called plant assets or property, plant, and equipment.

In business circles, following the accrual basis of accounting, fixed assets have been viewed as long-term prepaid expenses, because their acquisition entails an advance payment for years of future service. Like prepaid expenses, fixed assets provide benefits for only a certain period of time. As a result businesses record the purchase of fixed assets as a long-term asset (capitalization) and gradually reduce the asset on the books, via a process called depreciation. Depreciation is the allocation of cost over the service life of the fixed asset. Various methods exist, including the popular straight-line method, which spreads the cost of a depreciable asset equally over its estimated service life. Therefore each accounting period that benefits from the fixed asset's use shares a portion of its costs, which results in properly determined business income.

In church circles, the procedures relating to fixed assets have been dramatically different. First, following the cash basis of accounting, many churches have not recorded fixed assets on their books as assets. Moneys spent for equipment have been treated like expenditures for salaries and utilities. Both have been considered expenses of the period. Remember that on a cash basis, all cash payments made are expenses. Thus the fact that equipment has had a service life extending beyond the current accounting period has been ignored. Second, because few churches have capitalized the cost of fixed assets at the time of acquisition, there has been nothing to depreciate. This has bothered few church treasurers, because the purpose of church accounting has not been to measure profits, as it has been in the profit sector. Stated differently, businesses have been motivated to maintain their capital and earn a profit. Correctly or incorrectly, churches have paid no attention to maintaining their capital. They have existed to raise money for operations and special projects and to spend it. Third, unlike businesses, where the calculation of depreciation has been pivotal to determine income tax liability, nonprofit organizations have generally been exempt from income taxation. They have not needed to determine income tax liability.

In an attempt to bring accounting in the nonprofit sector closer to accounting in the profit sector, the AICPA statement provides that fixed assets be capitalized at their cost. In those instances where the entity does not have historical cost information for assets in its possession, other reasonable bases may be used, such as cost-based appraisals, insurance appraisals, replacement costs, or property tax appraisals adjusted for market. The AICPA recommends this treatment for fixed assets, because they are a major asset group of many organizations. Failure to include such assets on a balance sheet is considered misleading. Further, the AICPA statement requires that fixed assets be depreciated over their useful lives. The reasoning behind recommending taking depreciation is that the statement of activity should reflect the cost of operations for the period so that the reader can better judge financial results. Buildings and equipment wear out. To accurately measure cost, the portion worn out within the accounting period needs to be considered. Interestingly, the AICPA statement excluded the requirement for the depreciation of structures used primarily as houses of worship and for so-called inexhaustible assets, which includes cathedrals. Thus, many churches have not recognized depreciation expense on their books. To bring religious institutions into compliance with other entities, the Financial Accounting Standards Board (FASB), a rule making body recognized by the AICPA, issued a directive in 1987 that churches recognize depreciation on *all* of their long-lived properties.[2] The rationale for making depreciation mandatory for churches following GAAP is that church buildings, for instance, wear out and are affected by the same pollutants, vibrations, and so forth as anyone else's buildings. However, immediately after the directive was issued, the FASB received strong objections to the new rule from church leaders who found the figuring of depreciation unnecessary and the costs of compliance high. Faced with such opposition, the FASB has delayed putting into effect its controversial rule for churches until fiscal years beginning on or after January 1, 1990.[3]

With depreciation, a church would be in a better position to know the full costs of its various operations and programs. This information would be useful to management and to establish charges for the use of church facilities for weddings, receptions, recreation, and so on. Traditionally churches have either arbitrarily made up charges or have based the charges solely on direct costs for utilities, security, and so on. These direct costs may represent only a small part of actual total costs.

---

[2] See "Recognition of Depreciation by Not-for-Profit Organizations," *Statement of Financial Accounting Standards, No. 93,* (Stamford, CT: Financial Accounting Standards Board, 1987).

[3] See "Deferral of the Effective Date of Recognition of Depreciation by Not-for-Profit Organizations," *Statement of Financial Accounting Standards, No. 99,* (Stamford, CT: Financial Accounting Standards Board, 1988).

### Expense Reporting

Within the statement of activity, expenses should be reported on a functional or program basis that discloses the purposes for which expenses have been incurred. Expenses supporting programs should be reported separately from direct program expenses. Supporting services expenses normally include management and general expenses as well as fundraising expenses. Management and general expenses are expenses that are not identifiable with any single program but are indispensable to the conduct of all of the church's activities. It is important for a church to record carefully the administration of its programs so that appropriate allocations of staff time and the associated costs can be made both among the various programs and between programs, management, and general expenses. The allocation of time and associated costs includes those of the pastor and the office staff.

Functional reporting seems especially appropriate for churches that view themselves as entities committed to carrying out programs. Functional reporting forces the church to identify specific programs and the costs of those programs.

### Example Financial Statements

Two financial statements prepared in accordance with GAAP are presented on the following pages. Exhibit B-1 illustrates a balance sheet and exhibit B-2 presents a statement of activity. Observe that the House of Worship is not being depreciated. As noted, starting in 1990, the accounting regulations have been revised to include depreciation on all church property, plant, and equipment.

### Expectation of Change

Like most professions, the accounting profession is continually trying to improve its product—in this case, those regulations constituting GAAP. This is quite evident in the area of accounting and financial reporting by nonprofit entities. Committees of the profession meet regularly with representatives of various sectors, including religious organizations, to discuss alternative accounting practices. Over time, you can expect change in some elements of GAAP. These changes may come this year or in five years. They may be insignificant or profound. At the time of this writing, the accounting profession was studying, among other items, the accounting and financial reporting for 1) pledges receivable, 2) restricted gifts, 3) depreciation of fixed assets, 4) grants, 5) donated services, 6) the adequacy of fund accounting to communicate

## St. Francis Church Balance Sheet—6/30/8X

| Assets | | Expendable funds | | Plant funds | Nonexpendable funds | | Total all funds |
|---|---|---|---|---|---|---|---|
| | | Operating | Other | | Endowment | Other | |
| Cash | | $ 5,000 | $1,000 | $20,000 | $15,000 | $2,000 | $ 43,000 |
| Accounts receivable, less allowance for doubtful accounts | $ 2,200 / 200 | 2,000 | | | | | 2,000 |
| Pledges receivable, less allowance for doubtful accounts | $ 4,000 / 1,000 | 3,000 | | | | | 3,000 |
| Investments, at lower of cost or market ($3,750 cost) | | 5,000 | | 5,000 | | | 10,000 |
| Buildings and equipment, less accumulated depreciation | $300,000 / 50,000 | 250,000 | | | | | 250,000 |
| House of worship | | 150,000 | | | | | 150,000 |
| Land | | 50,000 | | | | | 50,000 |
| Total assets | | $465,000 | $1,000 | $25,000 | $15,000 | $2,000 | $508,000 |

| Liabilities and fund balance | Operating | Other | Plant funds | Endowment | Other | Total all funds |
|---|---|---|---|---|---|---|
| Accounts payable | $ 3,000 | | | | | $ 3,000 |
| Deferred payables | | | | | | |
|   Restricted | 5,000 | | | | | 5,000 |
|   Unrestricted | 2,000 | | | | | 2,000 |
| Long-term liabilities | 350,000 | | | | | 350,000 |
|   Total liabilities | 360,000 | | | | | 360,000 |
| Fund balance | | | | | | |
|   Restricted | 62,000 | | | 15,000 | | 62,000 |
|   Unrestricted | 43,000 | 1,000 | 25,000 | | 2,000 | 86,000 |
| Total liabilities and fund balance | $465,000 | $1,000 | $25,000 | $15,000 | $2,000 | $508,000 |

**Exhibit B-1 GAAP—Balance Sheet**

Source: Reprinted from an article by Terry L. Arndt and Richard W. Jones "Closing the GAAP in Church Accounting," *Management Accounting,* USA, August 1982, p. 27. Copyright by National Association of Accountants, Montvale, N.J. 07645. All rights reserved.

**St. Francis Church**
**Statement of Activity—Period Ending 6/30/8X**

| | | | | Programs | | |
|---|---|---|---|---|---|---|
| **Revenues** | **Total** | **Support** | **School** | **Parish projects** | **Women's aux.** | **Missions** |
| Sunday collection | $25,000 | $19,000 | $ 6,000 | | | |
| Pledges | 10,000 | 8,000 | 2,000 | | | |
| School tuition | 10,000 | | 10,000 | | | |
| Missions | 4,000 | | | | | $4,000 |
| Parish projects | 3,000 | | | $3,000 | | |
| Investments | 2,000 | 2,000 | | | | |
| Donated | 2,000 | 2,000 | | | | |
| Books | 1,000 | | 1,000 | | | |
| Women's auxiliary | 1,000 | | | | $1,000 | |
| Miscellaneous | 1,000 | 1,000 | | | | |
| Total revenues | $59,000 | $32,000 | $ 19,000 | $3,000 | $1,000 | $4,000 |
| **Expenses** | | | | | | |
| Salaries | $20,000 | $ 8,000 | $ 12,000 | | | |
| School | 10,000 | | 10,000 | | | |
| Interest | 8,000 | 4,000 | 4,000 | | | |
| Taxes | 4,500 | 1,500 | 3,000 | | | |
| Missions | 4,000 | | | | | $4,000 |
| Depreciation | 2,000 | 1,000 | 1,000 | | | |
| Parish projects | 1,000 | | | $1,000 | | |
| Women's auxiliary | 500 | | | | $ 500 | |
| Miscellaneous | 1,000 | 1,000 | | | | |
| Total expenses | $51,000 | $15,500 | $ 30,000 | $1,000 | $ 500 | $4,000 |
| **Excess of revenues over (under) expenses** | $ 8,000 | $16,500 | $(11,000) | $2,000 | $ 500 | $ -0- |

Source: Reprinted from an article by Terry L. Arndt and Richard W. Jones "Closing the GAAP in Church Accounting," *Management Accounting,* USA, August 1982, p. 27. Copyright by National Association of Accountants, Montvale, N.J. 07645. All rights reserved.

**Exhibit B-2  GAAP—Statement of Activity**

information, and 7) methods of aggregating funds for disclosure purposes.

Churches who prepare their financial statements in accordance with GAAP, either for purposes of an annual audit or because of what GAAP represents, should ask their certified public accountant to keep them abreast of changes in GAAP.

# CHAPTER 6

# *Concluding Comments*

## *Your Commitment*

The preceding chapters have covered the essentials of effective church accounting. At this point you may be one of a tiny group of people bursting with pride because of the exemplary manner in which your church does its accounting. Your church may be one of a handful of churches that needs no improvement. Assuming that the dreaded disease psychosclerosis, or hardening of the attitudes, was not a factor in arriving at your conclusion, it is possible that all the ideas advanced in this book are already integrated into your church's accounting affairs. If this is the case, I share in your joy. This means that your church has, among other attributes, 1) definitive short-term and long-term goals, 2) programs that can be objectively measured for success, 3) timely, effective budgets, 4) extensive internal controls of cash, 5) an efficient approach to the processing of accounting information, probably computerized, 6) easily understood financial reports, and 7) an accountant involved in each of these activities.

For most readers, however, the preceding chapters have exposed a variety of accounting deficiencies in your church. Some deficiencies may be major and others minor. Some problems may be fixed quickly; others may need a long-term commitment. For example, many readers would probably state that their church handles its resource allocation/budgeting process imperfectly, but somehow the church manages to muddle through year after year. Further, changing this process is not an easy task because of intrachurch politics. That doesn't mean that the advantage of change is ignored, just that the realities of the situation are recognized. And some deficiencies, like those that may exist in internal control or information processing, may need immediate correction and be easier to remedy. In fact, you may be able to make improvements in this area without consulting others. Thus the first step in improving your church's accounting and financial reporting is to identify and categorize deficiencies. The format presented in exhibit 6-1 is useful in this. Problems are assigned to one of four sections, two for important deficiencies and two for minor deficiencies. Further, each type of deficiency is categorized into those that are easy to correct and those that are difficult to correct. Space is provided for four deficiencies in each section. Your church's deficiency list, however, may have ten or twenty problems listed in one or two sections and perhaps nothing in the remaining sections. The analysis of deficiencies by type is the critical element of the exercise.

I advocate this approach because I want you to be successful in making improvements in your church's accounting and financial reporting process. Early success in correcting those important deficiencies that are easy to fix will boost your self-confidence and the confidence of others in you. You will find it easier to suggest and then implement more difficult changes. It serves little purpose for you read this book, get excited about becoming an effective church accountant, propose several improvements, and then meet stiff resistance and have to back off. Your ego could be so bruised that you might never again suggest changes. You need to develop your skills over time. Therefore, as you proceed to remedy the easy-to-correct deficiencies, first important and then minor, your track record should be impeccable, your reputation as an effective church accountant should be growing, and your ability to influence change should increase. These factors will assist you greatly in tackling those deficiencies that are difficult to change because of tradition, politics, personality, or their long-term nature. Further, in the unlikely event that you fail to correct the deficiencies labeled difficult to correct, you can still take pride in those important improvements that you did bring about.

The catalyst for improving your church's accounting and financial reporting process is you—not the pastor, not someone else. The pastor may be supportive of your ideas, but probably does not have the skill to explain, recommend, respond to objections, and then implement detailed accounting procedures. Likewise, leaving it up to someone else, whoever that might be, is a sure way to preserve the status quo. Effective church accounting comes from people who desire to be effective accountants. You are in the best position to influence improvement and change. After all, you have just prepared a complete defi-

Exhibit 6-1   The Overall Deficiency List

**Important Deficiencies—**
**Easy to Correct**

1.

2.

3.

4.

**Important Deficiencies—**
**Difficult to Correct**

1.

2.

3.

4.

**Minor Deficiencies—**
**Easy to Correct**

1.

2.

3.

4.

**Minor Deficiencies—**
**Difficult to Correct**

1.

2.

3.

4.

ciency list for the church's accounting process! Share your concerns; share your wisdom; share your enthusiasm. Your church will benefit from your efforts.

### My Commitment

As noted in chapter 1, time-sensitive materials, such as income tax regulations and specific computer systems for churches, have been purposely omitted from the book. Yet you may need some of this information to fulfill your responsibilities to your church. For up-to-date information on time-sensitive topics, you may elect to receive two issues of the *Effective Church Accounting Newsletter*. This handy newsletter will be published annually in January by Harper & Row, Publishers. In order to receive this newsletter, complete and mail the information card at the back of this book.

I recognize that effective church accounting will demand a lot of your energy. When you need inspiration, remember the words of Frederick William Robertson, who said:

> It is not the possession of extraordinary gifts that makes extraordinary usefulness, but the dedication of what we have to the service of God.

# Index

**Yes, please send me a copy of the next two**
*Effective Church Accounting* **newsletters,**
**full of helpful, up-to-date information!**

Mail to: *Effective Church Accounting*
          Harper & Row, Publishers
          Icehouse One—401
          151 Union St.
          San Francisco, CA 94111-1299

Name
_____

Street or P.O. Box
_____

City
_____

State _____ Zip _____

I am affiliated with (name and location of your local church):

_____

_____

_____

I am (check)
      ☐ church accountant
      ☐ treasurer
      ☐ financial secretary
      ☐ pastor
      ☐ other (please describe) _____